DATE DUE

THE
SIBERIAN
SEVEN

THE
SIBERIAN
SEVEN

John Pollock

WORD BOOKS
PUBLISHER
WACO, TEXAS

THE SIBERIAN SEVEN

Copyright © 1979, 1980 by John Pollock.
All rights reserved. No part of this book may be reproduced in any form whatever, except for brief quotations in reviews, without the written permission of the publisher, Word Books, Waco, Texas 76703.

ISBN 0–8499–0262–2
Library of Congress catalog card number: 79–57352
Printed in the United States of America

This true story of a few
is dedicated to the nameless thousands
who have suffered likewise
for their faith

Contents

Preface   9
Prologue   11

PART ONE: THE SETTING

1. The Prisoner of War   21
2. "A Believer Grown Cold"   29
3. Chernogorsk Revival   38

PART TWO: "THE STRIFE IS FIERCE"

4. The Great Persecution   57
5. The State Steals the Children   65
6. Letter from a Stranger   76
7. Moscow Adventure   84
8. The Thirty-Two   92
9. A Third Attempt   101
10. Peter in Prison   111
11. The Achinsk Desert   120
12. *Interlude:* Timothy   128
13. Sent to the Madhouse   135
14. Augustina's Calvary   148
15. Lida the Comforter   159
16. Prison through the Eyes of a Child   170
17. "Let My People Go!"   181
18. Aaron   193
19. The Ultimate Horror   204

20.	Lyuba's Feet	217
21.	Sasha's Trial	227

PART THREE: SUSPENSE

22.	The Selma Invitation	239
23.	"Who Shall Deliver Us?"	248
	Appendix I	262
	Appendix II	265

MAPS

Map 1.	The U.S.S.R.	20
Map 2.	Krasnoyarsk Territory	39
Map 3.	Chernogorsk	40

Preface

I WISH TO THANK most warmly the Vashchenko and Chmykhalov families for inviting me to tell their story. Many people have helped whom I may not name, and in the book itself I have disguised or omitted the names of believers other than those of the immediate families, or of known leaders. Soviet officials, on the other hand, are given their true names throughout, whether KGB or policemen, bureaucrats, prison governors, etc.

I was extremely fortunate to secure in Dr. Norvell Robertson an outstanding translator for the Russian source materials, who at considerable personal sacrifice gave the work priority. Speed, skill in deciphering Russian handwriting, and wide knowledge were just a few of the qualities which combined to produce an excellent translation, and I shall always remain grateful for a very happy collaboration. However, I am solely responsible for the final English form of all material quoted. We have used the transliteration system of the U.S. Board on Geographical Names, slightly adapted, but where a forename has an obvious English equivalent we have normally used it (i.e., Timothy, not Timofei, Peter not Pyotr, etc.). The aim has been to make Russian names easy for the ordinary English reader. A note on their construction will be found at the head of the list of principal persons, in the appendix.

Among others I would specially thank the director of Keston College, Kent, England (the Reverend Michael Bourdeaux), and the head of Soviet Studies at Keston (Mr. Michael Rowe), who gave me material about the Vashchenkos received in the West in earlier years, and advice, encouragement and some background material; Mr. Eugene Bresenden of California, USA, formerly of Nakhodka, USSR, who wrote me a long and most valuable memorandum about the Christians of Chernogorsk from his personal knowledge of the people and the place; and the Venerable Timothy Dudley-Smith, Archdeacon of Norwich, England, the well-known hymn writer, who kindly paraphrased a Russian hymn and part of the verses written by Sasha Vashchenko on the night before his trial in December 1977.

JOHN POLLOCK

Prologue

THE CHRISTIANS from Siberia walked towards the American Embassy on Moscow's inner ring road, a street so wide that the opposite side seems almost another part of the city.

Their leader, on this 27 June 1978, was Peter Pavlovich Vashchenko, a man of medium height in his mid-fifties with dark hair and moustache, wearing a neat dark suit. He held papers in his hand. With him walked his wife, fair-haired Augustina Vashchenko, their eldest daughter Lida, who was twenty-seven, and two of Lida's sisters, Lyuba and Lila. Their younger brother, John, was seventeen and looked older, being tall and strong beside the other boy, Timothy, who came with his mother, Maria Chmykhalov.

They wanted to emigrate from the Soviet Union, to live in a country where they could keep the laws of God without breaking the laws of the State. All the adults had memories of persecution: three had been in prison for their faith, one in a psychiatric hospital though perfectly sane. Lida and Lyuba as children had experienced the horror of abduction from home in an official attempt to educate them forcibly into atheism. It was this that had turned Peter Vashchenko to seek emigration. In 1962 he went all the way from his home in the coal mining city of Chernogorsk, Siberia, to Moscow, and in innocence applied at the Kremlin for permission to take his family abroad. Kremlin officials rated him crazy. They sent him home; he was arrested at the mine and put in prison.

Soon afterward, in January 1963, Augustina his wife had been among thirty-two Siberians who rushed past the police and into the American Embassy in Moscow, to plead for immediate emigration for all their families. They had been persuaded to leave after a few hours. Removed in a bus by the Soviet authorities the Thirty-

Two had vanished into the void, but not before the Western press had blazened their story round the world, to reveal that Christianity in the atheist Soviet Union was more alive than the general public in the West had realized.

The Vashchenkos had never abandoned hope of emigration nor weakened in their faith. As this book will show, fifteen long hard years with many adventures, hopes and sorrows lay between that winter day of 1963 when they disappeared into the void, and the summer morning of June 1978 when once again they walked towards the American Embassy. They walked calmly but with a sense of urgency. Their eldest son, Sasha, was in labor camp for his faith; John, the next son, might soon be arrested in his turn. But the Vashchenkos now carried a formal invitation to emigrate to Selma, Alabama. Their papers were all in order except for the Soviet exit visa which had been refused again and again. They had traveled the long journey to Moscow to seek American advice and help. They came with no intention of asking for asylum.

Peter walked up to the Soviet militiaman (civil policeman) standing in his smart gray uniform in front of one of the archway entrances to the Embassy, and showed his papers. By Soviet law a citizen has the right, as in most countries, to enter a foreign consulate on business; by Soviet practice no one may enter without a document from his local authority permitting him to do so. Peter had been unable to obtain it. He was not surprised therefore when the policeman brusquely waved them away with a *nyet*—no!

Peter had laid his plans. The two families surged forward and with a rush reached diplomatic territory, but the policeman reacted with the speed of long training and caught young John, who brought up the rear, and felled him to the asphalt.

At his cries the Vashchenkos looked round and were horrified to see their boy under the policeman, who was kneeling on John's chest with hands round his throat, apparently choking his life out. The seven Siberians rushed into the Embassy courtyard shouting and crying in great distress, to the astonishment of employees and officials happening to be about, who at first could not understand what was their trouble.

A diplomat took them into the consular waiting room and calmed them a little. The distraught parents begged and urged the Americans to rescue their boy. At first no one would go, for this was an internal matter over which foreigners held no jurisdiction. By the time an American officer went outside to inquire, John had been removed from the police booth and no one would say where he had been taken.

The Siberians refused to leave the Embassy until they knew his fate; instead they began a prayer fast. The Embassy staff urged them to leave but did not force them out, and allowed them to sit on the waiting-room divans, where the Western press interviewed them and volunteers from the American community in Moscow brought food which they welcomed after their fast.

Days and nights ticked by. The Siberian Seven began to write about their lives. They wanted the West to understand more fully the repressions and handicaps suffered by believers in the Soviet Union, and were sure that their own case would be resolved quickly if they might publicize the facts. Not knowing how long they would be allowed to stay, the writers among them put their energy into this work each evening after the consulate offices closed and they could move about and talk. Maria Chmykhalov spent a whole night writing in the toilet where the light could be kept on without disturbing the others.

Such time that they did not spend writing they read the Bible and prayed, and focused their prayers particularly on their absent families and on the missing John. After more than two weeks the Americans managed to make telephone contact with Chernogorsk. The Vashchenkos spoke with their daughter Vera, and heard to their horror that John had been brought home a few days before after being beaten and tortured, "the full treatment, almost the electric chair." He was in too much pain from internal injuries to come to the post and telephone office, she whispered. Then they heard Vera's voice come through strongly in a quick desperate plea: "Don't leave the Embassy!" she urged. "If they treated a minor like that, what will they do to you? Don't leave."

Peter knew she was right. Several years earlier he had been told by the Soviet authorities that if he stayed more than three hours in the Embassy he would be treated as a traitor to his country. He had long passed this point of no return. They must ask for asylum. Thus began the long sit-in of the Vashchenko and Chmykhalov families, which would stretch into weeks, then into month after month, into a year, and more.

Their best hope was to waken world opinion. They had brought with them a mass of official documents—copies of court sentences, prison discharge papers, official reports and demands, receipts from government departments, birth and death certificates and much else. They showed these to Americans who befriended them, together with the first beginnings of their autobiographies. Among these friends was a couple who became much moved by their plight and shared their concern that the widest public in the West should be told their story. The American wife longed to do something herself, but the husband, at that stage, was not sure whether he wished to be involved.

Some days after the Siberians had taken refuge in the Embassy a parcel reached this couple, mailed by themselves while on leave in the United States that spring. They had bought many books and had dispatched them to Moscow unread. They opened the parcel and the wife picked out to read first a paperback edition of a book of mine, bought cheap because it had been long in the shop. She began reading. The title was *The Faith of The Russian Evangelicals.*[1]

My story opened with the incident of the Thirty-Two Siberians who had rushed into the Embassy in 1963, but I mentioned no names before embarking on the historical and more general parts. Two publishers, an American and a British, had commissioned me to find out all I could about the Thirty-Two. I had been unable to meet them. Instead, my wife and I had traveled widely among believers and my book was the first to place before the nonspecialist

---

1. Hardback edition, New York, McGraw Hill, 1964. Paperback edition, Zondervan, 1969 (reissued 1972 as *Faith and Freedom in Russia*). British title: *The Christians from Siberia*, Hodder and Stoughton, 1964. Translated into five languages.

public the surprising extent and virility of Russian evangelical Christianity after nearly half a century of militantly atheist rule.

The American woman read on and reached the final two chapters in which I bring the book to a climax by describing all I could discover of the actual story of the Thirty-Two Siberians of 1963. And there before her eyes lay the name Vashchenko. She suddenly realized that some of the very people she read about were languishing at that moment in the consular section of the Embassy—that she had been talking daily to the heroes of the story.

Even though I was a complete stranger to her, and she knew nothing of my present whereabouts, she decided at once to send a cable to the town in England named on the little piece about me on the back of the jacket. Her husband was still not sure about involvement; the initiative was hers.

Many cables from the Soviet Union never make their destination. Hers, however, reached my town, with no further address. The postmaster looked at it, then called me at the nearby village where I lived, to ask whether it might be for me. He read it out: "Urgently request your immediate return to Moscow to continue story. Part of Thirty-Two are here. . . ."

I had noticed in *The Times* of London a brief mention of the incident of 27 June. This included the name of the home city of the Seven which I recognized from 1963, but that had been a long time ago. After completing the book about Russian Evangelicals I had resumed my more usual work as a biographer. The next fifteen years were spent writing about the Apostle Paul, Billy Graham, William Wilberforce and others, and I had just completed the first draft of a book on John Newton when the cable arrived.

I began to make a few inquiries. The cable might be a hoax, or a trap, or entangle me in events I could not control. A few days later a telephone call from overseas asked if I had received the cable. On the following Sunday afternoon, a wet, blustery day, I was about to go out for a walk when the telephone rang again. An American voice identified himself as the husband of the woman who had sent the cable. He said his work had taken him from

Moscow at short notice for a very brief stay in another European capital, and would I fly out at once? I had half an hour to make up my mind. I caught the night sleeper from the West Country and flew next morning.

Later my wife and I visited Moscow and through the courtesy of the American Embassy I was able to meet the Siberian Seven and talk with them through an interpreter. We sat in the courtyard on a rather cold day; everybody caught colds except me. I was impressed by their genuineness, gentleness, courage, and sterling Christian faith; and also by a half-hidden sense of humor despite their troubles, though I was touched to learn afterwards that they had worried a little lest their terrible situation might have made them seem to me gloomy and humorless.

I knew now that they had a remarkable story. At first it looked as if I must write a short account, using imagination and general information to put flesh on the skeleton of their autobiographies. But as their stay in the Embassy lengthened, so did their writings, especially as they came to realize which aspects were the more important, and that details about life in Siberia, too commonplace to remember at first, provided essential background. Eventually they wrote between them during their months in the Embassy many hundreds of pages, amounting to more than two hundred twenty-five thousand words in English translation. This is the fullest single account in manuscript of such matters ever to be received in the West.

Their testimony is supported all the way through by the documents they brought. There is no space for full verbatim reproduction but the authentication is available and in safe custody.

The scraps of evidence which have filtered from all over the Soviet Union for years past show a remarkable similarity as evidence of repression and discrimination against believers, yet never before has it been possible to follow in close detail the fortunes of one group among the thousands upon thousands who have experienced the full force of the State's determination to make atheism supreme. The sufferings of the Vashchenkos and Chmykhalovs reveal the truth in its starkness as no general assessment, no patchwork of evidence, may hope to do; the Siberian Seven have a significance far beyond the thrill and pain of their own adventures. They wrote with a full realization of the risk to themselves if their hope of emigration be denied. They wrote for the sake of all believers; wherever the Seven's future lies, in the West or still in the Soviet Union, their story demands attention.

The manuscripts presented a problem in that 225,000 words are far too much for one book. I have therefore made the story of Peter Vashchenko and his family the main theme of the present work, since everything that happened derives, in a sense, from them. I have drawn on the accounts of Maria Chmykhalov and her son Timothy, who at the age of sixteen shows himself a natural writer and provides some of the light relief, and I hope to follow this book with a second, the autobiography of the Chmykhalovs, because Maria, though not very literate, has produced a long account of peasant life and Christian faith among the very poor in Russia which has a Tolstoyan realism.

The task of sorting the material and welding it into good reading, much of it in their own words, has been formidable. I have sought to be true to the facts and the spirit of their writings but the responsibility for what is selected, and for the treatment of the theme, is entirely mine: the Siberians themselves were not in a position to check the finished product and cannot be held liable for any misunderstandings or mistakes.

The book became a far larger enterprise than I had imagined when I took the night sleeper and the plane to meet a man from Moscow, but I am deeply grateful to the Vashchenkos and Chmykhalovs for entrusting me with their story, and I warmly welcome a part in making it known. As Pope John Paul II said in his first encyclical, *The Redeemer of Man:* "It is difficult to accept a position that gives only atheism the right of citizenship in public and social life while believers are, as though by principle, barely tolerated or are treated as second-class citizens."

The Vashchenkos and Chmykhalovs are, at the moment of going to press, still guests of the Embassy, unable to leave the Soviet Union. The key to unlock the door may be the outcry which should follow publication of this their story. If, however, they have reached the haven where they would be, their past sufferings will force attention on the courage, faith and hope of all Soviet believers. Either way, no one may ignore them.

Part One

THE SETTING

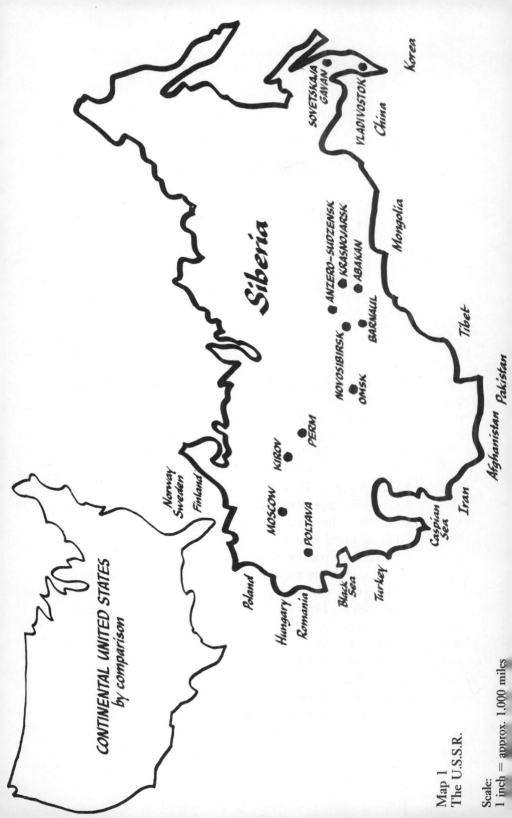

CONTINENTAL UNITED STATES
by comparison

Norway
Sweden
Finland
Poland
Hungary
Romania
Black Sea
Turkey
Caspian Sea
Iran
Afghanistan Pakistan
Tibet
Mongolia
China
Korea

Siberia

POLTAVA
MOSCOW
KIROV
PERM
OMSK
NOVOSIBIRSK
BARNAUL
ABAKAN
KRASNOJARSK
ANZERO-SUDZENSK
VLADIVOSTOK
SOVETSKAJA GAVAN

Map 1
The U.S.S.R.

Scale:
1 inch = approx. 1,000 miles

1

The Prisoner of War

THE STORY GOES back to the First World War when a Russian prisoner of war named Pavel (Paul) Antonovich Vashchenko, a peasant from the Ukraine, was put to work on a farm in Austria-Hungary.

Paul was born on 28 July 1888 in the village of Vaski near Poltava, the city famous for Peter the Great's victory in 1709 over Charles XII of Sweden. He was still active in Siberia in 1979, at over ninety years of age. Paul's mother died when he was seven. With four brothers he grew up to the typical life of a peasant; like his father he loved raising cattle on the local barm's rich black lands. They lived in a reed-thatched cabin of timber, and in winter they shared its one living room and the warmth of the great clay stove with their own cow, pigs and chickens.

Of average height, black-haired with light blue eyes, a straight nose and ruddy cheeks, Paul was calm and rather silent, a slow, thorough worker. In 1912, after completing his six years conscript service, he married Anna Svirdovna Vashchenko (no relation, but most Vaski families bore that surname), and they were expecting their first child when Paul was recalled to the colors in 1914 to be an insignificant cog in the cumbrous war machine which the

Allies hopefully dubbed the "Russian steam roller." He marched with a hundred thousand others into Austrian Galicia for a campaign of swift victory followed by defeat and stalemate.

He survived by refusing to obey a foolish order. The enemy had entrenched behind a wall on a ridge when Paul's captain shouted orders to each skirmish line to advance up the hill. File after file "were cut down in turn from the slaughterhouse and rolled down from the wall dead," until only Paul and the three men behind him were left. Hearing the order to advance, he stayed where he was and stopped the other three. Retreat sounded soon after and they were captured, the only survivors of a hundred men.

Paul spent seven years as a prisoner of war. The farming family to whom he was assigned, possibly in southern Hungary, were German-speaking evangelical Christians. Paul looked after their cattle and lived in the homestead. Here believers gathered to pray. The kindly farmer secured him a Russian Bible which the hitherto illiterate Paul taught himself to read so that, in his son's words, "He came to know in detail the teachings of Christ."

In childhood and youth Paul had been Russian Orthodox, like all in Vaski. He had attended the village church every Sunday and on the twelve great feast days and, above all, had joined in the unforgettable ceremonies and hymns of Easter. At home he had been taught to pray before the icon shelf with its smoke-grimed metal likenesses of Christ and of patron saints. Orthodoxy had laid for him a deep foundation. Yet in that period before its great renewal in the fires of persecution, Russian Orthodox devotion was much a matter of prayers recited by rote, and genuflections while the priest sang or droned the liturgy in an unknown tongue beyond the closed doors of the iconostasis. God the All-Terrible, the All-Merciful lived far away. Out of church the villagers drank, wenched, thieved and lied as if He did not exist.

As a prisoner of war Paul had discovered instead that God could be a Friend close at hand. When the Revolution and Civil War engulfed his fatherland, and defeat brought chaos to the land of his captivity, the farm remained a haven where Paul grew into a strong faith. Having declined the farmer's invitation to settle permanently, he was repatriated to the Ukraine early in 1921 at the age of thirty-three.

Civil war had flowed back and forth in the Poltava province, with countless battle casualties, executions and murders and famine had added to the misery, but Anna his wife had survived, with their girl he had never seen, Natalia (Natasha). At the end of that year a second child, Ivan, was born in Vaski, followed in 1924 by a boy to whom they gave the good peasant name of Khariton. On 30 September 1926 Anna gave birth to Peter.

Paul Vashchenko had returned from the wars rejoicing in his faith. Anna soon became his fellow disciple. She was tall and well proportioned with black hair which never turned gray though she lived to the age of eighty-four, dying in 1977. She had a Roman nose and gray eyes. She worked as hard as Paul but in contrast to his quieter pace she worked fast. She could be fiery but would quickly recover her calm. Paul read the Bible to Anna, who remained illiterate all her days, and they prayed together and sought to shape their lives according to Christ and to bring up their children to love him.

The household's cleanliness, Paul's chivalry to Anna, their freedom from alcohol and argument, all this made something new to Vaski. Paul's father disapproved of his ceasing to keep the Church fasts, but he was not persecuted as evangelicals had often been in Tsarist times. Lenin's Constitution of 1917 which separated the Church from the State and the school from the Church brought a few short years of freedom of conscience, for it had recognized, "as the right of every citizen," freedom of religious as well as of antireligious propaganda. Baptists, however, were scarce in the Poltava region; and during the six years he lived at Vaski after returning from the War Paul made few converts other than a younger brother and his wife, Lavrenty and Fekla.

In the spring of 1927, when Peter was six months old, Paul's circumstances altered dramatically.

It was the result of a disaster. The broad acres of the Tsarist landlord had been confiscated and divided among the villagers. They became owner-farmers, unaware of the horrors of collectivization to come, and each would put his harvest under his own roof. The village owned a steam threshing engine which the farmers used in turn. One April evening, at a little distance from Paul's thatched roof with its carved cockerel's head jutting above the street, the engine's big wheel whirred and the stack belched merrily as Paul and Anna, helped by Natasha and several relations, worked hard to get their corn threshed and stored before dark. They stoked the fire-box with straw.

"Suddenly," records Peter, "a flame shot out of the engine and engulfed everything around: straw, the roof and all that was stored under it, and a pile of grain. The family house, the flax, the stables with the livestock, all were lost because everyone rushed to save the community thresher which was on cast-iron wheels. We were not able to get the stock out of their stalls or the things out of the house. The well was far away and with buckets the people couldn't put out the flames. Everything burned; even the potatoes were baked in the cellar. After the fire my father offered all who were present some baked potatoes to eat. The people stood amazed by his calmness. They gathered together what they could to help our family." [1]

Thus Paul reached his fortieth year destitute except for this charity and his unshakable faith that God had a good purpose in every test of life. After prayer, Paul decided what to do. Since the hated compulsory collectivization of farms had begun in the Ukraine but not in Siberia, the Vashchenkos applied for a State grant of virgin land. In May 1927, at State expense, they moved to Omsk province in Western Siberia, to the village of Desyaty (tenth) Kusumys, near Issilkul, the last main station on the Trans-Siberian railway before Omsk city, where Dostoyevsky wrote *The House of the Dead.*

Unlike the eastern regions with their extensive *taiga* or forest, the steppes of Western Siberia were almost treeless. Paul therefore made a house of sods cut from the ground around, with dirt floors.

---

1. The children's birth certificates were burnt and not replaced until 1940, when the record office, ZAGS, used incorrect information. Officially, Ivan, Khariton and Peter are all one year younger than in fact they are.

Peter recalls the huge clay stove, heated with briquettes of dried manure, and the wooden barrel which, as in all Russian peasant houses of the time, served as bath; if Peter was chilled o suffering from a cold the family would heat the stove, rake out the briquettes and cover the base with straw to make a great steam, and sit him right inside the stove.

The land was rich, harvests good and the Vashchenkos lived well in those few calm years of the early nineteen-thirties. The sparse population in the neighborhood contained a mixture of Moslem Khirgiz and Russian emigrants, among whom were some sixty Baptists. They elected Paul presbyter. Peter especially remembers the family prayers when they sang together and his father expounded Scripture. Soon Paul's younger brother and sister-in-law, Lavrenty and Fekla, with several children including Grigory, who was less than a year younger than Peter, left the Ukraine and built a house next door. In contrast to Paul, Uncle Lavrenty was redheaded with light blue eyes, and "you could never see a smile on his face." He was strict and demanding, but Aunt Fekla was cheerful and reasonable; she was tall, with light brown hair and a beautiful voice.

Aunt Fekla loved to sing hymns and religious songs and to pray; and once when she was praying aloud she was suddenly baptized in the Spirit like the Apostles of old and began to speak in tongues. The Vashchenkos had no contacts with Russian Pentecostals; the charismatic movement in other denominations throughout the world would not begin for another quarter century; so Fekla's experience seems to have been a spontaneous invasion of the Spirit. None of the others followed her at that time, though in the end, long after her death from tuberculosis, she would profoundly influence them all.

Peter remembers her "praying in the Spirit" (as Russians translate "speaking in tongues"), and it impressed him profoundly. Soon all the Vashchenkos were to need the Spirit's strength in full measure.

In 1931 the Collectivization Program reached Siberia. A peasant must no longer work for himself and his family but for a *kolkhoz*, a collective farm, and any who had built up their own good farms and refused to join were denounced as *kulaks* (prosperous peasants) to be liquidated or expelled. Throughout the Soviet Union in these next years, fifteen million peasants, by Solzhenitsyn's count, died as a direct result of the program.

Collectivization was voluntary, in theory. Paul Vashchenko received a summons from the chairman of the rural soviet who asked him, because of his influence as presbyter, to apply in writing to join the *kolkhoz* and to conduct propaganda to persuade other believers. Paul refused, quoting the passage in the Book of Proverbs concerning bad men who tempt into robbery "and say . . . 'We shall take rich treasure of every sort and fill our homes with booty; throw in your lot with us, and we will have a common purse.' My son, do not go along with them, keep clear of their ways; they hasten hot foot into crime." Collectivization, in Paul's view, was robbery—and a swift road to inefficient farming and, as indeed it turned out, to famine.

At that stage in the program those who declined to join could take up internal passports, hitherto not needed, and leave their district: many local believers had gone already, but many remained and Paul, as presbyter, refused to desert them. "For the time being," he said, "I stay. I rely on God. Whatever he ordains, that will come to pass." Lavrenty stayed too.

Paul was deprived of the right to vote or stand for any election. And a presbyter now was a marked man. Atheism being intrinsic to Marxist-Leninism, a Party member had to be an atheist; religion should already have withered away, yet evangelical Christianity in particular had grown much stronger since 1917. Therefore Stalin's Constitution of 1929 had removed the citizen's right to conduct religious propaganda and forbade believers to extol or explain their faith except to adults in the context of worship within a church building. Everywhere else anti-God propaganda ran unlimited with the full support of the State.

Like thousands of other Baptist pastors, Paul had carried on his ministry. He was not surprised, therefore, when the chairman of the rural soviet came to the hut, followed by two or three henchmen. He felt nothing personal against Paul. "I told your husband," he said to Anna, "to take his passports and leave, and he replied, 'Whatever God gives.' And now let him rely on God because I cannot issue him a passport now. My own family would be punished if I did. I cannot help you at all."

The henchmen started to strip the place. "They took a pair of horses," continues Peter, "a heifer, a bullock, two pigs, and about twenty chickens. They emptied the barn of all the grain, took *everything*, everything except the clothes we were wearing. When they had thrown everyone out onto the street, they asked: Do you have anything left? My father replied: 'As you said, we have come to the end of the road, but above the oven a pood [36 lb.] of wheat is drying and behind the oven is a calf.' And they shoveled up the wheat and took the calf. And we were left with absolutely nothing, as in the Ukraine after the fire. They even took the plow and the harrow, the wheels, the shovels, and the spades because at that time these things were precious."

Uncle Lavrenty's goods were not confiscated, perhaps because he was not a presbyter. He therefore sold everything and managed to buy one horse. "Since we had nothing left, and since Uncle had a horse, we decided to move on together deeper into Siberia without documents for our family or his," hoping to reach at the last a friend from the Ukraine who lived in the hilly Karatuzk region beyond the Yenisei river.[2] The distance would be about nine hundred miles, but the Trans-Siberian railway was barred to them without papers, even if they could afford the fares.

The journey took two years. The first night Anna had a vivid dream in which she heard a voice say: "You are artisan people and you can subsist that way." They set off, the adults walking, the children sharing the horse and the infants carried; in Siberia Anna had borne Maria and Daniel. When they needed food or winter shelter Paul and his family would ride and walk ahead to the next village while the Lavrentys waited. Natasha was now seventeen, a hard worker who had been "nanny" to her younger brothers and sisters; and if the village did not chase them away because

---

2. See Map 2, p. 39.

they had no papers and were believers, she was adept at finding work for all who were old enough. Paul would ride back to bring in the other family.

The women and girls would spin flax, weave, and wash. The men and teenage sons would put up roofs or fences, repair barns, chop firewood, or do other jobs. They might stay as much as two months in winter, but then the rural soviet would discover their existence "and despite the weather we would have to move on within twenty-four hours. They would notify the surrounding villages and the local authorities would come out to meet us and forbid us to stop. Because each village was surrounded by fences for several kilometers to keep the livestock out of the fields beyond, we had to detour right round. Sometimes in winter it was minus fifty degrees centigrade and our clothes were bad. There would be much snow and the snowdrifts caused hardship."

Like Peter, Grigory and the smaller children were carried in woven baskets, normally used for manure, which the parents had lined with straw. "We were covered with rags but the wind cut through. When a village would not allow us to stop we were forced despite the snow and cold to continue our journey at night. We children were in the baskets; how the grown-ups whiled away the night in the cold, we did not know."

Both mothers lost babies. In the second winter Peter's small brother Daniel died, "unable to stand the terrible cold of Siberia." Round the little grave they mourned him with a funeral hymn, and then struggled on, a few among the millions who suffered in those terrible years, whether in labor camps of the frozen north, in prisons throughout the Soviet Union or by deportation and forced destitution.

2

"A Believer Grown Cold"

ON THE BANKS of the Kazyr river, which flows into the Tuba and thence to the mighty River Yenisei, which divides Siberia, stood two abandoned peasant huts or *izbas*. They were the last relics of the original village of Gorlovka, destroyed by flood in 1916 and rebuilt on higher ground.

The Vashchenkos heard about these *izbas* while lodging with Ukrainian exiles some thirty kilometers west whom they had reached after spending several months that summer on an isolated farm in the mountainous southern part of the Krasnoyarsk Territory of Siberia. Once more they were discovered and expelled, and they moved eastward until they found these fellow-Ukrainians. However, their new hosts suffered from tuberculosis and the Vashchenkos must move again. Desperately weary of wandering, Paul went to investigate.

While he was gone Anna had a dream. She found him sitting on the stove in a riverside *izba* preparing dumplings and soup, and he told her he had bought the *izba*. Then, in her dream, two men and an officious woman marched in, smoking, who ordered them to be gone because without passports they had no right to buy property. And Anna replied: "We have nowhere left to go.

There is the river! Throw us in or kill us in the house, but we will never leave here." The officials left and Anna awoke.

After she had recounted the dream to the children, she walked to Gorlovka with Ivan and discovered the *izba* and Paul sitting on the stove beside a steaming iron pot, just as in the dream. She told him the dream, and then returned to collect the rest of the children and the family's small possessions; but hardly had they moved in when the second part of the dream unfolded before their eyes. Arestova, chairman of the local soviet, and two men ordered them out. Anna thereupon spoke as she had dreamed. Arestova shrugged her shoulders and departed.

Lavrenty bought the *izba* next door. Paul's little hut, a mere three and a half by five meters (about eleven by sixteen feet) plus a lean-to entrance, remained the family home for nineteen years. Gorlovka was in the Karatusk region in the foothills of the Sayan mountains, about a hundred and eighty kilometers (over one hundred ten miles) east of Chernogorsk where eventually they all settled.

These were years of hardship. The great famine of the thirties reduced them sometimes to birch roots and toadstools. Peter has a vivid boyhood memory of walking through the *taiga* one sunny late March day to the construction site downriver where his mother and Ivan worked and might have something for the starving youngsters at home. He was singing a favorite hymn, "Don't be sad, dear soul, but joyful, And rely on the Lord your God." He had just sung the closing line, "Your Savior is watching you with love," when he noticed a little roadside knoll where the sun had melted some of the ice. Under the melting ice he thought he saw meal. Scooping a handful out, he found indeed a heap of meal preserved all winter, and "was ecstatic because I was hungry." He took off his shirt and filled it, ran home and cooked flat cakes and carried them to his mother at the logging harbor site. "When she saw me she said: 'Son, you have come for bread and we have nothing.' I told her what had happened, and that I had brought the cakes. Together we gave God thanks for his great mercy."

Peter's father at this time was incarcerated in a labor camp. There was nothing voluntary about the *kolkhoz* now. First, the chairman had played a cruel joke on Paul by saying an exception would be made: he would be given a plan, and grain, and could fulfill the plan on his own. When Paul asked where, the chairman said that the *kolkhoz* had no land to spare, that any place untilled belonged to the State, but—looking at the ceiling—"You have good Soviet soil on your dirt roof and can sow it there!"

Paul was tried and sentenced to one year, and then to another. After that he was allowed to farm with the *kolkhoz* without formally joining, but no worker received more than a pittance because nothing could be shared until the harvest had been transported downriver and the annual debt to the State paid off.

When at home Paul would always gather the family after work and read aloud from their single copy of the Bible. Peter says, "The Bible is a wonderful book. I have loved it since my youth." They would sing psalms and hymns in the slow Russian style, taking different parts to form a family choir, and then all pray aloud, each addressing his own petitions to God but allowing the head of the household to finish last. Then they would say together the Lord's Prayer and, as they rose from their knees, would cross themselves in the manner of the Orthodox. This has been the Vashchenko way of family prayers right through the story.

Two other believer families in Gorlovka joined them for meetings in Paul's *izba*, which being by the river and road became known far and wide for its Christian welcome.

Stalin, however, repressed believers of every persuasion with increasing rigor. Throughout the Soviet Union it became more difficult and dangerous to meet for worship; many parents no longer dared teach their children Christian truth; Bibles were scarce. Yet when Peter started school in 1935 at the age of nine (and only about half the children of rural Russia went to school in those years) he was not mocked as a believer's child except by a few sons of Party officials, and the program did not aim to force him into an atheist mold. He escaped the tensions which would make his own children's school days a misery in the Khrushchev and Brezhnev eras. But it was wiser to be a secret Christian.

In 1939 Peter went out to work as a plowboy. Next he helped

transport the grain down the river to the big town; then he worked on the *kolkhoz* again. He has a hilarious but painful memory of a wartime May when the remaining horses had become so feeble after a starvation winter that the *kolkhoz* told everyone to bring their cows, almost the only private possession allowed, to draw the harrows. Peter brought Manka, the hornless cow shared between the two Vashchenko households, and being by now a brigade leader he was ordered to make the first experiment "to see how a cow could harrow."

He put Manka into a collar and traces and began on a level field, sown with oats, at the top of a high hill. Manka behaved well until he had to lead her near the edge, when she saw cattle in the ravine and took off. Before he knew what had happened Peter was flying through the air down the slope, his left hand jammed in the reins, his shoulder plowing the ground. When the traces broke and Manka ran free, Peter cannonaded into the earth and dislocated his shoulder. Painfully he picked himself up and followed Manka into the ravine where she calmly left the cattle and came to greet him; "and in this way private cows escaped working on *kolkhoz* fields!"

That same year of 1942 Peter's cousins were orphaned. Aunt Fekla, fervent to the last, died of tuberculosis at Easter. Before her death she saw in a dream a crown prepared for her and also a martyr's crown for one of her children, who pressed her to say for which, but she replied: "I know, but I will not tell." Her dream was fulfilled twenty-four years later.

Fekla had had ten children, but only two daughters survived and two sons: Grigory, now aged fifteen, and Andrei, who was three. Paul and Anna became Andrei's foster parents because Uncle Lavrenty had been carried off into the Labor Army. Soon after Fekla's death he was selected for the front and arrived at the territorial capital, Krasnoyarsk. Understanding that he had several days before medical examination, Lavrenty went absent without leave and made his way south to Gorlovka to see his motherless children and Fekla's grave.

His squad was summoned out of turn; arrested as a deserter,

he was sent to a slave camp in the frozen north and never seen again. His exact fate remains a mystery to this day.

*   *   *

In 1944 Peter was called up into the Army before his eighteenth birthday; his brothers Ivan and Khariton had already gone to the front. He transferred to the Navy but did not see action, serving seven years in coastal defense of the Seventh Pacific Ocean Fleet, at Scvetskaya Gavan, a port on the Tatar Strait.

Deep in his heart Peter remained a believer, but he kept quiet. "If a believer in civil life is very scorned," he says, looking on those years with some shame, "how much worse it is in the ranks of the Soviet army and navy." He satisfied conscience by his manner of life—not smoking or drinking, swearing or womanizing, but working hard. He had a kindly captain who did not press him, as many might, to join atheist organizations or speak against religion.

After the War Peter reenlisted for a second term and was placed in charge of the Vehicle Repair and Fuel Station. He had grown into a good-looking young man with dark hair, deepset grey eyes and high cheekbones. His happy nature and sense of humor, his efficiency, and a native intelligence which offset his bare four years in a rural school, put him on friendly terms with the officers. Thus it happened in the summer of 1948 that one day, when Peter was filling up the car of an officer who was taking a small mixed party on an outing to pick forest raspberries, Peter was invited to join.

With the officers' wives was a girl of nineteen, a civilian who had just arrived on the naval station. Augustina Vasilevna Konovalov was petite, fair-haired and pretty, with an open, friendly nature, Augustina, Peter and three of the others missed the car ride for the return journey and walked back. "This," says Peter, "was a great pleasure, walking back with her. I found out about her life in detail."

Shortly afterwards Augustina was transferred to Peter's vehicle repair shop as a bookkeeping clerk, and they fell in love. She was aware that many servicemen married their girls and got them with

child, then disappeared when reposted, often leaving behind a heavy
suitcase to imply an early return, which in fact was filled with
stones. A girl would retaliate by dumping the baby, when it arrived,
on the commanding officer's table. Augustina felt she could trust
Peter. She knew nothing about his being a believer but considered
him a "calm" man, who would not deceive her, nor get drunk,
nor fly into a Russian rage.

Augustina came from a peasant family in Peter's region of Siberia,
born in a forest area nearer Chernogorsk, their eventual home.
Her father suffered ill health and had retired young from the
kolkhoz, though he was still alive at 88 when Augustina and Peter
entered the American Embassy in 1978. With her mother and
sisters she suffered much hunger in her childhood and schooldays,
as everyone did, until she got a job in the postal department. At
first she walked a rather terrifying postal round through the deep
taiga, but later, joining her sister at Krasnoyarsk, she worked as a
postal clerk on the railway, effecting the exchange of mail at each
station down to Abakan. She rose to be chief of the postal car
though somewhat embarrassed by her smallness and insignificant
physique.

In summer she helped take the mails by steamship up and down
the Yenisei, through "very beautiful places. There were high rocky
cliffs and above them large flocks of birds would hover and circle:
black kites, hawks, swallows, pinefinches and jackdaws, whose
screech rang out along the river beneath the cliffs. Seagulls dived
quickly into the water and rose holding fish in their beaks. The
banks were dotted with large fir, spruce, pine, birch, asp and poplar.
Between all the trees could be seen guelder-roses (snowball trees)
and raspberries. There were both calm and swift places in the
current, and rapids, and rocks jutting out to the water."

In the postwar years it was difficult to get enough food in overcrowded, industrial Krasnoyarsk, so when a young relative and her
baby who roomed with them received an invitation to live with a
couple at Sovetskaya Gavan in the Far East, she persuaded Augustina to come too. They arrived in June 1948.

Augustina was "not at all a believer," recalls Peter, "and I was a believer who had grown cold. However, I saw that she *should* be a believer."

Augustina's parents were Orthodox and had not abandoned their practice of praying before the icons, but her father swore, smoked, drank vodka, "and there was never any peace in our family." They forbade her to join the Pioneers (the Party's organization for children) because it taught atheism, but they would not give her the reason for the prohibition, so she joined, and later the Komsomol (Young Communists).

She remembers how at school one Eastertime a teacher told the story of the Passion and the Resurrection and then said: "All this is a myth, an invented fairy tale," and made them sing mocking songs. But Augustina cried all the way home for the One who had hung on that cross. She asked her parents who was this Jesus Christ. They could not remember.

"Then why do you believe?"

"Everyone believes and we also believe," replied her mother. "We are not literate and do not know anything, but literate people believe also. Earlier there were many believers and they went to churches, and now there are no churches and the believers have hidden; they are few."

These childhood memories were in the back of her mind when Augustina and Peter discussed religion. This was dangerous ground for Soviet citizens. Peter says, "She knew it was something very important and interesting, but I said little and hid many matters because it is not possible to understand everything about God right away."

On New Year's Day 1949 they were married in a brief military ceremony before eight guests, and were given an apartment. Peter continued to lead Augustina very gently towards faith He had no Bible, for copies had become rarities in Stalin's Russia, but he explained what he could and she particularly liked some of the hymns he sang when no strangers could hear.

After fifteen months of married life they went on leave in April

1950. Peter's brothers, Ivan, now married, and Khariton, had settled in the newly developed coal mining area of Chernogorsk because Khariton, wounded in the right leg in the War, had been trained as a doctor's assistant (paramedical) and assigned to Mine 16. Peter and Augustina spent twelve days traveling by train from the Pacific Coast to Chernogorsk, having failed to secure tickets for a Trans-Siberian express, and arrived at Ivan's about 1:00 A.M. on 19 April 1950. They were shocked to learn that the very day previous, he and four other leading Baptists had been jailed after a show trial; Ivan had been given ten years in labor camps for preaching, and for encouraging the young to be believers.

This shook Peter, a comfortable secret Christian, while Augustina was deeply impressed. After three days they started for his home at Gorlovka in the mountains. With very few cars about they walked the 180 kilometers carrying their suitcases and staying where they could.

At Paul and Anna's, Augustina saw a Bible for the first time, and was fascinated by what she read. Paul could not spare his only copy so she memorized as much as she could in the few days they were home, before floating down the Kazyr river on a homemade raft to the railway and thence back to the Far East.

Peter had once exclaimed to Augustina, soon after they became acquainted, that he would never marry a member of the Komsomol (because Komsomols are required to be atheists; he had not told her the reason) but had changed his mind! She now stopped going to meetings, complaining that they always degraded the innocent while justifying the guilty, and that it was boring "because there is only discord." However, she had not become a Christian by 6 March 1951, the day that their first child, Lida, was born and Peter was demobilized.

For a further year they continued to live in Sovetskaya Gavan. In May 1952 Peter's parents left Gorlovka for good and moved northwestward to Chernogorsk to build a little house next door to Khariton and his young wife Anastasia (Styura) in the new settlement growing up at Mine 16. Peter's two sisters and their cousin Alexandra Lavrentovna had joined Khariton already. In September

Peter, Augustina and their baby left the Pacific coast to make their home there too. Peter found a job in Mine 16.

Thus in 1952, when Peter was twenty-six and Augustina twenty-three, they came to Chernogorsk, unaware of the discoveries, triumphs and persecutions ahead.

3

Chernogorsk Revival

CHERNOGORSK, THE CENTRAL setting of this story, means "Black Mountain," but its small coalfield was only developed after the Second World War. It lies in the hilly basin formed by the confluence of the Abakan and Yenisei rivers in southern Siberia and is almost surrounded by uplands of rolling steppe, and beyond them the mountains; the Sayan range to the south, where the tops are under snow except in high summer, is visible from fourth floors of the newer buildings.

Eighteen kilometers—approximately eleven miles—southwest of Chernogorsk is the larger and older city of Abakan on a promontory. Round it, on every side but the north, flows the Abakan river, swift, pure, and sparkling cold, straight from the mountains to join the mighty Yenisei, the world's fifteenth longest river, as it proceeds north to the Arctic Ocean. Beyond the Yenisei stands the important city of Minusinsk, famous for its museum in Tsarist times and in Stalin's for its prison, which would obtrude into the lives of the Seven.

Abakan is capital of the Khakassian autonomous region. The Khakassians are Turkic speakers of Mongolian type, whose women wear long dresses and colorful embroidered blouses; they twist their

Map 2 Krasnoyarsk Territory

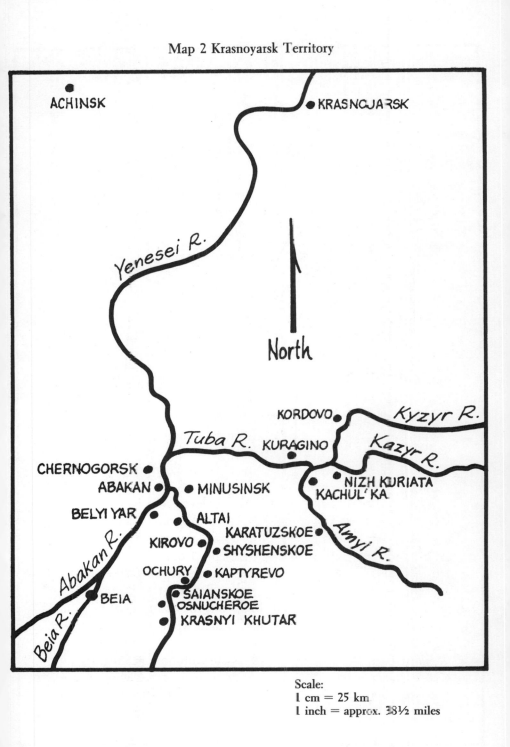

Scale:
1 cm = 25 km
1 inch = approx. 38½ miles

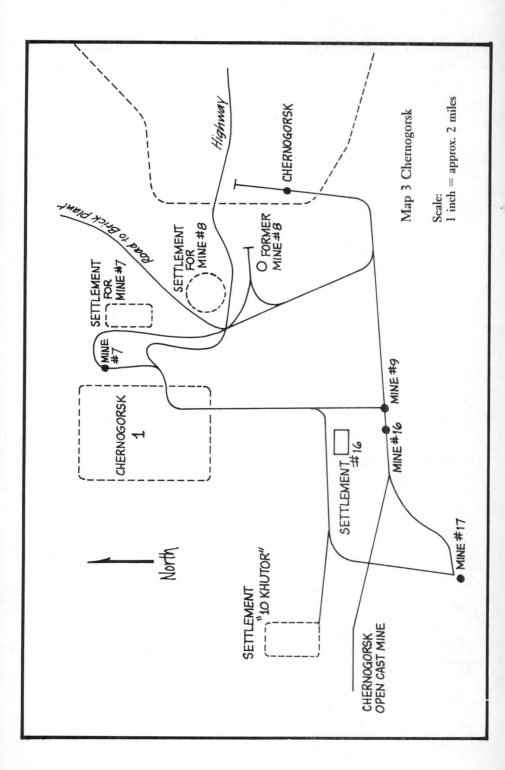

North

Road to Brick Plant

SETTLEMENT FOR MINE #7

SETTLEMENT FOR MINE #8

Highway

CHERNOGORSK

○ FORMER MINE #8

MINE #7

CHERNOGORSK 1

MINE #9

MINE #16

SETTLEMENT #16

MINE #17

SETTLEMENT "10 KHUTOR"

CHERNOGORSK OPEN CAST MINE

Map 3 Chernogorsk

Scale:
1 inch = approx. 2 miles

straight jet-black hair into high coils, and delight in beads and large earrings The main population of Chernogorsk is Russian, and when Ivan and Khariton Vashchenko went to live there in 1948, most of their neighbors had not come by choice. The mines were being opened up by convicts and victims of forced migration. One large camp housed the *banderevtsi*, expelled from the Ukraine and the Volga region after the Nazi retreat. Another had prisoners given twenty-five years for political crimes, and others held men and women serving varied sentences. Japanese prisoners of war, rounded up by Stalin's nine-day excursion which stripped Manchuria between the dropping of the atomic bomb and the surrender, lived in yet another camp. They were always cold, hungry and listless and used to be slapped by the Russian women workers underground. All except shorter term prisoners had left by the time Peter and Augustina arrived in 1952.

Mine 9, the biggest and deepest, later renamed the Yenisei Mine, had a vertical shaft. Another mine was open-cast, and the rest were reached by inclines from the surface. Most of these were worked out during the period covered by this story. The mines still used primitive equipment when Peter first went underground, and were dangerous to health because of accidents. They were bitterly cold in winter and the pay was small.

Contrary to widespread Western belief about Siberia, much of the countryside surrounding Chernogorsk is beautiful, including forested ravines, and high cliffs above one bank of the Abakan river and above the Yenisei, and the artificial lake for hydroelectricity, known as the Krasnoyarsk Sea; in 1969 the dam broke and flooded much of Abakan. The climate was pleasant enough when the Vashchenkos first settled; in Tsarist times indeed the basin was known as "Siberia's granary" or "Siberia's Italy," for its climate and crops.

The disastrous Virgin Lands scheme changed the climate for the worse after 1955 because they plowed the steppes, avoiding the numerous burial mounds of the old nomad chieftains, and did not plant trees except in the cities. The soil blew away in the winds from the west, and the absence of vegetation brought droughts; despite numerous rivers, water is poorly distributed and the people suffer shortages. The soil cracks from heat in summer and from deep frost in winter when the winds blow away the snow, and always the coal dust hangs in the air.

Chernogorsk city grew steadily. Most of the buildings had one story, wooden or brick, but concrete blocks of four or five stories were built as the years went by, with parks and a square. The main street, Soviet Street, has a pleasant lane of acacia shade trees down the center, with benches. At first the free miners all lived in the city. Then settlements *(poselki)* started near each mine. At Mine 16 Settlement, twelve kilometers (seven and a half miles) west, Khariton Vashchenko built his home. There were only two streets, First Line and Second Line. Khariton and Styura built on First Line. Ivan's wife had returned to her village near Gorlovka after his imprisonment, and he rejoined her there on his release, but the Vashchenko sisters, Natasha and Maria, lived with the Kharitons.

It was to First Line Street at Mine 16 that the Vashchenko parents, Paul and Anna, came to live early in 1952, followed in September by Peter and Augustina.

*   *   *

Chernogorsk church life had been nearly extinguished by the clampdown after the trial and imprisonment of Ivan and the other preachers. There was no Orthodox church nearer than Minusinsk, though a few Baptists would creep away to Abakan where a prayer house, as Baptist church buildings are called, had been registered by the State under the usual severe conditions, and drew about two hundred people from a wide area of surrounding villages and towns. Others stopped meeting and some of the younger believers had left the church altogether. It was the same everywhere; even Paul and Anna upcountry at Gorlovka had ceased to hold regular services in the later days of Stalin's repression, since most of the family were scattered and to believe openly brought dangers indeed.

By the time Peter brought his family to live at Chernogorsk his father had begun regular meetings again, the only open Christian witness on the Chernogorsk coal field. At first there were merely ten adult Vashchenkos, including Peter's older sister Natasha, now in her late thirties. In the days when faith had grown cold at Gorlovka she had married an unbeliever and had a daughter, Katia. Her husband had tried to force her to drink and dance; he beat her, there had been "tremendous scenes," says Peter, and the man divorced her and married again. Natasha and her Katia lived with Paul.

Augustina attended the Christian services as she lived in the house where they were held. Nor was this simple politeness; Paul's Bible had become her favorite reading. She pored over it, and compared its teaching with the lying, fighting, selfishness and drunkenness so common among unbelievers all around. She longed to know the secret of Paul's gentle Christian character and to unravel the mysteries of life and, tells Peter, "The Bible answered all her questions." In her own words: "In January 1953, I came to the Lord and repented."

Grigory Vashchenko at this time, with his young wife Olga from a Baptist family,[1] lived about four hundred kilometers (two hundred forty-odd miles) northwest on the Trans-Siberian railway; he had been a miner in Chernogorsk with his cousins but had left after the death of his firstborn; they now had another baby, Alexander. Their city of Anzhero-Sudzhensk was a center of the Pentecostal church, which thrived there despite Stalin, and Grigory had joined it and had been "baptized in the Spirit" like his mother Fekla long before. Peter's sisters Natasha and Maria went to stay with him, and when they returned to Chernogorsk early in 1953 they too had been baptized in the Spirit.

Thenceforth their supreme delight was Christ. Maria, with her dark grey eyes and rather reserved ways, did not talk much but she lived so openly for him that in April 1953 Augustina was baptized in the Spirit also; she began to "speak in other tongues," the "language of prayer." Peter did not oppose but did not follow

---

1. Ivan's wife, Panna, is from the more conservative branch of the Russian Orthodox Church.

her. Then Grigory brought his family back to Chernogorsk in the summer of 1953 and got a job in the mines. Peter and he together built near Paul's a one-story *zalivnaia* or "poured" house: they mixed clay with straw and poured it between boards. When one row dried they moved the boards upwards and poured in another. It was only 23 x 16 feet (approximately) and six feet high, with two south facing windows; the Grigory Vashchenkos lived in one half and the Peter Vashchenkos in the other, with a party wall.

Grigory was twenty-five. He had light brown hair, blue eyes and a thin face. Like his father he was a man of intensity inclined to be grave; he had that touch of steel needed by Peter, who was moved by his cousin's words and the change in Augustina and his sisters. A day came in 1954 when Peter read the passage in Acts 19 where the Apostle Paul meets some disciples at Ephesus and asks, "Did you receive the Holy Spirit when you believed?" And they say, "No, we have never even heard that there is a Holy Spirit." Those twelve men had been baptized with water by John's baptism of repentance. Paul then preaches the One who was to come after John, that is, Jesus; whereupon they are baptized in the name of the Lord Jesus. "And when Paul had laid his hands upon them, the Holy Spirit came on them; and they spoke with tongues and prophesied."

Peter says: "I prayed in this manner and received the Holy Spirit and now I pray in other tongues as it is written in God's Word in Mark 16:17: 'And these signs shall follow them that believe; In my name shall they cast out devils; they shall speak with new tongues.'" In the words of one of his favorite hymns, Christ's boundless love caught fire in his heart.

Peter sees his experience in strictly biblical terms. He had been a disciple since childhood but now he was born again, "born of the Spirit," by that new birth which Jesus spoke about to Nicodemus. The coming of the Spirit who guides into all truth, as Christ told the Eleven in the upper room, and the pouring out of the gifts of the Spirit which are folly to the men of the world, as described by Paul in 1 Corinthians 2, were likewise part of Peter's renewal. The gift of tongues being part of it, Peter henceforth used this "language of prayer," but he does not judge, as being less Christian, those who do not speak with tongues, for the Apostle says: "There are varieties of gifts, but the same Spirit. . . . Do all speak with tongues?" And, with the Apostle, he recognizes the importance of reaching an unbeliever in words easily understood, until "the secrets of his heart are disclosed; and so, falling on his face, he will worship God and declare that God is really among you." [2]

In the late autumn of 1954 Peter and Augustina went to Anzhero-Sudzhesk and were baptized by the Pentecostal pastor in a river. It was a frosty day and particles of ice floated on the water, so that the shock of total immersion emphasized the symbolism of the drowning of the old life and the rising again to the new.

By now there were some twenty-five to thirty believers meeting together at Mine 16 Settlement. Timid Baptists had emerged from secrecy, and imprisoned Baptists, following the death of Stalin, were returning from hard labor. The Vashchenko family had made a practice of visiting the local prison camps (closed down since then in the Chernogorsk area) with packages of food and clothes for any Christians whom they discovered. Thus they became acquainted with a young man from the Ukraine who, on his release in 1955, as a voluntary settler to work in the mines, married Maria, Peter's younger sister; later he was sentenced to exile for conscientious objection against service in the armed forces, and she followed him until they settled again at Chernogorsk.

Meanwhile, the elderly Baptist pastor from Abakan suggested that those who spoke in tongues had better meet separately from those who did not. Grigory was elected pastor, and thus the Vashchenkos and their friends ceased to be Evangelical Christians Baptists (members of the united sects formed by the union of

---

2. 1 Corinthians 12:4, 30; 14:25. *Glossolalia*, or speaking in tongues, has become familiar in the great denominations throughout the world since the rise of the charismatic movement, whether personally practiced or not. Therefore I do not discuss its place in Christian tradition.

1944) and became Pentecostals or, as the denomination is called in Russian, *Khristiane Evangelskoi very* (literally, "Christians of Evangelical Faith").

They were Christians first and Pentecostals second. Russia has always had its fringe of sects with peculiar views and practices, and Peter certainly would meet some odd believers when he was in prison, but the Pentecostals of Chernogorsk were firmly within the cornerstones of authentic Christian tradition and theology. They carried over several Orthodox customs such as the Watchnight on Easter Eve until dawn is marked by joyful Resurrection hymns and the ancient greeting and answer: "Christ is risen! . . . He is risen indeed!" They were young, mostly in their twenties or early thirties, a standing denial of the well-worn Soviet claim that only old women believe. Youthfulness and inexperience led a few to strange ideas, but the leadership sifted and rejected whatever was unbiblical.

They could secure no books of theology or devotion, no commentaries, and a family was fortunate to possess more than one Bible. Yet that Bible they studied and learned until it became the dominant intellectual force in their minds, the lamp to their path and the light which showed up the falsehoods of the Soviet propaganda surrounding them.

They had radios and listened avidly to Christian programs in Russian from missions such as the Far East Broadcasting Company transmitting by shortwave from Manila. As the years went by, programs came in from Sweden, Korea and North America. Many Soviet citizens listen to the Voice of America; believers listen also to exposition and evangelism and all the range of Gospel song and sermon, a spiritual lifeline which constant jamming cannot spoil.

The congregation grew steadily until they had a roll of about two hundred by 1961. It was a singing church, with that marvelous sense of harmony which is native to Russians. Small children and their grandparents, and the young marrieds who formed the majority came to the frequent and unhurried meetings ("without which we would die spiritually") and spent almost as long in singing as at prayer or listening to sermons. They used metrical psalms and a wide range of hymns and sang "How Great Thou Art" when it was still almost unknown in the West.[3] The sound floated out towards the mines, a proof that years of atheist propaganda and violent suppression of belief could not quench the Spirit.

And who could not be touched by the harmony of unaccompanied voices, from deep bass to high treble, as these miner families sang in the slow, measured tempo usual to Russian church music?

> *Help me to rest my weight on You, depend*
> *On Him who suffered as the sinner's Friend,*
> *Whose cross for me sufficed;*
> *Whom now I love, whose love I freely share,*
> *Happy indeed to follow You, and bear*
> *The easy yoke of Christ.*[4]

It was a pastorally minded church. Old Paul, and Grigory and Peter, and the four young sons of a Lutheran widow were particularly to the fore in this, spending hours with new believers. The coming of the Spirit had given a strong urge to evangelize, and the church grew fast until the Great Persecution. Atheists became Christians, such as the young wife next door to Peter and Augustina; she used to take refuge with them when her husband was drunk and abused her, or vodka parties grew violent. Two notorious drunks became notable converts. However, Grigory's brother-in-law resisted the gospel and made his wife's life a misery until he died in an accident in the mine, splitting his head on a hacking machine, leaving her with six children.

A vivid description of the Chernogorsk church is given by Evgeny Bresenden, a young believer from Nakhodka in the Soviet Far East who in 1975 became one of the very few Pentecostals allowed to emigrate. He had visited the city ten times and was a close friend

---

3. The English version published in 1948, and not well known before 1955, was a translation from the Russian, itself translated from the German in 1912. "How Great Thou Art" was originally written in Swedish in 1885.

4. The last verse of "I Want to Follow You," English paraphrase kindly written for this book by Timothy Dudley-Smith.

of Grigory Vashchenko. "I was always amazed by their hospitality and their cordiality," writes Bresenden. "They are mostly very poor people. However, they are capable of giving the last of what they have for those who visit them and who labor in some church work. I would say that their type of life in many ways is like the early apostolic church which held all things in common."

Grigory's wartime youth after his parents' deaths with starvation never far away, had taught him, says Bresenden, "a rule in his life and in the lives of his flock, to help those in need not just when you have something extra, but to give away the last even if there is nothing left for yourself." He taught that a believer's life must be a contrast to the unbeliever's in everything, and love must be shown to all, and close communion be kept with God and with each other.

Chernogorsk became renowned for dedication, willingness to bear sorrow and suffering, and for love. Looking back on the years of persecution which followed the revival, Bresenden goes so far as to say that "the believers in Chernogorsk are more active and zealous in their preaching amidst unbelievers and are more steadfast under persecution than the believers of other cities of the USSR. I have heard repeatedly from various cities of reports that they deserve to be imitated in their staunchness and zealousness for God. Believers often come to this city and have a look at their form of Christian life."

*   *   *

Among the new believers were Maria Petrovna Chmykhalov, one of the Siberian Seven in the Embassy in 1978; her husband, Peter; and all her own family, the Makarenkos.

Maria was born in 1922, the second child of two illiterate peasants who had met and married in Siberia before the Revolution; her father had been born in the southern Ukraine and her mother near Kursk. Despite little education, Maria has described her early life in great detail, and recounted her parents' stories about theirs, in her autobiography which I hope to edit and publish later. The present book has space only to summarize.

She had been brought up near Ochury in the countryside south of Chernogorsk during the terrible times of hunger and distress. After brief schooling she worked in a grain warehouse. Her younger sister Anna had come to the Chernogorsk coal mines in 1943, about the time their father died, and Maria had joined her in February 1946, getting a job below ground in Mine 9, as a *motoriskaya* who operates the conveyor belts which carry the coal from the face.

Maria's parents had not been religious but she had been brought up strictly, with such strong principles derived from the Christian ethic that even before her conversion the miners nicknamed her "the Baptist." She recalls praying in times of distress when she was young, and there was a period in the grain warehouse when she contemplated suicide until a kindly janitor and his wife lent her their New Testament; reading it held her back.

In the early years at the mine from 1946 to '48, when food and clothing were desperately short in Chernogorsk, she frequently prayed to God that she might die. Then she made a happy marriage in 1950 to a man four years her junior, a war veteran and miner called Peter (or Petro) Chmykhalov.[5]

By 1954 the Chmykhalovs had a girl and a boy and were living in a house they had built themselves, 40 Twentieth Khakassian Year Street, in the Mine 9 Settlement. This settlement was nearest to the city and gradually grew into a township, renamed Chernogorsk 1; there is now only a brief bus ride of countryside between the two built-up areas. Maria's mother, Mrs. Makarenko, and the two younger sisters, Anna and Katia, lived with them; Katia later married a man who had been crippled in the mine.

It was Katia, then aged twenty-three, who was the first to go to the church meetings. Next she tried to get Anna to come. "Anna," tells Maria, "made fun of her, and Mother did not want to go at all; she had a brother who was a Baptist and she went when she lived with them, and she said that things were worse

---

5. To save confusion with the principal Peter in the story (Vashchenko) I will normally call Chmykhalov *Petro*, a form which Maria frequently uses herself.

with them than with the atheists. All the same, my husband and I got interested and we went to a meeting with Katia to listen. And we liked it very much. And Petro and I decided to serve God."

Maria can still recall the details of that meeting. People gathered at the appointed home as soon as they were free from work and had washed and fed; several were present already when the Chmykhalovs entered. During this preliminary period Grigory Vashchenko read aloud from the Scriptures, a few prayed, others talked quietly among themselves, but gossip among the women was discouraged: "Go outside for your chat and then come back!" And to the men he would say, "Come earlier and talk things out before the meeting."

When enough had arrived, with others squeezing into the room for quite a while, the service proper began with two hymns: "Tell me, Savior, to Whom shall I go?" and "Long I Wandered in Spiritual Gloom." Someone read a passage of Scripture and then Grigory expounded the sixth chapter of Romans, with its great conclusion: "The wages of sin is death; but the gift of God is eternal life through Jesus Christ our Lord."

After this first sermon everyone knelt for prayer, praying individually and simultaneously as in their homes, with the preacher continuing after others ceased and then leading them in the Lord's Prayer. Next came a hymn urging repentance, followed by another which voices the penitent's cry: "In Your love and mercy hear the plea of my soul."

A full hour had now passed but no one wished to leave. The babies slept peacefully, held in a cocoon of swaddling clothes by their mothers, and the smaller children tried not to fidget. Another preacher—perhaps Paul or Peter Vashchenko or his brother-in-law, the ex-prisoner—preached from Isaiah 12: "Behold, God is my salvation; I will trust and not be afraid," linking it with verses from 1 John 3: "Hereby perceive we the love of God: because he laid down his life for us."

Once again they prayed as before, then sang a hymn seated:

"Christ's Church is a gathering of those redeemed by the Cross, Who have found forgiveness from the burden of sin." Its last line was a prayer: "Accept me like a son, O God, into the Church." They sang a closing hymn of praise, of gratitude for salvation and for all that Christ brings: "We belong to You, Lord, with all our soul."

The time now was late, and since their meeting was unlawful in the Soviet Union, they remained standing a little longer to thank God for his protection, before sitting down for conversation and counseling.

Maria comments: "The service made a big impact on us. The explanations by the brethren who preached, and the singing of the hymns, deeply touched our sinful souls, that the Savior had redeemed us at such a costly price with his sufferings and that he did so for us all; that he forgives all our sins and promises to give us peace and salvation. And therefore we surrendered fully to Christ, and soon afterwards accepted water baptism. From that time we have tried to keep his commandments although we often transgress, sin and fall, but with God's help we stand up and go ever forward."

The Chmykhalovs received the baptism of the Spirit. Before 1954, had ended, all Maria's family had joined the church—Anna soon; then Mrs. Makarenko in her sixty-first year, who watched the change in her daughters and followed them into faith. Their eldest sister became a believer and their brother, Alexander; but his wife resisted and made his life a misery until she too became a Christian. In 1956 Alexander was accidentally killed at the mine face.

*   *   *

One Sunday in 1955 Peter Vashchenko was using his motorcycle to transport candidates for baptism to a lake about eighteen kilometers (about eleven miles) away. The road passed Mine 17 which was being built at the time and was guarded by dogs. Peter was returning alone to fetch another candidate when a dog ran out and made for his legs and he swerved into a pole. A passing car rescued him, and he could not work in the mine for weeks while his foot was in plaster.

It had been difficult enough to keep a growing family on one wage and since this now stopped, Augustina sought work. She was taken on at Mine 15 as an assistant blaster and did fifteen days' technical training. When the manager learned that she did not wish to join the "voluntary" trade union, which would involve her in atheist reeducation classes, he refused to take her on—and did not pay her for the fifteen days. The family survived by selling milk from their cow until Peter could go back to work, this time at Mine 7: working underground he had been variously coal hewer and loader, bore hole driller, and motor mechanic for conveyor equipment.

They now had three girls. Lida had been followed by Lyubov in 1952 (the name means *Love*, and her diminutive is Lyuba), then Nadezhda in 1954 *(Hope*, whose diminutive is Nadya). In 1956 came Vera *(Faith)* so that they had Faith, Hope and Love. Their fifth child, in July 1957, was again a girl, whom they christened Lilia (Lila).

"Each new child was greeted with joy," recalls Lida. "Mother would sometimes say that they already had enough children, but father would calm her and say it didn't matter. He did not mind that the first five were girls and sometimes when he played with one he would call her 'my little boy.' Mother would laugh, but Peter would say it didn't matter. But he was very happy when his first son was born. All of us children wanted to name him Sasha, and that is what he was named."

Sasha, or to give him his formal name, Alexander, was born on 7 April 1959, and his mother fell seriously ill soon afterwards. Eight-year-old Lida took charge. Once when Sasha had been crying so lustily that Lida was reduced to tears, her mother took him as she sat weakly in the rocking chair. "She said: 'Lida, if I suddenly die, what would you do with Sasha?' Apparently, she wanted to see what I would say. I thought for a long time and then I said: 'If you die I will not allow them to bury you. You will lie there and lie there, get tired of that, and get up! Sasha will cry and we will too, and you don't want to die.' Such a conception of death amused her, and she began to explain that you do not get up when you die."

When Augustina recovered her health they decided to live in Chernogorsk city. Peter left the mines in 1959 at the age of thirty-three to work at the automobile factory. Selling his share in the house he had built, he had just enough to buy a small house on Airfield Street, built with bricks of earth and straw—one story, five windows, simply a kitchen-living room and a bedroom. To the children's delight the new home had a little garden planted with rennet apple trees. The Khariton Vashchenkos moved next door and the brothers made a wicket gate between the gardens, where both families played outside all day in summer. The children planted their own flower beds and Peter built a swing under a lean-to, so that they could still play when it rained.

The purchase price had left Peter nothing for new furniture. They were hard put to make ends meet. The saying in the Soviet Union is, "If you don't steal you can't live." A believer, who by his faith may not deceive or cheat or embezzle, and has a growing family to support on his wages alone, will be poor, and must depend on the truth of the Scripture, "My God shall supply all your need. . . ." The parents fasted often as they brought needs before God in prayer, but each evening after his work and their play, Peter and Augustina formed the children into a joyful choir and Peter would read the Bible to them.

Despite poverty, these years were wonderful, with a vigorous faith and a spreading revival. The local press put out the occasional slander which, as in propaganda articles from any part of the Soviet Union, accused the believers of tying their children to beds with wire and thrashing them, or forbidding them to play, or throwing babies under trains, or putting out the lights at meetings to make love in the dark, so that conceptions often were incestuous. Apart from this dreary run of nonsense the authorities interfered little during the later 1950s.

Then, around 1960, far away in the Kremlin, Khrushchev awoke to the fact that Christianity, which by Marxist-Leninist theory should have withered away, had spread rapidly in many parts of the Soviet Union. He began to tighten the screw.

In Chernogorsk the first sign was a demand that the Pentecostal church should register with the State, as the Baptists in the city had registered and were allowed a prayer house. Registration involved acceptance of stringent conditions.

Grigory, Paul and the other church members looked at the list of these conditions, such as the limitations on who may preach and what he may preach and for how long; and the requirement to report visitors to the authorities. Then they saw one condition which so appalled them that they did not bother to discuss the rest.

If they registered, they must not let their children join the church before the age of eighteen and must never organize special meetings for them—a condition, they felt, which ran counter to the Word of God and the duty of a Christian parent.

The virile, young and expanding Pentecostal church of Chernogorsk rejected registration.

With prayer they awaited events.

Part Two

"THE STRIFE IS FIERCE"

4

The Great Persecution

In the spring of 1961 Grigory Vashchenko and his assistant pastor, Andrei Miller, were arrested.

While they were held in jail under investigation, the head of the KGB (the political or State security police) in Chernogorsk, Ivan Romanovich Ikonnikov, summoned various believers to the procurator's office and ordered them to give evidence against the accused at the forthcoming trial. All refused. Ikonnikov fined some and forced others to clean trash holes in the city.

Khariton Vashchenko, who suffered from bronchial asthma, was not summoned for investigation but they stripped him of h s military pension and ordered his wife, Styura, although nursing a baby, to clean sidewalks for fifteen days, unpaid. She worked ten, then fell ill and refused to do more, saying they could put her on trial if they wished.

When Grigory's and Andrei's case came on at last, this first trial of believers since Ivan's in 1950 created such public interest that the court convened in the *Mir* (Peace, or World) Cinema, and loudspeakers carried the proceedings to an overflow crowd outside. Grigory was senior presbyter of the unregistered Pentecostals for the whole vast Krasnoyarsk Territory and had encouraged and founded many churches. He received a sentence of ten years: two to be in prison, three in labor camp and five in exile. Andrei received less but his sufferings affected his hearing; he had been choirmaster of the church but on his release he could not resume the post.

Persecution now began in full measure.

On a sunny Sunday morning some seventy believers of all ages were at worship, crowded into a little house in Settlement 7. The sermon had begun. Suddenly Sokolov, the mine rescue and fire brigade chief, pushed his way in. "Disperse!" he yelled. "Disperse!" No one moved. "I declare war on you!" he shouted, and waddled out—he had a decided paunch. The congregation began to sing and pray.

A few moments later the wall nearest the road, though within a little garden, shook with an impact so severe that the glass fell out of the window frames with a crash, plaster showered down, a crack appeared, and a mirror and framed texts such as "God is Love" fell to the floor: Sokolov had ordered the mine rescue truck to ram the place.

The believers thought this would be all and continued their service, grateful at least that the excitement had drawn a crowd of neighbors within sound of the preaching and singing; but after several minutes they heard the howl of a siren and a fire engine drove up. Trampling over the vegetable beds, where the seeds had not yet sprouted, firemen quickly uncoiled their hoses and removed the frame of the unbroken window. Children screamed as powerful jets flooded the room indiscriminately, and brethren jumped up to block the empty window spaces with their backs, though the force of the water inflicted painful bruises so that they took this punishment in turns; as one man staggered, another replaced him.

"Then another fire engine pulled up," recalls Peter Vashchenko. "The children wailed and choked from the cold water. Several nonbelievers began to shout at the firemen: 'Why are you doing this? Don't you realize these are living people?' Others enjoyed it and laughed. They said: 'They need it. Don't let them pray.' When they had emptied one fire engine, the second refused to soak the people, but drove off. No matter what, no one left the house while they shot in the water, and when they had gone we all went outside and quickly dried out in the sun. We went back into the house to thank the Lord that he had given us the strength to persevere and not to grow afraid of this violence. Of course they thought when they were soaking us that we would run out of the house, but not a soul ran out.

"The next Sunday the authorities took different measures. The church service was at another apartment and during the service the mine rescue squad arrived under Sokolov's command. They began to shout and disturb the meeting, but no one paid any attention. Then one of them went to the front, stood for a little bit, and waved his hand. In a few seconds tears began to roll out of everyone's eyes and our noses to itch. But no one left. They began forcibly to drag out those people in the back who were on their knees, saying, 'Get on out, can't you see you are choking?' and several of them cursed us freely. (There would always be about fifteen who came to disperse us, until they realized that they weren't achieving anything.) Everyone was on their knees praying. Some were dragged out and forced to get into a vehicle. They were taken to the police. Those who were left came out of the house and for a long time could not look at the sunlight because each person was crying so.

"Those who were taken away were detained until dark and then allowed home. The householder and his family were unable to live in the house for three days; as they did not know what sort of powder it was, they had swept it into the cellar and from there its effects could still be felt; they just could not live in the house."

Persecution had begun throughout the Soviet Union. Unknown to the West, Khrushchev's government intended to destroy the churches within ten years as hindrances to total socialism. For the time being, the brunt would fall on unregistered groups, and in Chernogorsk, I. R. Ikonnikov of the KGB carried out the order with zeal. Tall, dark-haired, "he was not afraid of anyone," says Maria Chmykhalov. "What he wanted to do he did." He arrived at one meeting in Khlebozavod ("Bread Factory") Street with a bus, interrupted the service and ordered all believers to get on it,

"But no one moved from their places," writes Peter Vashchenko. "Everyone was on their knees in prayer. Then he gave the order to seize us by the arms and drag us outside to the bus. If someone resisted they took hold of his arms and legs and dragged him outside. They were put in the bus and taken to the police," who levied a stiff fine on the preacher and the host, lesser fines on the rest. This fining became a regular practice. Nor was that all. One meeting place was a home near the cemetery. When the service finished the worshipers had to run a gauntlet of town thugs wielding wooden crosses looted from old graves while others screamed abuse.

At another meeting KGB henchmen drove up with a freight truck, and seized all the young people, including several girls, and the older men who were nearest the door, and forced them to crawl into the back of the truck; the recalcitrant were thrown in bodily. The truck drove off with about forty, and though a few of the men jumped out as it drove slowly through the city, the rest were taken far into the countryside where the first was pushed out about fifteen kilometers away, and the rest one by one at intervals. Since night was coming, each victim sensibly walked in the direction the truck had gone until almost all were reunited, and gave thanks to God together before trudging back to the city. But two girls, dropped the farthest, got lost and did not arrive home until morning.

By now the authorities had stirred up the local populace against the believers. "Reeducation" lecturers in their regular sessions at mines and factories taught the workers that believers were enemies to socialism, agents of imperialism, that they were deluded, even clinically mad; they must be struggled against. The populace had no means to assess this, for apart from illicit overseas broadcasts the Soviet citizen has virtually no news or information uncontrolled by the State, which shapes it to conform to Party dogma.

The people of Chernogorsk therefore harassed the church. An open window in summer attracted youths who threw in rolls of burning celluloid film or magnetic tape, which did not blaze but smoldered with a choking smoke; believers threw them out. Yet, recalls Lida Vashchenko, who was then a girl of ten, 'if we shut the windows the people would knock on them from the street. Again they would be opened, and then they screamed and made fun of those trying to preach, especially if any had a physical defect. Wherever there was to be a meeting they would stand around, and, as the Christians arrived, call them fools, and throw stones and spit."

Her father takes up the story: "On our religious holy day of Easter in 1962 Ikonnikov arrived with five other people during a church service and began to rip Bibles and hymnbooks out of the hands of the preacher. He then tipped the table on which were resting books and psalteries and everything fell on the floor. He stopped the service and, having chased people outside, forced several to sweep the street."

*   *   *

The Chmykhalovs have equally harrowing memories of the Great Persecution and of Ivan Romanovich Ikonnikov. At a Bread Factory Street meeting he arrived with a detachment of armed workers. Maria remembers him dragging her sister, Anna Makarenko, by the sleeve "until her dress ripped at the shoulder. My little daughter Nadya was clinging to Anna's hand and screamed. Ivan Romanovich swung his hand and hit my little daughter. This is just what happened.

"Early one Sunday morning I got up, milked the cow, and began to shoo her out to the herd. All of a sudden an ambulance pulls up to our place, the gate opens, and in walks Ivan Romanovich followed by a nurse. I asked him where he was going, for everyone was asleep. He pushed me aside and walked into the house. My mother and sister were sleeping in the entryway. He walked up to Anna's cot, grabbed hold of the blanket and jerked it off. Since Anna was sleeping with my little son Shura and did not know who had come in when he yanked the blanket, she grabbed hold of it because she only had her shirt on after a bath. He screamed: 'Get up!' Mamma got up, as did the children. There was noise.

The nurse came up to Anna: 'Come on, we will have a walk.' And my sister said to her: 'Why should I go for a walk with you?' She couldn't understand what was going on."

The nurse said that Anna was not right in the head. Realizing that they intended to remove her to a psychiatric hospital, the family argued with Ikonnikov and the nurse until they left without her.

At a meeting in Settlement 7 the mine rescue team "arrived in a van and opened war. They pulled some people by the collar, ripped the shirts of some, the sleeves of others. One person's dress hung loosely ripped. They even became so brazen as to take one woman's underpants off; a man pulled her by the head, and another pulled off her underpants and they put her in a car. Hymnbooks and Gospels were ripped out of hands. They knocked down benches and tipped over tables. Children screamed, but the meeting continued. This time they took us to the police and put us in jail. There were many such instances."

Released after paying their fines, Maria and another woman were walking to a meeting in the Mine 16 Settlement when they saw ahead a scrum of men milling around something or someone on the ground. "When we approached we found they were choking Oleg Igorevich. We screamed. They had already tied his hands behind his back with a belt and were choking him. When we intensified our screaming they abandoned him and we went to him. We arrived at the meeting. Andrei Vashchenko had been hit in the eye. Despite the knocking about they gave him he came with his black eye." Andrei, then twenty-three, had taken over as choirmaster and had a glorious voice.

A few of the weaker or more shallow members of the church ceased attendance; one or two, to cries of triumph from the KGB and the city soviet, openly renounced their faith. Evangelism grew more difficult but the large majority of the settled members, including teenagers and the younger men and women, stayed steadfast, meeting in small groups when necessary. Life became wretched materially as fines increased, jobs were scarce or refused, and wages arbitrarily reduced, but they rejoiced "that they were counted worthy to suffer shame for his name." This joy was not insensitive: they felt their sorrows acutely. In the phrases of a hymn they often sang, briars grew across their difficult path but something beckoned them on. They looked to Christ.

His Word was their support. If hymnbooks and Bibles or manuscript sheets of Scripture were confiscated or torn up, someone would recite a passage and give out the hymns line by line from memory, though in homes where the only Bible had gone to swell the basket in the KGB office, they felt the loss acutely.

In all this, no matter how many complaints they wrote to the Kremlin, there was never any answer or defense. Instead, the authorities began to take criminal proceedings against more of the leaders, putting them in prison three or four at a time. While the two months' investigation continued, the rest would prepare the next four to be arrested. Twenty-one in all went to prison camp or exile.

As leaders disappeared, others less able but no less valiant took their places. And thus came a Sunday in 1962 which the Chmykhalovs will never forget.

The meeting was in the home of a believer already in prison and Petro Chmykhalov had taken over, though he was not very literate. He was reading the Scriptures aloud, picking out the words slowly, with his two-year-old Shura sitting beside him, when Ikonnikov and his henchmen drove up in a van and sprang into the *izba.* He pushed people around, and tipped over the benches. The children screamed. He rushed up to the table and seized Petro by the throat as he read, and began to choke him and pull him outside. Shura started shouting and tried to pull away the ogre who manhandled his papa. As Maria, carrying baby Timothy, hurried into the passageway, Ikonnikov seized Shura, who screamed.

"Ivan Romanovich," cried Maria, "Is this allowed? Why are you choking him and frightening a child?"

He pulled Petro outside. Maria managed to get her foot over the threshold as he tried to shut the door. He swung his arm and hit her baby. The force of the blow sent her reeling but she redoubled her hold on Timothy and pressed him to her chest as she fell down. From the floor she tried to restrain Ikonnikov, and when she attempted to rise he shook her arm above the elbow and almost broke it; the doctor next day found it black.

Protected by his cocoon of swaddling clothes, Timothy was uninjured except for being stunned briefly. Maria struggled outside, where Ikonnikov was writing out summonses for the brethren. She went up to him. "Where do you have a law which allows you to beat a child like this?" she said.

"When the brethren were put into the vehicle," relates Maria, "and Ikonnikov was still shouting, there were many neighbors around. I walked by, got my son, and then put him down, and began to read the Gospel loudly. The windows were open and the people outside began to laugh at Ikonnikov and they said: 'See what he does to a woman!' Then he waved his arm and they took away the brethren. We who remained prayed, read, and when we had finished I gathered food and walked to the police station with the children." Here the doors were shut. She walked around, looking in at the windows, and the believers saw her and shouted. She gave them the food and went home. They were released the next day.

Almost every Sunday the first meeting was conducted with a battle. The KGB seldom interfered with the second service, which started after an interval spent in chatting or taking food while the young people made music. The church members felt they were winning this war.

Already, however, the authorities had begun to attack where believers were most vulnerable—the welfare and future of their children.

5

The State Steals the Children

Lida Vashchenko had started school at the normal age of seven in 1958.

The Soviet school system is deliberately, definitively atheist. A socialist, "scientfic atheist" philosophy and the Kremlin's view of the world are worked into each subject in the curriculum, creating a conflict of conscience for an intelligent Christian child at every turn. As the eldest and thus the first of the family to experience postwar education, Lida had the hardest time, but her next sister, Lyuba, puts it well: "It is very difficult to bear when at home it is one way and at school just the opposite. It is like a sudden change in the weather for a sick person." The teachers know who are the believer children and consider it a duty to destroy their faith.

Every humiliation and trick was legitimate. Vova Chmykhalov, for instance, was a bright boy who always got his sums right, but the teacher would mark him down a grade. His sister was put to shame by teachers who mockingly kneeled before her. Lida's cousin Valya, Khariton's eldest daughter, with a defiance which in retrospect looks a little pathetic in view of what happened to her faith, stood to ask God's blessing before a lesson. The pupils chanted,

"Pray Baby!" The teacher gently told her there was no God—he was invented by the landlords to make the serfs more docile. She forced her to recite a poem:

> No one gives us salvation,
> Not God, not the Tsar, not the Hero.
> We achieve freedom by ourselves.

The teacher said: "We wanted a revolution and we did it ourselves. God did not help us, nor did the Tsar, and you can't find a hero." (Stalin had been debunked and perhaps she took Lenin for granted; his picture dominated the classroom.)

Valya replied: "No! There is a God. And there is a Tsar."

"Who is the Tsar?" asked the teacher.

"Khrushchev!" In this Valya spoke truer than she knew but class and teacher derided her.

Her cousin Lida had a quick mind, but the teachers' campaign of "reeducation" and discrimination had an unsettling effect. And her father, unaware at first of these handicaps, punished her if she came back with low marks.

Peter Vashchenko took education seriously, all the more because his own had been checked by poverty and the unsettled state of the country. "Therefore," recalls Lida, "I left home for school as for an execution to which I was compelled to go, and came from school as to a place of punishment. . . . Several times I thought about throwing myself under a train because the line was on my way home. But evidently God saw my poor strength and said that He would not allow me to be tested above that which I was able to bear."

Peter was intelligent, if poorly educated, and his two greatest interests being the study of the Bible and the raising of his children, he always wanted to know what Lida learned. He would test it against the Bible, and steadily became more horrified. As Lida says, "There is a constant struggle between what the teacher is telling the children and what the parent is saying, and sometimes the teachers win." Peter was determined that they should not.

The battle raged fiercest at two points: the "voluntary" organizations; and the singing classes. The Little Octobrists and the Pioneers wearing red tie or scarf formed the first steps towards the Komsomol League and Communist Party membership, both of which require open loyalty to atheism. Believers looked on joining the Pioneers as putting Mammon before God, for no man can serve two masters; and the teachers, in their own way, saw this too. A Pioneer was more likely to abandon Christ. They put intense pressure on the girls to join.

As for the other center of conflict, Peter and Augustina and all the Vashchenkos loved singing, but the school sang in praise of Lenin, and the class struggle, and carrying rifles to push forward the power of the Soviets; sometimes the songs mocked God and Christ. Peter asked that his daughters Lida and Lyuba, and later Nadya, be excused. The school principal refused. Peter told the girls to stay out The teachers retaliated by ordering other pupils to hold them to their desks or even throw them to the floor. Or they tried trickery: a language class would be announced, and then swiftly changed to singing.

The girls tried hiding in the toilet, in winter jumping up and down to keep warm. If the class were last of the day, the teachers warned the cloakroom attendant not to issue their coats early. Lida arrived home one winter afternoon in nothing but her school uniform, almost frozen despite running all the way. Once Lyuba and Nadya ran off, and the other pupils gave chase and caught little Nadya. Another time the girls waited until the teacher turned to the blackboard and then dashed to the door and ran home.

Peter wrote to the ministry of education in Moscow to say he could not approve the songs and requesting the permission refused by the principal. The ministry replied that the Soviet Union had a single educational program which his children must follow.

By now Peter knew that this single program was atheistic at every turn, and he concluded, after special study and prayer, that Christ must come first: "He who loves father and mother more than me is not worthy of me; and he who loves son or daughter more than me is not worthy of me." If children or parents should suffer, Christ knew all about it. It was not accidental that his words about taking up the cross and following him were uttered in the context of the family.

Before New Year 1962 Peter and Augustina withdrew their three children of school age, to educate them at home. It was slightly easier for Lida because she had been in the hospital since November with swollen legs. At first the doctors had diagnosed a form of tuberculosis and isolated her until they found it to be rheumatism, which was not surprising since the school had not issued her with the usual free pair of *valenki* (felt boots) and she had to use rubber boots in the bitter cold. That was deliberate discrimination against a believer child, but when the Vashchenkos were not admitted to the school dining room for *pirogs* (a kind of filled bun) and broth and a hot drink, this arose simply from their being too poor to pay: a Soviet commentary on Marx's dictum, "From each according to his capacity, to each according to his need."

Lida's legs improved, she left the hospital, and Peter made her knee-high boots of sheepskin. After that he asked her, "Do you want to go to school?" She was afraid at first to say no, because he had punished her previously when she had tried to beg off; but now, "with great joy I received his permission not to go."

Peter also stopped accepting children's allowances, since the authorities stated plainly that these conferred on the State the right to direct the lives and thoughts of the children it thus subsidized.

Khariton and several other believer parents followed Peter's example in withdrawing. Maria Chmykhalov, who formed a little class in her house, remembers "those days of sore trial when we would not let our children go to school. I was not able to sleep at night, but pleaded to God constantly that he himself would help and defend my children, and guide me how I should act. After praying, I would walk up to the cots where they were sleeping and my heart would sink. I would see how peacefully and sweetly they slept, and I would stroke their heads. I passed many such sleepless nights. I would ask the Lord to help my precious treasures and to defend them for his glory so that my children could always glorify God and serve him of their own free will and freely love God." Her prayers were answered.

*   *   *

Teachers came round demanding every child's return. The city education department threatened to take Peter, Khariton and others to law; they would be deprived of parental rights and the children removed to an institution. On 28 February 1962 threat became fact for Peter and Augustina. Henceforth, in the eyes of the law, they were the parents no longer of Lida (eleven), Lyuba (ten) and Nadya (seven). The children were wards of the Soviet Union until the age of sixteen, to be brought up according to Marxist-Leninist dogma.

Policemen arrived at Airfield Street to take the three little girls to an institution, and searched all over the house in vain. Peter had made a hideout.

He had blocked up a narrow passage between two basement rooms which were little more than store places and made an entrance from a different room. He sealed it up with skins and made it warm and very comfortable. "The only trouble was," recalls Lida, "that it was gravelike. We slept there with the boards open and if they came to search in the night my parents would cover us up and we would sleep peacefully while the search took place. Sometimes we would wake up and it seemed that our hearts were beating so loudly that they must hear them upstairs. If they came in daytime we would sit there frozen with terror. The memory of it makes me shiver all over."

In daytime the girls could not play outside the house, for the police had told neighbors to report them at once. While it was winter this mattered little for they had the run of the home. A younger brother or sister kept guard by the window while the girls ate, or played with the others. If the guard shouted *"Bobik!"* (police car) the girls dropped whatever they were doing and rushed to their hiding place, secure while police searched rooms, basement and the outside storage areas.

Once police carried out two searches one after the other, hoping the family would be tricked and the girls emerge, which they did. But the "guards" went to their places by the windows and yelled: "Police!" The girls disappeared. "The police ran from room to room and searched everywhere," recalls Lyuba. "One policeman said: 'They are not needles, we will find them!' He looked under a child's bed and caught sight of a child's foot—it was my brother Sasha's—and he dragged him out frightened and crying. They were not able to find us this time no matter how hard they tried."

In March 1962, shortly before the birth of Jacob, Augustina's eighth, Peter sent the three girls to friends far out in the country, Lida to one village and the other two to another where no one knew them and the police showed no interest. Augustina soon found that a new baby and four children under six were hard to handle without her faithful "nanny," and at the end of May Peter brought Lida home secretly. The children played with Khariton's children and Lida took care not to go beyond the two gardens and at first no one noticed. Then her sisters begged to be allowed home briefly to see the new baby.

On June 15 they were all together again. "Day passed into evening," writes Lida, "and mother let us play outside. We went under the awning. Here we began to play and did not notice how time passed. A small boy arrived . . . and quickly left. Apparently he had been sent there specially by those people who were trying to follow us. A police car drove up and the police literally burst into the yard. There were many children—eight from our children and six from Uncle Khariton's. Lyuba and Nadya took off. One went between the legs of a policeman; the other under a policeman's arm, and managed to jump down into the hideout and cover up, but my way there was cut off; they had already closed it up anyway and wouldn't have opened it.

"Therefore, I ran to the cow's shed and crawled into a hollow— there was a box there and I managed to crawl under it except for one leg which I did not get under in time. A policeman jumped on my leg and grabbed it. I screamed and all the rest came and they took me."

*　　*　　*

In the Abakan Children's Detention Center,[1] an old building with crumbling walls, Lida was standing by a window on a midsummer evening. She was eleven years old. "It was a very difficult period of my life. I had always lived with my parents before and now I was with strangers. I did not try to find friends because I spent my days in secret loneliness for my home, and in tears. For me it was as if I had been buried alive.

"That evening the horizon was red from the last rays of the sun sinking into the distance. A little radio was hanging on the wall and a man was singing a song. At first I paid no attention because all my thoughts were about home, but little by little I began to listen. I have often relived these moments of homesickness and the words and melody of this song have always stayed with me, because many times I have been deprived of the joy of my home, poor though it was. This song was etched into my memory for a lifetime."

It was the song of an exile who is watching a flock of wild geese or cranes fly over the steppe as if "homeward to my beloved native fields." The singer yearns to have wings to join them, "to fly to the home where I lived and grew up"; he would give his soul to do "what my heart so longs." The birds fly in a flock, the exile is utterly alone.

> *My geese, my cranes, my brothers!*
> *O carry my song to my home!*
> *If only you knew my sorrow*
> *When torn away from the flock.*

"I too was torn from the flock and it was difficult to survive this period. I envied the little ones who had the opportunity to

---

1. *Detsky Priemnik:* a temporary holding place for children removed from their homes for some reason, criminal or civil, or temporarily without accommodation. Several might be awaiting trial for alleged offenses, others might be orphans on their way to an institution or have been removed from their parents as Lida had been.

be with their parents and I wondered why I had to be born to suffer, why I didn't immediately die. Much later I was to be in difficult situations in my life and many times this question has repeated itself in my head. . . . With the help of God I have understood why I should live, why I was bearing these hardships, with his help.

"If I had not sensed his hand near me I would not have been able to bear it; my heart would have stopped or burst asunder from the insufferable loneliness and grief which had fallen on an eleven-year-old child and which have accompanied me all my life.

"There have been times when I have not sensed God's hand and at such times I prayed and cried that he had abandoned me. 'If I have committed an offense, show me, but do not withdraw your hand from me,' I entreated God. Then I would sense anew his presence and joyfully continue. There have been times of despair when I wanted to leave this difficult path and live like the other believers who surround us, for whom it is easier to live, or like those who do not know God and do not want to know him. Then I pray once more and say: 'I do not want to go on. If you still have mercy on me, support me, support me, for I have no more strength to go on.' And once again, after the stormy agitation, peace comes and new strength to go forward, all those qualities which only God can give in this earthly life. An approving, joyful sensation comes to the heart and it is easy to bear new hardships.

"I believe that anyone who has not experienced difficult circumstances has been deprived of life's greatest joy—the awareness of God.

"The path of the believer, its purpose in earthly life have now become understandable to me. A man should condemn Satan who lives in the flesh, and strive to reflect Christ in his own life. And besides, all people, irrespective of whether they are believers or not, live for God. They all live for his glory: the big difference is that some give him honor and glory while living in the flesh, and others will give him honor and glory upon their death when they see that they have been deceived by Satan and they look upon the glory of Christ whom they rejected in their earthly life. Tardily, they will have to acknowledge his majesty and render him honor and glory.

"God does not compel a person to follow him in this life. He does not punish him immediately as is characteristic with men. But man condemns himself by his own acts and will reap the emptiness and the irretrievableness of his whole existence and there will be wailing and gnashing of teeth."

*   *   *

When a month had passed, Lida had the bittersweet experience one night, as the children slept on the floor in the tumbledown building, of waking up to see Lyuba and Nadya led in. "So they found you too!"

Peter had smuggled them back to his friends in the country, but after a time his mother, nearly seventy, had an urge to visit them. Granny bought a bus ticket and did not see a KGB man ask the clerk where the old woman had booked to. During the journey she noticed a car which never overtook the bus, never fell back, and always waited on the main road when the bus turned off to the villages. She guessed with alarm that it might be a *bobik*, but the desire to see the grandchildren outweighed her sense of danger and she went straight to their house.

The girls had spent the day as usual with other children playing on the banks of the broad and beautiful Yenisei. When they returned in the evening they saw and instantly recognized a *bobik*.

"We sensed immediately," writes Lyuba, "that they were after us. For many hours we wandered through the streets of the village and along the banks of the river, having decided not to enter the house. We met one of our village girlfriends and her brother. They were looking for their little calf which had not returned home from the pasture, so the four of us went to look for it. We found it at the other end of the village and Nadya and I accompanied them home, and we ourselves went wandering off further, still not intending to go home. It was already ridiculous and we just continued to walk and walk." Lyuba was about nine and a half and Nadya about eight, and by now both were tired out and ravenous.

"It had already become completely dark and I said to Nadya: 'Let's go home. If they are really after us, let them take us, especially since they have already taken Lida, and if they don't take us now, they will take us sooner or later anyway.' And sure enough the car was there; it had been there for several hours now. I had no doubts, but I calmed my sister by saying: 'Maybe they are not after us.'

"We went home. The house was a one-story long wooden barrack. In the middle of such a structure there is usually a long corridor with doors to apartments on both sides, and only one entrance, in the middle. The residents would take turns cleaning the corridor. When we entered the corridor we met our neighbor woman and she looked at us carefully and at the same time in surprise, as if this was the first time she had seen us, although we had lived there for a good long time already. She took a look at us and then her eyes shifted to the door of our apartment, and then she quickly disappeared behind her door. We both understood everything and without a word we opened the door to the room.

"Passing through the kitchen into the living room—it is also the bedroom—we saw many men sitting there. The light had not been turned on and they were all sitting in the dark. We did not see grandmother, or more accurately we did not notice her in the darkness, until she began to cry loudly when she saw us standing there on the threshold. The woman of the house who was tall and plump stood next to us and very soothingly smoothed first Nadya's head and then mine with her hand, and she also was crying. Her two daughters were grown up but were not married; their father, the man of the house, her husband, was at work. The only thing we could beg these KGB men was to let us pray one last time all together.

"I will never forget the prayer of my grandmother. And to her last day she considered it her fault that we were taken then. About two or three days before her death in October 1977 I was sitting by her bed and we were remembering past years and recalled this incident. I was trying to comfort her, saying that it did not make any difference, that they would have taken us sooner or later; that they accomplished nothing in their six years of 'reeducating' us, that we just found out more about life, about its difficulties, about their deceptions, and much else besides that we would not have seen had we not spent time with them. She agreed with my words and repeated: 'Just stand firm as you have been taught and do not retreat. God keeps track of everything. He knows everything. He will repay.'

"The KGB men put us in the same car in which they had followed grandmother. It was very stuffy in the car because they put the three of us in and there were five of them. It was extremely crowded to sit, and hot. Besides that, they smoked the entire way and made noise among themselves. What they were making a noise about, I don't remember, but I do remember their mocking glances at us and their loud laughter—the hysterical laughter in those five men's throats. We sat pressed between them, somber, silent, but we did not cry. From time to time grandmother would brush away the tears from our eyes and look at us with pity."

6

Letter from a Stranger

THE ABAKAN CHILDREN's Center allowed parental visits in the sti-
fling presence of staff. Peter and Augustina learned that the girls
had been going to doctors in the city, the usual preliminary to
enrollment in a boarding school *(internat)*. They hoped it would
be the one at Chernogorsk.

A day came in mid-August when a promised visit was denied;
the girls were out in the country, "visiting one last doctor." Peter
and Augustina smelled evil afoot and so indeed had the girls; they
had sobbed loudly as the car drove them, not to a doctor, but to
a little railway station on the steppe, where they were bundled
into a train.

The parents now met a blank wall of feigned ignorance at Abakan
and Chernogorsk as to their daughters' whereabouts, and were
treated as having no more rights than if the three girls had been
born into another family. Desperate, the Vashchenkos wrote to
the education departments of all the republics which form the
Soviet Union and each denied having the girls in their care. Peter
and Augustina had no means of contacting their children, of knowing their health or happiness.

Some among the neighbors and the workers at the mine thought this was right, "so that the Vashchenkos would not cripple their children with their God." Others were sorry. Some were silent lest the authorities be annoyed. "In an atheist country," comments Peter, "everyone is suspicious of everyone else; there is no trust." About six weeks passed. Then in mid-September a neighbor brought over a letter from a stranger.

A woman on the kitchen staff of the *internat* at Achinsk, a city 280 miles to the north where the railway line from Abakan joins the Trans-Siberian, wrote to say that the three girls were there. She had asked them why they were always crying. They told her of being taken forcibly from a beloved home, and that their parents did not know where they were. She had been drinking and being in a somewhat maudlin state and feeling pity had promised to write, but not directly to the parents; the girls gave her a neighbor's address.

Augustina, carrying baby Jacob, set out with Peter's mother for Achinsk the next weekend. The distance might be only 280 miles, but the mixed passenger and freight train drawn by a diesel locomotive crawled up and down a zigzag line for eighteen hours, including lengthy stops at numerous towns and shorter halts at wayside stations. It climbed mountain passes (beautiful with grass and wild flowers in springtime), ran through two tunnels (one very long), and wandered with the river Chulymn and past the great power station at Nazarovo and onwards through the *taiga* until at last it reached Achinsk, a city on a mountain, surrounded by forest.

On leaving the Achinsk railway station the Vashchenko women were uncertain how to proceed, since the school would not want them to meet the children. They decided to go to the address on the letter, where they found the cook. She took them to a birch grove, a disused graveyard, opposite the school, begging them never to reveal that she had written; she would lose her job.

She left them in the grove, and went to find the girls. "I was peeling potatoes in the kitchen," writes Lida, "when this woman who had sent the letter home came up to me and said: 'Your Mama is waiting for you in the grove opposite the *internat*.' I stopped dead because of the shock and was unable to take my surprised and frightened stare from her face. 'Well, what are you looking at? Go to her, but be careful or you and I will catch it!'

"I walked around the building for a long time and when I observed that no one was watching me I crossed the highway and entered the big iron gates of the grove, which were always open, and found Mama standing on a footpath under the trees. She had seen me at a distance when I had entered the grove and watched me approach her. I still could not believe that it was Mama; I had not believed that the letter would get there and that someone would come to us. It was a huge surprise.

"I just stood there in front of her and she began to cry; she bent over and kissed me. Ever since I was a child I have been ashamed to show my feelings. Mama said: 'What kind of a child are you? Others would run up and kiss but not you! You stand there and look, and one doesn't know if you are glad or not that we have come to you.' We talked for a little bit and I left to walk to the *internat* from the grove. Having sent Lyuba and Nadya there, I returned, but once again I could hardly believe that I had just spoken with Mama."

The girls told how they had been taken by train to this *internat* and straight to a Pioneer camp in the country until the school term began. They were unhappy. The other children mostly came from broken or violent homes—one even said she would knife her mother if ever they met—and were crude, and angry with all the world. They formed gangs which fought for supremacy but the Vashchenkos kept to themselves, which gave all the groups reason to mock, swear at and even occasionally beat them.

Mother and grandmother encouraged the children; they would never be forgotten and their father would come next time.

Peter arrived at Achinsk at the end of September and went to the cook's address, only to find she had fled the town before discovery of her "crime" in writing the letter. Disconsolate, praying silently, he walked in the direction of the *internat*, certain that the staff would not know him by sight but wondering how to make contact. As he neared the entrance he heard a sound of sad music, which grew louder, and a funeral procession came in view: brass band, coffin, the mourners. It was a sunny, warm autumn day and a crowd of children, teachers and "upbringers"[1] stood at the gates to watch it pass; and among them, the three girls. The cemetery lay beyond the old graveyard where Augustina had met them, and the street curved round this grove.

Some of the adults and children, including the Vashchenko girls, joined the procession. Masking his excitement Peter joined too. His children had spotted him but gave no sign of recognition either, and when the funeral passed inside the cemetery gates and stopped at the grave, Peter and the girls kept their instincts under control. Even little Nadya did not rush into her father's arms but knew, at eight years old, that she must be careful in all her actions—a bitter commentary on Soviet life.

Peter tells what happened. He took out a piece of candy, and "when they began to fill up the grave I went up to Nadya, and said: 'Little girl, come here.' She came over right away to me and I said to her: 'Here you see that a person has died. He has been put in a box and buried'—then I said—'I will wait for you all in the grove near the big gates across from the *internat.*' The teachers did not suspect who I was and Lida, Lyuba, and Nadya told them that they were going to run back to the *internat.*

"I went straight through the graveyard to the appointed place, and arrived before them in the grove because I did not have as far to go, but they soon ran up to me. This was the second secret meeting.

"Now that we had found out where they were we went almost every week. It was a difficult journey and I often had to work several shifts in a row to earn free days, but it was necessary to travel to see them in order to lift their spirits, to strengthen them spiritually. Half of the money I earned went for the tickets and on buying gifts to bring them—and not just for our own children. There were many orphans for whom I could bring gifts. Every

---

1. *Vospitatel,* responsible in a Soviet boarding school for pupils' physical welfare and morals, as distinct from *uchitel,* a classroom teacher. Both are expected to keep watch on ideological attitudes. For convenience I will use "teacher" interchangeably.

time we arrived other kids would meet us and go tell ours of our arrival, because there were gifts tied up for many. Our children divided up the gifts among those who did not have parents, who would always meet us just as if we were their parents. None of them ever told the teachers or the school director about our meeting."

Sometimes Peter and Augustina could go together but more often they took turns. On one occasion Peter had finished the day shift at 4:00 P.M. and just had time to rush home, wash and change and seize the bags of food which Augustina had prepared. He took a taxi to Chernogorsk station for the last train of the day—at that time the short line to Abakan still carried passengers— and arrived to hear the train's immediate departure announced.

He paid off the taxi and made a run for it. A policeman whose job was to stop citizens jumping on moving trains gave chase. As Peter leaped for the car handle the policeman seized a leg but a jar of jam fell out of the bags and smashed at the policeman's feet. He gave up and Peter was on.

"We did not begrudge this expense laid out for our little ones," say the Vashchenkos. "We knew the school would feed their bodies but cripple their souls." Eight years lay ahead before the youngest would be free to come home.

*   *   *

This adventure of faith, love, and endurance had only just begun that autumn of 1962, when Peter took a decision which profoundly affected his own and many lives, and made the name of the obscure Siberian town of Chernogorsk reverberate round the world.

Peter had come to realize that the Soviet Union was totally opposed to God. He had tried to be a good citizen and a good Christian: to "render unto Caesar the things that are Caesar's, and to God the things that are God's." But the State wanted all men to bow down to Caesar in all things. It rejected God and had placed its full authority and resources behind a long term campaign to destroy religion, while paying lip service in the constitution to freedom of belief and, under severe restrictions, tolerating it until "reeducation" should succeed. "They call the Word of God darkness and the Marxist doctrine light," stress Peter and Augustina, "and when a believer does good, the servants of man call this evil." Whoever seeks to render to God the things that are God's becomes the enemy of Caesar.

A Christian, however, may not put Christ second to any earthly authority or power. Believers in Russia are in the position of the Apostles Peter and John when the Sanhedrin ordered them not to teach in the name of Jesus, and Peter and John had replied: "We must obey God rather than men."

Christ's "first and great commandment," "You shall love the Lord your God with all your heart, and with all your soul, and with all your strength, and with all your mind," contravenes Soviet law. The law says, No children in church; but Christ said, Let the children come, do not stop them. Soviet law says, No open preaching; but Christ's command is, What you hear in private, proclaim on the housetops. The State forbids exposition of the Book of Revelation, but the Lord says that no part of the Word shall be removed. The State ordains that schools shall teach atheism, yet Jesus condemned any who deceived the little ones. And when the State promotes anyone to the humblest position of leadership, he or she is under an obligation to "reeducate" subordinates in the Soviet way of life, specifically including atheism.

The Vashchenkos comment: "Psalm 13:1 [2] reads, 'The fool says in his heart, There is no God.' If the fool just said it in his heart at that time, today you hear it everywhere—in the newspapers, the radio, in lectures, in schools."

There is one Scripture which Soviet authorities continually quote at believers who balk at atheistic commands of the State, the famous passage in the Epistle to the Romans condemning those who disobey secular authorities which are lawfully constituted: "Let every soul be subject unto the higher powers. For there is no power but of God: the powers that be are ordained of God" (KJV). *The New English Bible* translates it: "Every person must submit to the su-

---

2. Psalm 14:1 in the English Bible.

preme authorities. There is no authority but by act of God, and the existing authorities are instituted by him."

This passage exercises Peter as deeply as many in history who had suffered under ungodly tyrants. He argues from logic that it is inconceivable that God would ordain or institute a power which opposed Himself. Peter does not in fact deduce that the Soviet leaders are therefore usurpers who may be disobeyed. Instead he looks at the word which is translated in English "ordained" or "instituted," and in Russian as *ustanovleny*, from the verb *ustanovit*, to establish or install. He expounds this as if it meant "established *on* God" rather than *by* God. He asks, "Is there a godly establishment *(ustanovlenie)* in this Soviet power which muffles and eradicates every religion and terms it 'the opium of the people'?" Peter concludes that there is not. God foresaw it, but it is not established on Himself. No State which rejects God can be built on His foundation. In effect, Peter rewrote the verse to suggest that obedience is only obligatory if a "higher power" is founded on God, which the Soviet Union is not.

The Russian translation of the text does not entirely warrant this interpretation, though no one can deny that Peter's exegesis conforms with the general trend of Scripture as summarized by the Apostles before the Council: "We must obey God rather than man." And if Peter Vashchenko is wrong, he is wrong in a company which includes Oliver Cromwell and George Washington, not to mention Lenin who opposed a Tsar who, constitutionally and personally, regarded his authority as received from God.[3]

Peter, however, had no wish to rebel. In 1962 he was in a dilemma. Should he conform to the ungodly commands of the State? Should he become a martyr? Or should he—Peter kept finding one Russian word coming into his prayers: *Doroga*, the Road—take the Road, emigrate, leave the atheist State: "Come out of her [Babylon], my people, lest you take part in her sins" (Rev. 18:4). Peter, Augustina and many of their friends became pro-

---

3. I should emphasize that this is the translator's and my interpretation; Peter Vashchenko particularly wishes to emphasize that he cannot be held responsible if we have misunderstood him, since he was not present at the time of translation.

foundly convinced that they must heed the Word of God in 2 Corinthians 6: "What fellowship has righteousness with unrighteousness, and what communion has light with darkness? And what concord has Christ with Belial? . . . Wherefore, come out from among them and be separate, says the Lord."

Peter recognized that Russia could be won for Christ only by Russians. He believed profoundly the teaching of one of his favorite hymns:

> *We are not given life for empty dreams*
> *But to carry the sacred Word*
> *To those who languish in sin.*
> *So you and I should be ready*
> *To serve Christ in sorrow and tears.*

He recognized too that most believers are called to stay, doing what they can whether refusing to belong to a registered church or walking in the straitjacket of registration. Peter's dilemma was that of the Pilgrim Fathers, of the Huguenots, of any who have lived where the laws of the secular authority conflicted with the dictates of conscience.

He and Augustina would have been ready to suffer to the last drop of blood for Christ in once Holy Russia, but they could not stand idly by and see their children subjected to the overwhelming forces of atheism. They longed beyond all else to see them grow up as strong, happy believers leading a full life. Khariton, whose three elder children had been removed to an *internat*, felt the same.

The only answer was to take the Road.

7

Moscow Adventure

Determined to emigrate, Peter, Khariton, their father and many church members "sought a country." Their first choice was Israel. They knew it existed as an independent State because the Soviet Union had been the first (other than Britain) to give recognition, before turning to enmity. They had read in the Bible about the land and the prophecies that "outcasts of Israel" would return, and since the New Testament spoke of believers in Christ being true Israelites, there should be a welcome.

They were told in Chernogorsk, wrongly, that Israel had no embassy in Moscow. They then turned to the United States.

The KGB and local educators had taunted them often for holding a faith "imported from America," for Soviet theory insists that no man can discover ideas for himself. It excludes the power of the Word of God and therefore, argued the KGB, the influence which turned Soviet citizens into Pentecostals was that of the émigré Russian from America, I. E. Voronaev, who had founded the first Pentecostal churches in the early Soviet Union. Petro Chmykhalov could recall an occasion when KGB chief Ikonnikov was on the bus from Abakan, "and in front of everyone began to disgrace me, saying that I prayed to God, had connections with America, and he added: 'He is the sort of person who if they dropped a spy by parachute would certainly hide him.' " Petro had retorted with spirit, "You are a poor employee of the police if you haven't found the spy!"

The Chernogorsk believers did not naïvely confuse America with Israel or Zion or some biblical Land of Promise, as later reports in the West suggested. The only naïvety was their assumption that emigration would be allowed; at that time hardly any Soviet citizens could secure exit visas.

Peter's expectation was high. He sold the house in Airfield Street to finance the expedition, settled up and received final pay at the Auto Factory, and in mid-October 1962 bought tickets for Moscow for himself, Augustina and the five remaining children. Khariton was ill, but his wife, Styura, nursing a baby, came too. It was not a reconnaissance: their purpose was to complain to the Kremlin that their elder children had been abducted by force, to request permission to emigrate, and to hand letters in to the American Embassy asking for the necessary papers, so that all who wished in Chernogorsk might leave *en masse* for Israel or America as soon as formalities were complete. "At that time we simply believed the Soviet authorities and thought that what they said was true," that the country was run for the people. They expected to be received sympathetically; from time immemorial Russians had a touching faith in their Autocrat, that he had only to learn the facts to do justice.

They went first to Achinsk, where they had now discovered believers in the town. The three girls daringly absented themselves from the dormitory and spent the night with their parents and family in a joyful reunion. They said good-bye early in the morning, and the girls returned to the *internat* after the train had left for Moscow.

Their absence had been noticed. The director of the school, Sofia Grigorevna Ishchuk, ordered them to show a teacher the house where they had slept: the believers would certainly be punished.

To give their parents plenty of time to get far from Achinsk the girls displayed unchildlike cunning, of the kind that had been familiar among children in Nazi-occupied Europe. They walked about the streets as if they could not remember, and at last knocked at a house. When the door opened and the teacher asked, "Do you know these little girls?" a genuinely puzzled housewife answered, "Never seen them in my life." They played this trick at three or four houses until the teacher returned to the school exasperated.

At that, Sofia Grigorevna took them to the police. She asked that they be given a good fright; but the police, confronted by three small girls, felt irritated at such a request, and the Vashchenkos look back with amusement on an episode which seemed alarming at the time. "We were interrogated," writes Lyuba, "but they did not get anything. We were asked where we spent the night, but we did not want to tell. The policeman screamed, beat his fists on the table, and since he had not achieved anything in this manner, he said, 'Now we will put you in jail.' We didn't say anything. Then he tried to entertain us with candy! But we would not take it. We were taken back to the director of the *internat*."

Meanwhile their parents, Styura and the children were well on their way. After a total of three and a half days' travel from Chernogorsk they drew into Moscow's Kursky station early one October morning: none of them had seen Moscow before. At daybreak they all began the walk to the Kremlin, the babies carried in the usual way. They entered the Receiving Room of the Presidium of the Supreme Soviet but no one would receive them. They walked out across wide Revolution Square, passed the National Hotel and up Gorki Street and round to the American Embassy.

The Soviet policemen on guard outside, whose standing orders were to turn away Soviet citizens unless carrying official permission, refused to let them enter. "But a car came out of the gates," relates Augustina, "and we were standing not far from the arch. I went up to the car with Jacob in my arms in order to pass on the letter. I asked the person sitting in the car: 'Do you work in the American Embassy?' He answered that he did. I wanted to say that I had a written request to the American Embassy, when a policeman came up and pushed me away from the car and said:

'Get out of here. It is not permitted to be here near foreign cars.' It was an extremely cold day. Snow mixed with rain was falling. The policeman saw that I had a small baby in my arms and that there were four others besides and so did not talk to us for a long time. Therefore he did not know what we wanted to find out there." The children were cold, so the Vashchenkos found their way back to the Kursky station to spend the night in the huge waiting room with its air of faded Tsarist ballroom. Here they composed a letter to Khrushchev. Next morning they handed this in and waited in the receiving room.

Peter continues the story: "We were told that 'Peter Ivanovich' wanted to speak with us," writes Peter. "We still do not know who he was. He led us all into his office—Vera, Lila, Sasha, John, Jacob, ourselves and Khariton's wife and baby. He asked what we wanted to find out at the Presidium. Then he began to ask why we wanted to go abroad. He wrote everything down and said: 'Now go on home and then we will inform you about emigration abroad through the local authorities. We will tell them; and they will tell you.' Then he called somewhere by telephone. We went out and went to the train station in order to go home. We did not know Moscow and hardly where the train station was.

"There was a man who never left us, never passed us, never turned away from us. He arrived at the station with us. We understood that this was our guard—the KGB. At the station we were asked to get into two Volgas which pulled up. We were seated inside and driven to the procurator of the Kuibyshev district. He received us in his office. He asked where we wanted to go and why. He asked me where I worked. I said that three of my children had been taken because I was a believer and taught them God's law, and that I had decided to emigrate because then my children could study God's law in school.

"They laughed at us. Three other people came into the procurator's office. The procurator said to me: 'What, you have two wives?' I answered: 'No. This is the wife of my brother Khariton. He could not come because he is sick, but his wife has come to seek emigration abroad. Three of his children were also taken.'

"The procurator asked: 'Does your *ear* hurt now?' I said that it didn't. 'Did it hurt at one time?' I said: 'I don't remember. Maybe it did hurt sometime.' Then he said: 'And when you were in the mine, *didn't something hit you on the head?*' I said: 'No. I am completely healthy!' Then he wrote a note to one of the three men and we were once again seated in the same cars in which we had come. We were taken to the railway station, where they told a policeman to set aside a place in the corner and to let us sit there. The policeman moved two divans together and we sat down. We spent another night in the station and he guarded us.

"The station staff had noticed that we had slept there three nights. Next morning the station manager invited us to come to his office. He questioned us about everything. We told him that our children had been taken and that we wanted to emigrate from the USSR to Israel or to America. But this seemed funny to the station manager. He considered us to be crazy. When he found out that we were believers, he sent to the Baptist House for a believer leader, who also asked us where we were going and why: 'After all,' he said, 'you are free to believe in God here.' We explained everything to him, how we were oppressed. He listened and then left. Then we were led into a police room and later, when the train was to depart, they put us in the last compartment of a carriage and told the conductor that this was a family of crazy people and to be careful with them. The conductor, a woman, said: 'Oh, my! I'm afraid.' They told her we were being accompanied, but they just wanted her to know.

"My wife heard this conversation when she went to get boiling water for tea. The conversation took place in the conductor's little room. When my wife heard that they were talking about us, she listened for a little while as she got the hot water from the boiler. They did not see her. She came and said that we were being accompanied, but I did not believe it. Then, during the night, when our little boy Jacob was not sleeping, my wife got up and began walking up and down the car. She saw that our guard was not sleeping; he was keeping watch over us. She told me. At one station

I left to buy something and a man from our car went with me wherever I went. I did not believe that he was following me, but my wife insisted that we were being accompanied by two people.

"When we approached Achinsk, I began to gather up our things in order to get out and see our children in the *internat* Two policemen got on board and the two men left. One of the policemen came to us and the other sat down near us. He asked: 'Where are you heading for?' I said: 'I am getting off in Achinsk.' And he said: 'You aren't going anywhere. We are all going on further.' Only then did I understand that my wife was speaking the truth that we were being followed and accompanied, and had been since Moscow itself.

"We were transported to Abakan, led into a police room, and they began to phone Chernogorsk to find out where to take us and in what: they would not let us take a bus and be with other people. We waited for a *voronok*—a van in which prisoners are transported [1]—and it arrived at twelve midnight. When they opened the door to the car there was a lot of smoke, dirt, and spittle. They began to put us and the children into the car, but the policeman who was accompanying us said: 'Let the smoke out. After all, there are children here.' And thus at twelve midnight our family of five children, my wife and I, and my brother's wife Styura who was also nursing, and the two policemen, went by *voronok* to Chernogorsk.

"They brought us to the police station and summoned the KGB chief Ivan Romanovich Ikonnikov. He had been drinking. He said: 'You have gone and fallen on both knees in front of the Americans and they do not even want to see you.' We said that we had gone on our own business and, what difference did it make to him if we had fallen on two knees or one before the Americans? Ikonnikov said: I have guests at my table today and you are preventing me from being with them. But never mind, I will be taken

---

1. *Voronok* means "little raven." They used always to be black, hence the nickname, but are now of different colors with the word "Bread" or "Produce" painted on the windowless sides. Passers-by recognize a *voronok* by the soldier or policeman beside the driver.

home and then you. And tomorrow I will summon you.' It was already October, and there was snow on the ground. They took him home and then, in the same police car, they took us to my father at Mine 16 Settlement where my parents lived."

*   *   *

The journey to Moscow had failed. The path to emigration looked much more thorny and longer than they had supposed. Peter got another job, as a timberer reinforcing pitprops at Mine 9, and the Vashchenkos settled down, temporarily as they hoped, to live in the parents' crowded *izba*.

After the church meetings, everyone discussed the next move. They decided that they must throw themselves on the understanding and concern of the Americans; there was no one else to appeal to. A large party must go secretly to Moscow and make a dash for the American Embassy, finding safety in numbers.

Family by family, going at different times in order to fox the KGB, they began to buy tickets at the advance booking office.

Peter intended to lead the party. But on 14 December 1962: "I was working the day shift from 8:00 A.M. to 4:00 P.M. I had already left the mine and was walking home along the incline of the mountain. I saw a car. It stopped beside me and I was invited to get in with them. They took me in my dirty workclothes home, conducted a search in my presence, and then took me to the mine to the bath. I washed, put on clean underwear, which was at the bath. They waited for me and then took me to the police station, at first to the one in Chernogorsk, and then to Abakan. They interrogated me and put me in jail, into the basement of the KGB building where they have special preliminary detention cells (KPZ)."

He was transferred to Minusinsk, to the prison which had a horrible reputation in Stalin's time, while the KGB decided what clause of the criminal code should convict him. He was not allowed packages from home, which during the pretrial period are permitted only if the investigator thinks they will make the prisoner more pliable.

"The cell had fifty people in it. It was so filled with cigarette smoke that you could not recognize a friend with whom you were imprisoned if he was more than three meters away. It was a cold winter and since there were so many people the cell was terribly stuffy. I had to sit an entire day until Retreat below a high window with no glass. A full stream of cold air came straight down out of it to where I was sitting. I caught a cold in the head sitting there all the time under that stream of cold air."

While Peter sat in prison, thirty-two of his relatives and friends went to Moscow and made history.

8

The Thirty-Two

THE THIRTY-TWO CHERNOGORSK Pentecostals had bought one-way tickets, and went in small groups to the station at Abakan on 29 December 1962, deliberately choosing the New Year holiday so that their absence would not be noticed too quickly.

They threw the KGB off the scent by not getting on the train together. Those with children took their seats, the rest hung about outside the station ignoring each other until the last possible moment. The Abakan KGB did not notice them and the railway KGB did not know them by sight, but to avoid suspicion each group pretended to be strangers to the others in the through coach: in the 1960s, coaches were uncoupled at Achinsk and attached to the fast Trans-Siberian express, hauled by a powerful electric engine. Nowadays through trains run the whole way.

The party of six men, twelve women and fourteen children included the Vashchenko grandparents Anna and Paul, who was in his seventy-fifth year, and Augustina carrying baby Jacob in a tight cocoon of skins and swaddling clothes, with Vera, nearly seven, and Sasha, three and three quarters years old. "All," comments Peter, "were from families who were suffering in some way—if the husband was not in prison or the camps, then a son or brother was." Grigory's wife had visited him and returned frightened that he was dying of starvation. Those who could not go to Moscow fasted and prayed intensively. As Peter was in prison, the Thirty-Two, as they came to be known, were led by Khariton.[1]

The journey passed without incident although, as Augustina relates, "the children began to run from one compartment to the next to visit each other and the people traveling with us started to notice that we all knew one another. However, we arrived safely in Moscow," this time at the Kiev Station. "And there the Lord wondrously protected everyone."

It happened like this. They had arrived on 3 January 1963 at 3:00 A.M. (Moscow time is four hours behind Chernogorsk time) and those with children had gone up to the balcony as it was cold below in the huge waiting room. Everyone went to sleep, inconspicuous among the crowd on the divans and the floor. At 5:00 A.M. they were woken by a banging and locking of doors. The police began a routine check on travelers' documents.

The adults among the Thirty-Two realized the danger at once. If the police discovered so many from one city who said they wanted to visit an Embassy or to complain to the Kremlin, yet had no papers of authority from their local soviet, they would be taken to a police station for questioning and would get no further.

"When," continues Augustina, "we saw that they had begun a check of documents, we were keeping apart from each other. We could all see each other, and all began to pray wherever we were sitting that the Lord would not allow any conflict; and if it was pleasing to Him, that we might report about the repressions which they inflicted on believers, how the Soviet authorities pretended to see nothing and not know about the misfortunes of believers.

"And God heard our prayer and helped us. How did He help? A policeman was going down the row checking documents, but

---

1. In my earlier (1964) book, which wrongly gave Grigory Vashchenko as leader, I was misled by the inaccurate list put out by the Soviet *Novosti* agency. Several other details were wrong, the contemporary evidence being scrappy and often faulty.

before he had reached any of our believers he turned and went back the way he had come! Then he returned again and began to check, *but not the row in which he had not finished checking the documents,* but the row immediately behind us. We all rejoiced and understood that the Lord had given him some sort of urgent business and he had abandoned his check, and then when he started around the room again he remembered something and began to check the next row and not ours. It was the Lord's hand which accomplished this thing."

*   *   *

On the morning of 3 January 1963, dressed in their usual winter clothing of thick quilted or skin coats, knee-length felt *valenkis* and skin caps, they trudged along Tchaikovsky Street. At the entrance archway of the Embassy they turned, and by force of surprise and numbers rushed past the police on duty and reached diplomatic soil. Shouting, "If you believe in Christ and in God—help us!" they poured into every open door, causing astonishment and confusion.

Americans, quick to detect distress, did not try to force the invaders back into the street but shepherded them into the courtyard, which was more spacious in 1963 than later, and then into the community room, "and since there were children with us they suggested that we have a bite to eat." They served bacon and eggs while Khariton was taken upstairs to a Russian-speaking senior officer.

Khariton told the full tale of their complaints, supported by documents, and of their desire to emigrate to Israel or America or wherever they could serve God freely. They expected to complete the paperwork at once.

The American official expressed his deep sympathy but had to reply that the list for the current year (1962) had closed. They would be placed on that for the coming year (1963) and thus would not be able to go abroad at once. Khariton could not hide his distress at this answer.

Meanwhile the Moscow correspondents of the world's press had hastened to the Embassy. The Thirty-Two had torn aside the curtain. Next day banner headlines and front page dispatches throughout the West awoke the general public (as distinct from experts and a few churchmen) to the continued existence of a virile, persecuted Christianity within the Soviet Union.

The Americans had at once alerted the Ministry of Foreign Affairs. Minister Kuznetsov arrived with seven or eight assistants and apologized to the American officer: "We have no idea why the American Embassy was chosen for this demonstration. As is well known, religious freedom is guaranteed in the Soviet Union . . ."

The Americans took the minister to the Thirty-Two. In Augustina's words, "We began to tell why we were there, that it was because of the repression in Chernogorsk; and in front of the authorities he said: 'We knew nothing about your being soaked with water by fire trucks, poisoned with gas, or thrown out one by one from a truck into the fields. We will dispatch a commission. . . . We will reexamine the cases of the twenty-one who have been tried, and free them. We will allow the children back to their homes. And those who cannot serve in the Soviet Army may work out their term of service in industry.' "

The Vashchenkos were fairly certain that the persecution would not have continued without approval from Moscow. Though they knew nothing of Khrushchev's personal demand in 1961 that measures against religion should receive greater attention, they were not inclined to trust Minister Kuznetsov. However, he held out hope that emigration was not in the least impossible, but said that the paperwork must be done in Chernogorsk.

"In general," says Augustina, "they presented themselves as angels. Several people said: 'We will return to Chernogorsk *since the high Soviet authorities have promised*, and they would not deceive us.' "

The Vashchenkos had already lost faith in the Autocrat of the Kremlin. Others held to the traditional belief. The Thirty-Two were now divided in mind and uncertain.

Fifteen years later Augustina could recall it all factually, calmly, though she adds: "To remember this is like reliving a scene from the past which is buried deep within the heart, and if the Lord did not comfort with His Word and did not support us by His strength it would have been impossible to continue this path to the present day. Jesus said, 'Let him take up his cross and follow Me,' and therefore it is our desire to follow the Lord wherever He leads." On that January day of 1963 it looked a heavy cross indeed to be taken up by the Siberians who, appalled, faced the fact of no Western help and that they must go back into the jaws of the lion. Others, having believed the minister's promises, were ready to return to Chernogorsk. Some wanted to stay where they were.

"And so there was a disagreement. But there was not time then to get this matter straightened out because the Soviets drove a bus up and proposed that we get in. Some got in. Others did not want to. Everyone was in a defeated frame of mind, but the Americans said: 'You are Soviet citizens since you have Soviet passports. You need to reject Soviet citizenship and only then will it be possible to go abroad.' "

To the Americans the atmosphere in the yard suggested a crucifixion being prepared with all its agony and shame. Minister Kuznetsov poured out his promises. He emphasized that no reprisals would be taken, that no crime had been committed by entering the Embassy. Siberians cried out, "We don't believe you. Our requests have been ignored. You'll punish us."

An older man, perhaps Paul Vashchenko, turned to the Embassy officer, "*Please* let us emigrate. They will shoot us here!" The American sadly explained again that he could not ship them anywhere without Soviet exit visas.

The bus had high wooden panels to block the newsmen's view, and stood under the entrance archway. After four hours, in sorrow, and not without further argument, most of the Thirty-Two had agreed to board it. The older man shouted to the newsmen, "There is no place for believers in the Soviet Union!" and another begged all in earshot, "Help us! Those who believe in God and Christ, help us!"

A few wandered uncertainly in the snow across the yard, as if contemplating escape. They walked in grief and weariness, and when the bus, having started without them, stopped opposite the south entrance (right beside the little basement room which in 1978 became temporary home to the Vashchenkos and Chmykhalovs) they allowed themselves to be taken aboard without protest.

The Western public heard no more.

*   *   *

"They drove us round and round and up and down," recalls Augustina; perhaps the Soviet authorities needed time for decision, and to pass the problem from ministry to ministry. "And we arrived, as I remember, at Kursk train station.

"We were put into a large room. There were many important people gathered there and they began to talk with us. Someone shamed us for not complaining in the right place. Someone tried to explain that the Americans were our enemies and that there was nothing they could do to help us. Someone else tried to frighten us: 'For this you can be put in jail. You are Soviet citizens and yet you went to complain at the Embassy.' But we were not frightened that they would imprison us. We answered them: 'If the owner beats his dog in his garden, then the dog is going to run away. It is the same with us. If you had not mocked us, we would not have gone to the American Embassy.'

"After they had talked to us for a long time they said: 'We will send a commission there. If it is true, we will punish your authorities. If you are lying, we will punish you.' "

Kuznetsov had assured the American diplomats that the Siberians should receive medical attention as required, and then spend the night in a hotel before being returned home "in comfortable sleeping cars." Medical attention came, and money for fares was offered and refused: "We have our own money." But they were held at the station, then put into a general (saloon type) railway coach at the very last minute when it was full. "We wanted to get out but the train was already leaving. We all stood there in the entry way by the door with the small children in our arms because not only was there no place to sit but no place to stand; we traveled for a long time holding the children. I don't remember where it was that a woman with children yielded up a place for us. There were mainly soldiers traveling in this car and those who did not have far to go. Some got off and others would sit down. The car was stuffy and filled with smoke. There were many drunks on board. Seats were given to us right next to the doors and as these were often opened, the children were cold."

At Novosibirsk in Siberia three of the men who had interrogated them at the Moscow station boarded the train and proposed that one of the Thirty-Two fly with them to Krasnoyarsk, where their two presbyters were held in jail: Grigory's broken health had been one of the complaints voiced at the Embassy. No one would go, not trusting Soviet officials, and later when the Moscow men reached Chernogorsk and claimed to have seen Grigory fit and well, it was easy to see they had been duped by the prison governor, for they said the senior presbyter's hair was very dark instead of Grigory's light brown.

The weary homeward journey continued. "When we arrived in Achinsk everyone was collected together in a room; they would not let us go into the station with the people. Then two men and a woman came and said: 'We will accompany you to Abakan.' They put us into a carriage by ourselves. Later one family from the next carriage came into ours but they would not let anyone else in. As we traveled along we sang, prayed and read, and these three people did not forbid it. When we arrived in Abakan we were met at the station by many plainclothes KGB men, and led to a bus in which again there was no one except us. They drove us to Chernogorsk and everyone went to their homes.

"The next day they began to summon and question us at the police station. 'How did you go? Who suggested that you go to the Embassy? What did you say there? What were you told at the Embassy?' . . . No one wanted to talk with them. All the city knew about the mockery which the authorities had inflicted on us since the middle of 1961, because they and the head of the KGB, Ikonnikov, acted without restraint."

*   *   *

The commission from Moscow arrived. Maria Chmykhalov recalls the visit of one of them when Petro was out at work. "It was already evening; someone came to our place and knocked on the wicket gate. My sister Yelena was spending the night with us. I said: 'Yelena, go and ask who it is, but don't open the gate.' She left and asked: 'Who is there?' Immediately the answer came: 'Maria Petrovna, please open up.' My sister said: 'I am not Maria. I will go and get her.' She came into the house and said: 'Come. Someone is calling you by your patronymic. He probably knows you.'

"I went out and opened the gate. He took off his hat, and bowed, and asked: 'Can I come in?' I said: 'We lock ourselves in because drunks come to us and use foul language. They show their Party cards and say, 'We will strangle you devils.' And you can't get rid of them. We can't let the children out into the yard if youths are cycling by because they turn towards the gate. Tolik once was kicked so hard that his eyebrow was cut. That's why we lock the gate.' "

The man politely offered to come next day, as it was late, but Maria invited him in and to take a seat, apologizing that there were no chairs, only benches, cots or a trunk. He chose the trunk. Maria's mother, who had been sick, lay on her cot, and Yelena came in and lay down on another. The man cleared his throat and announced that he had come to find out how their supplies in store were, at which Yelena began to say that they had not had chicken in the store for a long time.

Maria interrupted her and turned to the man: "You did not come about provisions, but because we are believers, to find out how we are persecuted here. I like it when people speak frankly."

"Why did you determine that?"

"Because you are so businesslike. You even said that since it was late, if I would not permit you to come in, you would not come in."

The man got out his documents, headed Central Committee,

and a long sheet of paper, remarking that he had flown in that morning and theirs was the eighth home he had visited, and he had several more that night. He asked how they were treated. Old Mrs. Makarenko told how Ikonnikov had ripped Anna's dress and how he would come to their home and scream, "You are Americans. Your faith is taken from America."

"He wrote it down," continues Maria, "on one side of the paper. My sister Yelena said that he also wrote on the other side as well. I said to him: 'You are wasting your time going house to house. It would be better if you go from our place to the rescue station and there you will find out more than going from house to house.' He said, 'Maria Petrovna, who is going to tell against himself?' "

But Maria, remembering the folly of Haman in the Book of Esther, cannily said: "You hold a high post from Moscow. Tell them that you have come regarding the believers, to find out what can be done to disperse them. They will tell you all the methods they used and everything they did, how they beat, dragged, ripped; they will even tell you things you will not be told in the homes. They will boast."

He left the Chmykhalovs and went straight to the rescue station, "and everything turned out just as I had predicted. In a friendly way they told every detail, and boasted. When he had written everything down, he explained why he had come! They were frightened, and dispersed." He also collected information from the police.

Petro Chmykhalov, having been absent that night, was summoned for interrogation by the local procurator, Volkov, in the presence of the KGB chief. Petro suggested that Ikonnikov speak first and then not interrupt, and when Ikonnikov started interrupting, Petro exclaimed with spirit: "Ivan Romanovich, if it is going to be like this I will not talk. You talk." Volkov said sternly to the KGB man: "If you interrupt I will have you led out." Petro began, and Ivan Romanovich "just fidgeted and twisted his head."

Shortly after this I. R. Ikonnikov was replaced by Kazarin and transferred to Abakan, to watch all the westbound trains and spot any Chernogorsk believer setting off for Moscow, since he knew them all by sight—a job in which he proved singularly inept.

9

A Third Attempt

Moscow had investigated the complaints because of the uproar in the world's press. But the Chernogorsk police went to absurd lengths to shadow believers, instead of tracking down crime, of which there was—and is—"a great deal in Chernogorsk; there are murders and robbery and crimes of every sort."

A Vashchenko describes a comic incident during the intensive shadowing: "There was always a man at our place the first days. One would sit there until dinner, then another would come. Once the children were playing around and it was very noisy. Mother told them several times to calm down but they did not listen. She wanted to frighten them, so she said: 'Beyond that door stands a policeman and he will come in now and take you.' The door quietly opened and a policeman really came in.

"He timidly came into the room feeling awkward before mother. The children looked at him in amazement and quietened at once— they had not foreseen that her words would turn out to be true. And mother was more surprised than all of them and everyone stared at each other in confusion. He had come to relieve the other policeman but had decided to listen behind the door, and when mother had wanted to scare the kids by saying that the policeman was standing behind the door, he thought that she had seen him while he had been eavesdropping. That is why he was embarrassed."

It was not funny, however, when Augustina was continually refused a job though her husband was in prison and she had his aged parents and five of her eight children to support. As soon as she gave her name the employment office would tell her they had no vacancies, and that being a believer woman she would frequently be absent having babies (since believers never allow abortions, the usual form of birth control in the Soviet Union). Only when she threatened to complain to Moscow did they find her a job at the mine, at a reduced wage because she did not belong to a trade union.

Investigators came and went. The authorities granted two small concessions which will be mentioned later, but no children returned from *internats*, no men from prison or labor camps; and although the KGB ceased to break up the worship services, they tried to stop them starting: miners were brought by cars straight from their shift to the house where a service was expected, to stand shoulder to shoulder in a human wall in front of the door.

The request to be allowed to emigrate was ignored. They had followed American suggestions and rejected Soviet citizenship by renouncing their internal passports; some of the ex-soldiers had already done so. They were now conscientious objectors, and the executive committee of the local soviet had warned them that possession of a passport rendered them liable to recall to the colors.

Lack of a passport prevented legal traveling and had other disadvantages. Several times during the next five years the authorities tried to return the passports, without success. The believers found themselves caught in a vicious circle—vicious indeed because it served no purpose except delay, until applicants should give up in despair. Minister Kuznetsov had kept none of his promises except not to punish the Thirty-Two.

Early in March, refusing to give up, the believers decided to send a smaller delegation to the American Embassy carrying written details. Very secretly, for fear of interception, Khariton, his sister

Natasha, Anna Makarenko, and Augustina with six-year-old Vera, returned to Moscow by air, at more than double the cost of the train tickets (60 rubles instead of 28).[1] Augustina would just have time to return before Peter's trial.

Thus on a March morning of 1963 an American diplomat emerging from a barber shop opposite the Embassy, on the far side of the wide street, noticed a knot of five very ordinary Russians: a man, three women and a child. They stood too far from the Embassy for the police to identify or even to notice them unless they began a long colloquy with a Western diplomat; but the KGB had at least one man shadowing them. The Siberians had seen the diplomat leave the Embassy and enter the barber shop and had waited. They followed him down the pedestrian subway which emerges a few yards west of the Embassy past the bus and trolley bus stop, and spoke to him. On hearing who they were, he made a rendezvous for 9:00 P.M. that evening at a suburban station beyond the metro.

They met him as planned at the Ismailovsky station and handed him their manuscripts and documents. He promised to talk to the Ministry of Foreign Affairs and to ensure that they were not arrested, and suggested that one of them meet him the next evening at the same time and place. He drove away, shadowed by a KGB car.

Since they too were followed by the KGB, somewhat aggressively, they decided among themselves that Khariton should stay and the others fly home. In their efforts in the metro to shake off their shadows Natasha got lost, and since Khariton carried her plane ticket she decided to go home by train. She shook off the KGB by sleeping the night between two Ukrainian grannies in the waiting room at the Kiev station, then went to the Kursk station. When at long last her train neared Abakan, she alighted early, at Tasheba, as she did not know what the situation might be. She walked the twenty-five kilometers (about fifteen miles) home, arriving at 2:00 A.M.

---

1. By 1979 the plane ticket from Abakan to Moscow had risen to 72 rubles for an adult.

Khariton took the rest of the party that same night to the airport and waited with them until their plane left at 3:00 A.M. He had the whole of the day to fill in, knowing the KGB shadowed him all the time.

In an hour or two he returned to the center of Moscow and hung around until the opening of the department store GUM, a series of separate booths on two floors with a covered concourse down the center, which stands slightly down hill from Red Square and Lenin's Tomb. Khariton was dressed in a brown leather coat which the KGB could spot easily. They followed him in but the crowd of shoppers enabled him to give them the slip. Buying a quilted jacket, he went into a fitting room and put it on, wrapping his old leather coat in paper. He left GUM unobserved.

"Until evening he went to a lot of places," tells Peter. "He was at the zoo and in the Tretyakov Gallery. The time came for him to go by metro to the agreed station. He had to come out on to the street. On the escalator there were many important people, apparently KGB bosses, looking at each person closely, but all were expecting him to be in a leather coat. He knew that they wanted to apprehend him and decided to bend further over and pass by them. But right in front of the exit, in the doorway, they recognized him and wanted to stop him. However, the door opened and the American diplomat drove right up to the exit and saw Khariton, who got into the car. They drove around Moscow and had a talk; there were many interesting questions on both sides.

"The diplomat said: 'You will not be imprisoned. Tomorrow you can go to the Ministry of Foreign Affairs.' Khariton spent the night in the train station and in the morning he went to the Ministry and talked there with someone—I don't know with whom—about the return of the children from the *internat* and about emigration from the USSR. But this man got so angry that his shirt shook! He told Khariton: 'You can go home and then your matter will be resolved, but while you are in Moscow it will not be resolved.' Khariton went home that very day."

Augustina, Anna and little Vera had had their own adventure, as Augustina describes: "When we got off the plane in Krasnoyarsk we were met by the airport head and two other people. All the passengers went to the bus, but the three of us were led to the terminal and they began to interrogate us. 'Where have you been? Why? Who have you met?' Then we were placed on a supplemental flight because the plane on which we should have flown had already left. At the Abakan airport we were also met, by a police car. The new chief of the Chernogorsk KGB, Kazarin, and his assistant, Ignatov, and still another person whom we did not know were sitting inside. They invited us to get into the car and they took us in to Abakan for interrogation.

"Here we were separated into different offices; Kazarin interrogated me and Ignatov questioned Anna Makarenko. I could hear Ignatov banging his fist on the table and shouting at Anna, 'Where have you been? Why? How many of you were there? What did they tell you?' They asked the same questions of me. But we refused to answer them. They held us from five in the evening until ten, and then, after the buses had already stopped running for the night between Abakan and Chernogorsk, they let us go. We went to a hotel, but it was full. From there we crossed the whole city in order to sleep in the train station. We sat there through the night and in the morning went home."

When Khariton returned to Chernogorsk, Kazarin summoned all four who had been to Moscow and interrogated them again and again.

"Why do you want to emigrate from the USSR?"

"Because we cannot let our children go to atheist schools where the law of God is not taught. Give us a believer teacher and our children will go to school."

Kazarin said sarcastically, "I think in such a situation they can only let you emigrate. They will not give you a believer teacher. Do you really want to return to 1917?"

They insisted: "We will not sign releases for putting our children into school. It is written in the Psalms, 'The madman says in his heart that there is no God.' All the books are designed to refute

God and you all teach that, and we are supposed to turn our children over to madmen, for God calls such people mad who say that there is no God."

One interrogator amused Augustina by claiming that the Thirty-Two had devoured a whole cow at the Embassy and that the Americans clamored for payment. She replied: "We have a large bullock. If you will let us, we will take it and give it to them."

He answered, "You really just want to return to the Embassy!"

"Well, then," replied Augustina, "don't slander the Americans by saying that they demand a cow from you, that your Soviet citizens have eaten the Americans out of house and home!"

*   *   *

Khariton had now been arrested; Minister Kuznetsov's assurance of no criminal proceedings against the Thirty-Two for going to the Embassy did not extend to the second visit. Khariton was ill with bronchial asthma so at Minusinsk they put him in a medical cell. Augustina was told she too would have gone to prison but was saved because baby Jacob had an accident.

It happened the day of Peter's trial. Augustina, Peter's parents, his sisters and his married niece were away from home all day, leaving ten children from three Vashchenko families to look after themselves. Vera, the eldest, was nearly seven. Lida describes how high spirits led to tragedy. "They had a merry time when the parents weren't home! Happy games commenced. They tie a scarf around somebody's eyes and he must try and catch the rest. All ran away except the tinies, who crawled along the floor. And if a two-year-old stumbled over one who could not walk and caught him, the baby would not understand anything and would not crawl away. This was all very funny. When you are having this much fun you don't notice how quickly time passes and then the parents knock at the door.

"But everything at home is a mess and there is general consternation with everyone running around and straightening things up. And the parents continue to knock. Finally, everything is arranged and they open the door to them. If there has been any scrapping during the parents' absence it is now that the tinies complain and, as always, the older ones get into trouble because order in the house depends on them when the parents aren't there. Vera was always in trouble with her parents!

"Mama returned from the trial and all the grown-ups arrived. She took little Jacob into her arms and he continued to cry. When she asked why he was crying, out came the story. It turned out that the children had begun to play and had not noticed that Jacob had crawled up on to a child's chair and it fell over, entangling him. He began to cry. Everyone rushed to free his legs, but they were unable to pull them out. Someone held him and someone else pulled the little chair, and thus, with everyone's help, they finally pulled his legs out of the chair. All this time he was screaming.

"By evening his leg had swollen up and he did not sleep at all that night, but just cried. A week passed. Water collected on his knee, which became inflamed. They put mama and the baby in the hospital and gave him penicillin, but his temperature did not drop. She lay with him in the hospital for two weeks. There was no bed in the hospital so he lay on a cart used for moving sick people. Mama would spend the night sitting on a chair next to him and would only sleep when he went to sleep, which of course happened rarely, so that by the end of the second week she was no longer in any condition to lie with him and began to ask to go home."

In the middle of this all-night nursing Augustina was summoned again to Abakan for interrogation. "The investigator seated me and said: 'Wait a bit while I write here in my book.' He began to write and in the meantime I sat there and went to sleep on the divan. He shouted at me: 'Vashchenko! What are you sleeping for?' And I said: 'What is there for me to do?' He looked at me and said: 'Really! What sort of a woman are you? Your husband is in prison. Your children have been taken away. And you come to an interrogation and sleep, instead of thinking out answers to give the investigator.'"

But the questions were always the same.

The doctors wanted to operate on Jacob's leg for tuberculosis of the bone. However, one of the women in the ward was certain that the baby simply had a dislocated knee. She offered the address of an old man who could reset it. So Augustina refused her permission for the operation, took Jacob away, and went by taxi into the countryside the next day to see the old man, who once had been a vet.

Jacob yelled and sweated, but the moment the leg was reset he fell asleep. The ex-vet warned Augustina that the delay of twenty days meant that the leg would get worse before recovery, and must be packed with steamed birch leaves. Since there were no birches near the Vashchenko home, his aged crone of a wife gave her leaves from a besom.

Jacob eventually recovered completely and learned to walk again.

*　　*　　*

Policemen or KGB agents continued to hover around and inside the houses of those who might try to return to Moscow. At last Peter's sister Natasha, her patience exhausted, "sat down in the entrance to the house and stretched her legs out. When the KGB Chief wanted to enter she said: 'I will not let a single one of you in. Why do you come here? You put our husbands in jail and you yourselves come here every day. That's what the people from the settlement say behind our backs. . . . You should be ashamed of yourself knowing that our husbands are not here and yet you come.' "

Eventually this form of persecution died down and it became easier to live, and to gather to pray for the prisoners that they would be steadfast.

The State tried a new tack. Grigory Vashchenko was released after serving two years of his ten-year sentence. They released the assistant presbyter and the two oldest of the convicted church members, all from prison at Krasnoyarsk.

Undoubtedly a prime factor was world opinion, alerted by the episode of the Thirty-Two into much more concern about freedom of religion in the Soviet Union. However, as Peter comments, Moscow "only made right those things which profited the Soviet authorities." The release was a calculated maneuver: the four men were made to promise to "maintain order in the church" and prevent further complaints to the Embassy. Under pressure and fear of the authorities they criticized the Thirty-Two for "defaming Soviet power" and persuaded several to write to the Presidium with apologies and an admission of guilt that their going to the Embassy had been wrong. Peter says darkly that "this did not bring profit to these people's lives; it was soon apparent to them that it did quite the opposite."

"Then," writes Peter, "discord arose among the believers. Satan found a place to divide the congregation. A spiritual malady arose among the people. Some held firm that we were right to complain; others opposed this," and felt that the four released men ascribed their homecoming to the generosity of the Soviet authorities, instead of to God and the initiative of the Thirty-Two.

The break came when Peter's father preached from the Book of Revelation, which is banned by the State from sermons in registered churches. He expounded chapter twelve with its vivid description of warfare between the forces of light and "the accuser of our brethren. . . . And they overcame him by the blood of the Lamb and by the word of their testimony. And they loved not their lives unto death." A KGB man being present on duty, Grigory was alarmed at the possible consequences. He stood up: "Uncle," he said to Paul, "since you expound this forthrightly, you can meet separately."

Most of the Thirty-Two, with their families and some others including the Chmykhalov household, joined this second church, despite Grigory's warning that they might be put in prison.

Friendship and mutual respect between the cousins survived, and Grigory's faith did not fail. And when, twelve years later, he submitted a record of his sufferings to the United Nations, he gave the credit for his early release in 1963 to "the protest of millions abroad connected with complaints about repression submitted by the believers in Chernogorsk." Peter was surprised when he learned about this; it revealed a change in Grigory's attitude, though in fact the KGB had told him in his prison cell that two million protests had been received by the Soviet government.

History has vindicated the Thirty-Two. Bresenden, the Pentecostal emigrant from Nakhodka, records "the fact that Chernogorsk believers were the pioneers in appealing to Western public opinion and thereby achieving success. Many believers from various cities have begun to utilize this method in order to guard themselves from unwarranted attacks from the authorities. Therefore, the authorities are faced with a dilemma: what methods are 'available' for suppressing believer activeness and to what degree can they be applied? How much will the believers tolerate without complaining? . . . The only issue which concerns the Soviets when dealing with these troublemakers is what effect taking action against them will have on *themselves:* will the West find out and what effect will it have if it does? They are now more careful about taking vengeance on those who damaged their reputation so that it will not be further damaged."

Peter can rightly claim that because of the Thirty-Two, "God sent help and a little bit of freedom, not only to Chernogorsk but to other places, and to all believers, not just to Pentecostals. In Minusinsk all the electrical wiring had already been ripped out and they had closed the Orthodox church, but after this trip it was restored and services are conducted there now. Yes, all those who refuse to accept that this atheist power was founded by God's will, by God's determination and Providence but rather is based on human lies which refute a godly foundation—these people experienced relief after this trip."

After the fall of Khrushchev in October 1964, the persecution lifted for a time throughout the Soviet Union. In Chernogorsk itself, church meetings had not been disrupted since the second trip to the Embassy, but the KGB chief had always attended or sent a deputy, to make sure that none slunk away to Moscow. Now he stopped coming, pretending he disliked being stared at. The church had rest.

10

Peter in Prison

BEFORE HIS TRIAL Peter had "sat" (the usual Russian euphemism for being confined in jail or labor camp) in Minusinsk, at first in the overcrowded, smoke-filled draughty cell. Here he benefited from one of the minor concessions granted by the Soviet authorities.

"After the Thirty-Two made the trip," he relates, "I began to receive food parcels in an unlimited number. But prisoners are suspicious of someone who receives parcels all the time; they reckon he is not to be trusted by those in the same cell, that he has been put there to report everything to the authorities, and the prisoners will be careful in their conduct with him.

"But when they found out why I received parcels so often they changed their views with respect to me; because thirty-two people had been in the American Embassy, that meant there would be some relief, even in the cell in which I sat. I shared with everyone with whom I was in prison. In this cell I prayed openly. My plank-bed was the last one in the row and I prayed in the corner. The prisoners had made fun of me when they heard, and shouted: 'Throw *sapogi* [high boots] at him to make him stop praying.' But now no one threw a boot at me. And later when they found out about me and my family situation, and after I shared my personal parcels with everyone, all this softened their opinions and people became well disposed towards me. But there were no new converts at all, nor were there any believers in the cell.

"The investigator kept saying to my wife: 'Don't bring parcels so often. He can't use them all and distributes them to other people. You can't feed everyone in prison. Feed your children better.' But she answered that the children had enough and it was necessary to bring food here. Then the administration decided to take me out of this common cell where there were fifty people and put me in a cell with two people who had been in it a long time and were mad, or pretending to be; they did not understand anything and were always under medical observation. Investigator Volkov said to me in this cell: 'You win over everyone to your side and people are at your disposal and come to your defense. Now we have put you in a cell where no one will come to your defense.'

"My first day in this cell when the day's meal came—bread and tea—they stood by the *kormyshka*.[1] And they took everything for themselves and left nothing for me. Having received the bread they crumbled it up on the floor into little pieces and then threw them all over the place. Then they collected them and ate them. They had taken both their own bread and mine. I went hungry that day. The next day I stood next to the little window myself and took both their bread and mine. Both these men were tall, but they were thin. On this second day when the "feeding-trough" opened they again rushed to it, but I was already standing there. One wanted to push me aside and thrust out his arm towards me, but I grabbed his hand and said to him: 'Now I am going to feed you!' The one I held by the hand stepped back and the second did not dare to move towards the little window. Each day I received the food and fed them and I did not let them throw the bread on the floor any more.

"But it was impossible to converse with them about anything:

---

1. Literally, *feeding-trough* for animals. Peter describes it as the little carved-out window in the door through which warders serve the food.

you couldn't understand a thing they said. When the investigator summoned me to his office again for questioning he asked: 'Well, how do you like the fellows?' I answered: 'They are better than those I worked with in the motor shop of the auto factory. If everybody there was like these two, it would not be necessary to carry your keys in your pocket, but as it is, if you put your keys on your workbench and turn around you will never know who took them.'

"They took me out of this cell and put me into a medical cell. The cell was very small. On both sides of the cell were two places for resting during the night, shaped like a real coffin covered with a roof. These four places were fastened with strips of iron set in the concrete floor. We slept in these coffins. The cell was clean. Everything was white-washed. There was a stove, but the fire-chamber was in the corridor. There was already one person there. I do not know who he was, but they brought him so much food that he gave me part of what he was brought. I had bread left over so I dried it on the stove and made *sukhari*—dried bread crumbs." Peter put these in a bag for future use.

*   *   *

Peter was sentenced on 21 March 1963 to two years' deprivation of freedom under Article 227 of the Criminal Code. Khariton received five years' exile.

This Article 227, which has sent countless believers to forced labor and exile, makes it a crime to organize or lead a group "whose activity, carried on under the guise of preaching religious doctrines and performing religious rituals, is connected with causing harm to citizens' health . . . or with inciting citizens to refuse to do social activity or to fulfill civic obligations, and likewise with enticing minors into such a group." Peter had taken his children to church services and prayer meetings, had withdrawn them from singing classes and then from school; thus he had been caught red-handed in the commission of a crime as understood by the Article. It was not necessary to prove any harm to health; the acts themselves were sufficient guilt. Nor did it matter that the minors were his own children, nor that he held his beliefs in sincerity from a good conscience. He had "crippled his children with God."

After his sentence on 21 March 1963 Peter was sent to the hard labor camp at Ingash. He was there only a week but had the interesting experience of meeting members of a sect totally opposed to the Communist state, the "True Orthodox." This sect arose soon after the Revolution, formed by priests and laymen who saw Communism as the Anti-Christ. Despite provoking much Soviet brutality, it reached its greatest influence in the years immediately following the Second World War, spreading throughout the Soviet Union until a severe repression in the late '50s.

Peter writes that there were about twelve True Orthodox Christians in the camp, "who were either middle-aged or young. They told me that they must not work for the Communists, for the Soviet power. They would not work in the camp, nor in industry when they were free. I had the occasion to hear a great deal about them in the camp. When free they lived by hiring themselves to do things like saw firewood, bring water, do some carpentry. They would not accept Soviet passports at all and for this they were punished. They would be recorded as parasites. One time they would be tried for parasitism, the next time for breaking the passport regulations. They would be given one year and when they had served their year would be imprisoned again for one year. They were in the camps all their lives, year after year. While the investigation took place they would be in prison for two months and then back to the camp for ten months. They would not work in the camp either, so they were given 400 grams of bread and nothing else—no soup, not even a cup of boiling water. The authorities always said to them: 'Go to work and we will give you soup, boiling water, and *kasha.*'

"They would not let them sleep in the barracks; day and night they were out in the cold. They would pray for an extremely long time—having taken their hats from their heads and standing outside somewhere behind the barracks for two to three hours.

"When the brigade of prisoners went out to work they would

be taken too. All the timber ready along the bank had to be rolled into the water, then dragged out of the water by a conveyer to be taken to the factory. The escorts led the True Orthodox to a stripped log which had fallen from a pile and forced them to roll this log into the water. They would put their hands on the log and say 'Roll it!' but they would not roll it. 'Push it!' but they would not push it. Then escorts would push them together with the log and press them so that they could not get away from it. But they could not train them to work.

"The escorts would push some of them off into the water and then pull them out and chase them back to the barracks zone. Near the zone was a lot of mud, even more where the vehicles pass and their wheels leave ruts. They would force them to these ruts and command: 'Lie down in the mud of this rut!' Some they pushed into the mud. Then they would get a truck and speed towards them. When the driver got close he would brake, but they would lie there and not get out of the ruts. Then the escorts screamed: 'Get up!' Some would get up, and others would be forced up from the ruts. The drivers were given instructions to frighten them to see if they would jump out of the ruts to escape being hit by the truck.

"When they arrived in the zone they would go right to the trash bins. These were large wooden boxes with lids. All sorts of slop from the kitchen and trash would be thrown in here. There they could find fish heads and also fish skin, and moldy crusts of bread. They would drag all this out of the box and put it in their pockets.

"When I arrived I had the opportunity to talk with them, although they do not wish to talk with anyone. I offered them the bread crumbs which I had dried when I was in the medical cell; I had about half a bag full. I returned to my barracks where I was temporarily located (they were going to transfer me to another camp further into the *taiga* to a medium regime camp, whereas this one was a strict regime camp) and the True Orthodox came into the barracks also. The duty person began to drive them out and I to stand up for them. The prisoners who had been here a long time threw themselves on me, but there were some with whom I had been in prison in Minusinsk and had arrived before me and these defended me. While they were all making noise, some for me and others against, I managed to give the two True Orthodox the dried bread crumbs and they immediately left the barracks. They were very glad."

*   *   *

A few days later, in bitter cold weather although it was already spring, Peter entered the medium regime camp of Lugovoi near Reshoty, about nine hundred kilometers (over five hundred fifty miles) east of Abakan on the main Moscow–Vladivostock Trans-Siberian main line. A narrow gauge railway led to a group of forced labor camps engaged in logging in the *taiga*.

Here he found his young cousin Andrei serving sentence for refusing to be drafted into the Army, and two other Chernogorsk believers, and two from Novosibirsk province, all Pentecostals. "We worked in different brigades, but we gathered together when we could to read the Gospel, pray, and discuss the Word of God."

The labor camp was less confined than the prison, for the living zone was large and in summer they could get away by themselves. The other prisoners never reported them but they had to be careful not to be spotted by anyone from the administration. "They are very severe in the camp if you pray, read the Gospels or have prayer services. They would punish you by depriving you of parcels or visits, or the right to buy things at the camp kiosk, or they would put you in the punishment cell, the *shizo*."[2]

A *shizo* is barely heated, with concrete floors; duckboards and the wearing of jackets are allowed only at night; in Solzhenitsyn's time in Stalin's camps those sentenced to a spell were stripped to their underwear, but regulations had become a little less harsh. "In the *shizo* you are fed meagerly," records Peter. "The first day they give you 400 grams [14 ounces] of bread and a glass of cold

---

2. Short for *shtrafnoi izoliator*, penal isolation. Vladimir Bukovsky in his memoirs calls it "the box." See *To Build a Castle: My Life as a Dissenter*, trans. Michael Scrammell (New York: Viking Press, 1979), pp. 257–58.

water. The second day you are given 400 grams of bread and hot soup in which there is only liquid; if a potato turns up, that's good. Then again 400 grams of bread and a glass of water the next day. Sometimes people sit there one, two, or three months and even up to six months for various crimes and they can no longer walk because they are weak. This is what a *shizo* is."

When Peter, Andrei and the others slipped away to read the Bible and pray, they knew what they risked, but "not once were we caught by the administration, although they all knew that we were believers. Now it has even become more strict. There are many young people serving time and in the mornings and in the evenings they teach them drilling like in the Army; in the past they did not do that in the camps." Peter's eldest son Sasha was a small boy at this time, but fifteen years later in September 1978, while serving time in a labor camp for his faith, Sasha was beaten and thrown into the *shizo* and kept there for fifteen days and nights because he possessed a Bible portion and allowed other prisoners to read it.

*   *   *

Peter served his sentence until December 1964 and returned to Chernogorsk stronger in his faith. For Khariton it was different, bringing the first break in the ranks.

In Minusinsk prison Khariton's asthma had become worse. He was sent to serve his five years' exile in the northern regions, first at Yeniseisk, and then a few kilometers northward at Ust-Kem, where the Kem river enters the wide Yenisei on its way to the Arctic Ocean. "He worked at a hospital, since he was a doctor's assistant," relates Peter. "I don't remember how long he lived there alone. He received an apartment, his family moved to him, but the three oldest children—Valya, Petya, Tanya—had been taken away and were in the Zaozern *internat.*

"They began to promote him in his work. He was a good worker and the supervisor of the hospital would always summon him anytime, day or night. The people liked him and began to treat him well. And since he was living there alone and there were no believers he began to accommodate himself to life and gradually left God. He was made supervisor himself when the other man left, and they forced him to educate the hospital personnel, to give lectures against God. At first he did not do it, but then he began to give the lectures. The children, seeing that only the mother held fast and prayed to God, but the father did not, started also to move away."

Valya's story was even sadder. When first taken to the *internat* she had written brave letters of faith and defiance which Khariton gave the Embassy at the time of the Thirty-Two: they were published in *Newsweek* and wrung many hearts in the West. But when Khariton was still free he and his wife had seldom visited the children, though they sent them money and parcels. After his sentence Augustina went whenever she could; she would visit her own children at Achinsk on the way to see Peter in the labor camp, and Khariton's at Zaozern on the way back, though an aunt cannot replace a mother.

"Somehow, somewhere," writes Peter, "she would see them and talk with them so that they did not lose hope. Having lived four years in the *internat*, Valya asked to be allowed to make a trip home. The director made a proposal to her: 'If you will speak on the radio, we will let you make a trip home.' For a long time she would not agree, but then, apparently, the desire to visit home overcame her conscience and she agreed to speak over the radio. They wrote down for her what she had to read. She sat silent for a long time, and then she said over the radio: 'Once I believed, but now I want to say, that there is no God whatsoever.'

"But they deceived her. They would not let her go home.

"Today Valya does not believe in God. She studied to become a doctor and is now working as a gynecologist in the city of Sverdlovsk. She married a nonbeliever and has become a nonbeliever herself."

After completion of sentence Khariton took Styura and their family to live in Georgia so that the southern mountain air of the Caucasus could help his asthma. Peter cannot understand how

Khariton can deny Christ. "Perhaps he still believes in his heart and that's all, but he has no association with believers."

All Khariton's children followed him into apostasy. The *internat* cooled their ardor and blinded their understanding, as it did the abducted children of another Chernogorsk family, whose forced "reeducation' destroyed their faith. The eldest son remained a believer long after he left the *internat*, but the arrest of his mother, and service in the Soviet army, weighted the scale and he went over to atheism.

Unlike Khariton's, Peter Vashchenko's children survived abduction and the State's efforts to destroy their love for Christ. How the three eldest daughters emerged from the *internat* with deep and sensitive Christian dedication, how this family held together at tremendous cost after their father's imprisonment, is one of the sagas of modern Siberia.

11

The Achinsk Desert

AUGUSTINA AT LAST received permission to see the girls in the *internat*. Until the return of the Thirty-Two the family's stream of letters of complaint to Moscow, the citizen's normal route of redress, had achieved nothing except the obligatory receipts. "However, Minister Kuznetsov's promise to let them come home was unfulfilled, although we did not cease bothering them with letters to free the children."

Augustina took her mother-in-law and little Jacob. When they reached Achinsk on its hill, they learned that these visits must be in the presence of the school director Sofia Grigorevna Ishchuk, a short plump woman of Jewish descent, or one of the teachers. "Each time we were warned to talk only about their studies or their health, and not to say a word about God—otherwise meetings would be stopped. The teachers sat next to us and a bit further away sat the children. The conversation would be through the teachers."

The Vashchenkos found this intolerable. So, under the very noses of the teachers, they fixed a secret rendezvous for the next day. They did it by using a private language they call "Pugachev," which is a very simple code yet unbreakable because it depends on the names the children used when too small to pronounce their actual names properly. This became normal practice at every official meeting. Since the teachers watched the girls sharply and never let them go into the city unaccompanied, each one would slip away in turn while the others, if asked a sister's whereabouts, would reply vaguely that she was running around somewhere.

Occasionally they slept with their mother at the home of whichever believer was her hostess. Once Lida was caught. The mother of one of her school friends, a day girl, worked at the *internat* as a janitor, and two teachers had given Lida permission to spend a night with her while the mother was on night duty although it was against the rules; neither they nor the girl's mother knew that Augustina stayed nearby.

Peter describes what happened: "At 1:00 A M. in this believer's apartment there was knocking. Everyone woke up and the woman of the house went outside to ask who had come. They talked for a long time and then came into the room. Lida and my wife were in the same bed and pretended to be asleep. The woman of the house persuaded the teachers to let Lida stay until morning." Director Ishchuk had discovered they had let Lida stay with the girl and she had phoned the address for evidence to put her on punishment report. The teachers, however, concealed that Lida had spent the night with her mother because they did not want their worker, the girl's mother, to be fired.

Director Ishchuk had been uneasy for some time at the Vashchenko girls' slow progress towards socialist attitudes, at their independence and contempt for atheist teaching; they acted as if they forgot that officially they were State orphans. In September 1964, after two years of the secret meetings, she discovered the reason by accident.

"Mama and Jacob had come," recalls Lyuba. "We were given an official meeting in the director's presence, and during it we fixed up an illegal meeting for the next day. This took place, but when mama boarded the bus to go to the railway station, the director happened to be in the bus. She immediately noticed mama and began to berate her with questions. 'You're still here. You didn't leave yesterday? You met with the children somewhere, right?' Mama answered yes, she had."

Sofia Grigorevna could not stop visits authorized by Moscow but her behavior became unpredictable. Once the girls' grandmother, seventy-three at the time, came alone and "we darted out into the corridor to greet her. She had brought candy, *prianiki* (little cakes), tomatoes. But the director shoved her out on to the porch, where she dropped all the presents for us and they rolled everywhere. Then she fell herself. Our hate of them became even greater, that they would push such an old woman until she fell. There were many such incidents."

One time, when Augustina brought eight-month-old Abel, Sofia Grigorevna won a tactical victory by taking her to the police station immediately after the official meeting saying, "This woman had been deprived of her parental rights, yet she comes to them all the time." The police kept her for interrogation until late at night, making sure that she caught the last train to Chernogorsk.

Lida has some trenchant comments on the incident. "The police asked, 'Why did you come? The children are not yours!' They tried to suggest an absurdity, as if the children were not hers, or they could force her to give them up. The authorities had created a law fit for beasts, but even if you take a piglet from a sow, she will attack you."

The Vashchenkos' form of attack, as Christians, was never to grudge the weary, expensive journeys which kept hope and love alive.

*   *   *

For the girls, the *internat*, a two-story building of classrooms and dining hall, with a three-story dormitory beside it, was a desert where they came to Christian maturity through loneliness and pain, inflicted by a State which placed its Godless philosophy above the happiness or freedom of a child. "We got very tired of this government atmosphere," writes Lyuba. "Besides, we felt humiliated because not only did the teachers follow our every step, but the children were forced to do the same. Nevertheless, despite the assignments they gave them, we were able occasionally to discover something in common, especially when they saw some unjust actions on the part of the teachers towards themselves. There was no one to say a word in their defense; then they sensed that we shared a common experience of injustice.

"They would help us when our parents came to see us and the visits were not allowed. Our parents could trust them completely to let us know that they were waiting in the grove, the cemetery, or some other place. But sometimes the teachers would set them completely against us and then it was difficult to find a quiet corner, some comfortable place to get settled in silence and rest where no one would see."

The Vashchenko girls missed their smaller sisters and brothers, although their mother always brought the latest arrival as soon as she and the new baby could travel; during the six years of the exile at Achinsk she bore Dinah, Abel and Paul—a baby each calendar year of 1965, '66, '67. They found something of a substitute for the family by "adopting" orphans of the preschool children's home opposite the *internat,* beside the grove. This was "always a source of joy for us," writes Lida. "It was as if we were seeing our little sisters and brothers. On Saturday we would gather up candy and cookies which we had received at lunch and dinner. Our appearance there on Sunday would delight the children and they would run to meet us. We would feed them and they would ask when we were coming again. Each of us picked a child, or two or three, as her own and took them by the hand outside and played with them. 'Mama, are you going to come again soon?' they would ask and we liked this.

"And if we had taken on two or three children it was necessary to collect goodies in the middle of the week, because on Saturday the one portion would not be enough. Now, fourteen years later I remember these children. . . . Sometimes it would happen that we could not restrain ourselves and would eat all the candy ourselves which we had saved up! Then with tears in our eyes we would look across the road and were ashamed to go with empty hands.

"The children were very thin and were always frightened if you suddenly raised your hand; they would think you were going to hit them. The older group said they were beaten and the little ones didn't say anything. I do not know how they were fed but we, certainly, had cooks who would not put everything into the kettle. We were older than some and therefore noticed if a cook left our dining room with her bag full of food. We complained about it, they would fire her, but then it began all over again.

"Once on a cold autumn day we arrived at the children's home and saw a group sorting potatoes in the yard. The husband of one of the teachers tied a bag of potatoes on to a bicycle. The children dropped their work and rushed over to us. A rebuke from the teacher compelled them to return to work and we were brusquely sent beyond the gate. This attracted our interest. Later we found out that the children's home bought the potatoes but one of the teachers simply took them for herself. This is a mundane story, but it brings a wider perspective to life.

"We had one man teacher who was on friendly terms with the woman in charge of linen and thus had opportunity to exchange his old linen for new, older underwear for new, etc. What could we do? If sometimes they were scared that we would realize what was going on, they had nothing really to be afraid of; the main idea was to select a collective of teachers and other workers whom they could rely on and then carry on."

In both children's home and *internat* many boys and girls came from broken homes; the father of one of Lida's friends had killed the mother with an axe. Teachers took a parent's place for their favorites while the rest grew up in a jungle of fights and bullies, and Lida adds: "A great many from the *internat* are sent on to a school for the mentally retarded, but what had affected them is hard to say. They are taught by educated people; why then do they turn out hysterical and mentally retarded? Some were already very lazy, and these simply needed the advice of those they could trust, who could support and encourage them in the difficulties of life; they were like hardworking children who had lost their way. Some were fortunate enough to meet such teachers and got their lives in order, but they were very few."

Others put all their faith in the benevolent State and Party "which cared for homeless children," but after leaving school were not allowed to do what they wanted. "The State lost so many gifted people who were capable of doing worthy things," writes Lida. "So many of these talented homeless children did not have the opportunity to develop, and perished in drunkenness, debauchery and in prison, disillusioned with life and society."

Lida, Lyuba and Nadya were forbidden to help unhappy or poorly guided schoolfriends in the only lasting way. Very occasionally an opportunity came to throw in a word. "Once during excavations in the old cemetery across from the *internat* some children found an icon and ran to a teacher and showed it to her. She said: 'Take it to the Vashchenkos. They have not prayed to it for a long time.' And since a grown-up gave permission they brought it. We said: 'We pray often. but not to an icon. Give this back to the teacher. We don't need it—and perhaps she prays to an icon!' For a long time after this the teacher was angry at us."

Not only were they forbidden to practice their religion, but every effort was made to wean them from it: "They try to instill into you a completely unreal person in opposition to your real self." In Lida's view that is to reduce you to slavery.

Both sides in the dispute recognized the red tie of the Pioneers as the symbol of surrender to the atheist State. At the school itself and at the Pioneer camps to which they were taken in the summer holidays the authorities hated to see parades spoiled because three girls lacked the red tie which stands out on the white blouse over the blue skirt. Lyuba says the teachers "resorted to every possible device to force me to put on a tie. They used flattery, deception, and encouragement. Right before we were to leave for the All-Union pioneer camp they said: "If you put on a tie, you may go." But I did not put on a tie and they gave the pass to another girl. They tried to threaten, but nothing came of that either. Then once again they began to propose going to the Pioneer camp in the Caucasus which is called 'Little Eagle.' All I had to do was just put on my tie, but again they were unable to bribe me. They gave me a lot of dolls and all types of toys, but this did not help them. Therefore, my teacher was extremely angry, especially on festive occasions when all the children were supposed to be dressed identically, with their ties, and I did not have one on, yet they had to put me in the formation. This infuriated them. 'What can we do with her?' Often they would say, 'Better ten hooligans to bring up than you three.' "

It was easy to gang up the class against a Vashchenko because the "collective," as in all areas of Soviet life, counted for much more than the individual. The others would be urged to humiliate a Vashchenko, to make her feel unwanted and a disgrace to the class because she was a believer; even those who took her part at other times would be swept into the struggle. Once they put a frozen rat in Lida's desk, and it so upset her that she refused to attend lessons for days. Another time "I had an argument with a teacher who told me that my parents did not need me and therefore did not take me away, although he knew very well that they were not allowed to, and if they did take me, I would be brought back again." Sometimes at night she would lie under her blanket and long to die: "Lord, take me to Yourself. If I go home they will only seize me back again but from you they cannot." Other children in their tears cry for mama but Lida's mama was helpless. "Seeing her as helpless, I never called for her. When I wept I cried, 'Lord, Lord.'

"One evening when the only staff left were the night nanny and the janitor I went down from the third floor and lay on the stone paving underneath the window in just my shirt. There was a lot of ice and I lay for a long time on my back; I wanted to catch cold and get sick so that I could die. Time passed and the nanny noticed that my bed was empty and she began to search. She came up to me and wanted to pick me up, but I resisted. For a long time she tried to persuade me to return to the dormitory and I only gave up when I was once and for all frozen. But I did not get sick or die. I got a little flu and that was all."

However, the secret meetings with parents or grandmother continued despite director Ishchuk's efforts. Pupils whom she set as guards to follow the girls took their side, delighted because Peter, back from labor camp, and Augustina always brought goodies, and sometimes money which the girls would share out so that their orphan friends, who never had visits from parents, could buy ice cream or fruit. The school authorities gave up; gradually they became less stric̄ at the official meetings because they knew they could not stop the clandestine ones which followed

The *internat* education was quite good in itself and all three Vashchenkos were intelligent. Lyuba enjoyed geometry, literature, Russian language, history, and especially domestic science; she dreamed of being a first-rate seamstress and then a dress designer. Nadya could have made a great career in music had the school allowed her to learn an instrument. Lida took a technical college course which could lead her to being director of clerks in a store. But when she was about to take her exams she was asked, as a matter of course, her religious views. She replied that she continued to believe in God. The careers interviewer said: "Then you will not enjoy success in your job assignment. Having graduated you would be entrusted with about twenty or thirty people. In such a position you would be required to deliver lectures on atheism, force those who are not members of the trades union or the Komsomol to join; and a boss should be a member of the Party." Lida realized that her training had been a waste of time.

The interviewer had been frank about a handicap which lies heavy, right across the Societ Union: an open Christian, whether Orthcdox, Catholic or Evangelical, whether belonging to a registered or an unregistered local church, is barred from any but the lower rungs of the ladder, not only in intellectual careers such as teaching, as the West is sometimes told by official religious leaders, but in all careers, because every boss must be a "reeducator."

Lida put on the red tie in the end, to ease the pressure which was hardest on her as eldest; she wore it in the spirit of Naaman when he bowed down in the house of Rimmon. Lyuba continued to refuse; she put one tie in the toilet pan. Nadya refused too.

Soon after putting on the tie Lida turned sixteen. on 6 March 1967. The State could not legally keep her in the *internat*. She did not wait to finish the course, but took her internal passport and went home to Chernogorsk.

12

Interlude: Timothy

TIMOTHY CHMYKHALOV WAS nearly nine months when the Thirty-Two returned from Moscow. His early memories therefore date from the years when life had become a little easier for the Christians of Chernogorsk. He gives a graphic and at times amusing and charming picture of growing up as the youngest of a close-knit believer family in the mid-1960s. His parents were in their early forties and his unmarried aunt Anna, whom he calls Nanny and who, like his father, worked in the coal mines, was a few years younger.

Timothy's three brothers and his sister all had diminutives; his own was Tima. Next above him in age was Alexander (Shura or Shurik); then came Anatoly (Tolik or Tolya) who was nearly four years older than Shura. Vladimir (Vova or Volodia) seemed a big brother, being eleven when Timothy first could remember him, and their only sister, Nadezhda (Nadya) was the eldest, a young teenager. Their beloved elderly grandmother, Yelena Fedorovna, completed the family circle in the little house in the Mine 9 Settlement on the street called Twentieth Khakassian Year.[1]

1. So named because it was laid out in 1950, twenty years after the nomad chieftains were replaced by a soviet-style government in Khakassia.

"Time passed," writes Timothy of his earliest memories, "and mother began to teach me to work. They took me to the fields from the time I was three, and I began to cry. Mother and all the children started weeding the potatoes and I ran on ahead crying and would not weed. Mother gave me a little spank and sent me home," where the old grannie would comfort him. He was her favorite and sometimes she would beg him off chores. He loved to listen to her stories of the famine and the terrible hardships of wartime.

The Chmykhalovs planted potatoes in the allotment provided by the mine. "In the summer when it was necessary to weed the potatoes mother would gather us all together and we would go to the fields. She immediately divided up the rows among us according to age; the older received more rows, the younger ones less, and since I was younger than everyone else I was given the least number of rows. When we finished weeding she would allot us more until all the potatoes were weeded, and when we had finished we went home with joy, because at home they would give us a present for good work. And if someone had been lazy, mother would punish at once and not put it off.

"In the autumn when the time came to dig the potatoes, we would pile them in the cart, everyone would get hitched up, and we pulled them homeward. People always made fun of us and called us 'Slaves of God,' but no one ever decided to help us in this hard work, because we are believers in Jesus Christ our Lord."

Each child had duties. The two smallest, Shura and Timothy, grazed the geese. And thereby hangs a tale, from 1965. "Shura and I grazed the geese together. One person alone did not do the grazing because the nonbeliever boys would gang together and beat us, so Shura and I would graze together. One time rainclouds appeared and a storm began. Mother sent Nadya, Vova, and Tolya to chase us home with the geese, which were still small so the rain could kill them. As we hurried home it was raining very hard, with thunder and lightning and a strong wind which kept blowing the geese over. The rain completely soaked us. When we got home we realized that the goose which we called 'Papa' was missing. We immediately all began to cry and went to search.

"Beyond the settlement were some holes for telephone posts, a meter deep. We immediately looked in these holes and out of one of them we heard the sound of our 'Papa' goose. We were overjoyed. His wings were stuck in the mud and he could not fly out. We tried to think of a way to pull him out of this deep hole, but there was nothing with which to pull him out. We came up with the idea of lowering our oldest brother Vova head first into the hole so that he could grab the goose with his hands. Then we would pull him out. This was because he was the tallest and thinnest. We held on to his legs and Vova began to descend into the hole. He grabbed hold of the goose and we started to pull him up, but in the heavy rain we could not keep our footing and kept falling because it was slippery."

The sight of three small boys slithering in the mud to rescue a goose from a Siberian bog must have been funny, but soon they were in trouble. The upshot shows their spirit, young as they were.

"We all got frightened, and in desperation began to scream because the hole was filling up with water and Vova was beginning to choke. But our Jesus Christ is Almighty and helped us and with all our strength we pulled Vova and our 'Papa' goose out.

"We were extremely happy and ran home with great glee carrying 'Papa' in our arms. We put him in with the other geese and they immediately began to cackle and were of course very glad. When we arrived home the rain fell even harder and turned into a downpour, and our town began to drown. Water rose knee-high in level places. Several people went about with shovels and unblocked the trenches so that the water could drain off more quickly, because our settlement is built in a low place. The downpour lasted about three hours or more, and when the rain stopped more water began to arrive and covered everything. When it dropped there was a great deal of material left in the gardens; the water had brought silt and grime. And the earth had turned into cement, ruining many of the plants. We had to drag out of the garden everything the water had left."

The Chmykhalovs, "in order to live and to be able to give to others," depended much on cattle. Often they had as many as nine head, including calves. They grazed them on waste ground which abounded in the neighborhood, butchered them and sold meat "and there would still be two or three milk cows left for us. Few people keep livestock in our area because of the hay which is difficult to obtain. Nadya would milk them, give them water, and chase them out with the children. And when she got a job, if she had to go in the morning, she would get up at five, milk the cows, and give them water, gather us boys to accompany the herd, and then go to work."

Grazing the cows brought plenty of fun. "When we were small," continues Timothy, "we would drive them to Mine 9 where we would bathe in the reservoir where the fine coal remained. And when we arrived home mama would immediately wash us because we were dirty from the coal and we looked like coal! We would have to bathe three or four times in order to get clean." With boys and girls from two other believer families they swam in the nude, though "Mama scolded us for taking off all our clothes when we went swimming." They were unashamed to swim in the nude, for no one saw them, but when they grew older the Chmykhalov boys looked back on the episode with embarrassment, "and we consider it very disgraceful."

Mine 9 was about two kilometers (a little over a mile) from home, and they swam there "for a long time until all our parents found out that it was miry there and you could drown. Then we began to go swimming on the sly. Mother spanked us and said: 'I won't see you near that filthy reservoir!'

"We switched over to another game. We took food and sugar from the house into the fields, lit a bonfire, heated the sugar, and when the sugar had dissolved we would cool it and eat it. It was very tasty. We also made little stores and sold in them what we had brought from home. Also, when autumn came we would gather mushrooms, fry them in a children's frying pan, make a dinner, and eat.

"Another family began to drive the cows with us—the Vashchenkos. They could take turns grazing their own cows because they had lots of children. Jacob would drive ours, or Abel with Paul; then John would graze, and all of a sudden there would be ten children. We started bringing a field pot and would cook soup made from potatoes and smoked meat. (We smoked meat for the summer so that we could take it to the fields, and so that it would not spoil at home.) Shura and I would bring smoked meat from home and the others would bring other things: some brought potatoes, others cabbage, and still others would bring cups, spoons and bread. This is how we spent the summer and the autumn."

Occasionally they played so hard that they forgot the cows, which wandered off on their own, "and we ran through the fields crying and looking for them. When we didn't find the cows we would run home and creep into the byre and look and see if the cows were in the place where we were supposed to drive them in the evening. If they were not there we would run crying to look for them again, and if we ran about all day and had not found them we would come home crying in the evening and say that we had lost the cows. Mother would say: 'Why didn't you come earlier and say that you had lost them?' Then we would all go out together and search and if we did not find them at night then in the morning we would go to search for the cows with buckets, because they had not been milked in the evening, and in the morning would be bursting with milk.

"When we found the cows we immediately milked them there in the field. Mother did not punish us for losing the cows because she was afraid that we would run off somewhere and not come home. She would always try to convince us we must watch the cows better and, if we did lose the cows, to come right home and tell them."

Sometimes kindly truck drivers, bringing coal refuse to the dump, would give one kid a ride to and from the mine while the other remained with the cows, but the mine officials did not like it when the cows wandered into the crops. "We had a cow named 'April' who was sly. She was always running off and causing damage in some meadow or field. There was no way you could graze her;

you could not hold her back and the others followed her. The cows were more clever than we were and always got into the crops to graze there.

"I climbed up on the edge of the dump area so that I could see the cows better, and then I saw that two people riding horses were coming through the planted fields. They wanted to chase the cows out. When they had come up close to our cows, 'April' all of a sudden raised her head and saw the horses which the men on duty were riding. She immediately stuck her rear in the air, and darted into the dump, and the others ran out of the crops after her. The duty men on their horses cantered after 'April,' but 'April' and all the calves and cows were already in the dump area. She was always the victor and they were never able to chase her out. And this is how I grazed the cattle until I reached school age."

Because the cows meant much to the family economy, finding hay for winter was very important. Petro would range as far as twenty kilometers (over twelve miles) in his search for grass on waste land which he might mow. In a bad year he would be reduced to cutting wayside verges, while Shura and Timothy pulled as much as they could. The grown-ups tied it all in sheaves and loaded their cart until it was full; then father, mother and nannie harnessed themselves to the cart and the five of us would go back."

The year when Timothy was eight they had been allowed to mow a field five kilometers away, where they went on foot because they had only one bicycle. "When the hay had been mown and had dried we would go again and rake and put it together in sheaves. Whoever was lazy was punished by mama immediately. Once I raked badly and mama forced me to rake again; I did not want to, then mama spanked me with the rake and the handle of the rake broke in two!

"When the hay had been put into sheaves, we found a tractor driver who agreed to help us transport it. During the evening we all gathered and when he arrived we immediately took a seat and left, everyone except Grandmother and Nadya. Grandmother was very ill and Nadya had to milk the cow and water the calves.

When we arrived at the field, had loaded the hay, and tied it down, we—Vova, Tolya, Shura, and I, Timothy—climbed onto the cart, dug ourselves a hole, got down in it, and then we began to move. Mother sat in the cabin with the tractor driver.

"As we were driving along and nearing the village we suddenly saw two lights across the field. They dazzled us and came closer. Our tractor kept going; then policemen in a Volga car pulled up and stopped our tractor. The driver crawled out. He was pale. They looked at the number and examined the wheels and the bumper. They wanted to take him into the police station, but one of them said: 'Let him go,' and asked: 'Have you seen a vehicle in the field?' The tractor driver said no, and asked: 'What is going on?' They answered: 'A vehicle ran over a man and we are now looking for it.'

"They left to look in the fields and we went home and when we arrived at home the tractor driver said: 'You did the right thing by not looking out from the hay. Otherwise, I could have been put in jail for hauling you in the hay.' The tractor driver helped us unload and then we gave him money so that he could buy his kids some sweets, but he said: 'Buy your own kids sweets with this money.'

"Then he left and all night we lugged hay to the hayloft. When we finished we washed and went to bed. When people woke up and saw that there was no hay beyond the garden they were very amazed that we had dragged it all in during one night and had finished by five in the morning." The Chmykhalovs had a rule always to put hay in their loft at once. "If we left the hay until morning then somebody could throw in nails or glass. This is a rule we have had since we were small and have until this day."

Timothy has memories of other harassments of believers. He describes much else: the Pentecostal services of worship; his schooldays and the trouble they brought him; and many sidelights on life's enjoyments and sufferings. But he covers much the same ground as the Vashchenkos and therefore must wait, or this book will grow too long.

Instead, it must return to the main story.

13

Sent to the Madhouse

DURING THE HOLIDAY celebrating the fiftieth anniversary of the Communist "October Revolution," 7 November 1967, Lyuba ran away from the Achinsk *internat*, five weeks before her fifteenth birthday, and thus more than a year before she would be free legally.

She had been intensely homesick yet never was allowed a visit to her home, which officially did not exist. The school let her stay the previous new year holiday with another girl, whose parents welcomed her warmly and showed their concern by many questions, so that at the festive meal "I felt that I was in a family and not in the *internat* where I was so sick of everything. But it was not *my* family. This feeling swept over me with even greater force later: they drank a lot of vodka and wine and tried to persuade me to drink with them, but I did not drink anything. After this family dinner my girl friend's father went to visit some neighbors, the sister and her husband went to a club, the mother lay down to rest, and my friend and I began to clear the table of dishes.

"When we had finished cleaning the house she and I went to sleigh down the little hill on the street. It was already evening when we returned home and I saw the following scene: the neighbors had dragged her father home drunk because he had begun to make a noise and fight. He continued to do this in his own house, and when he saw us his swear words were hurled at me and at all the stories which I had told him during the first day of my stay with them. He cursed horribly, cursed everyone and everything, and threw himself forward for a fight. I scurried outside, stood for a little bit on the porch and thought: 'Where can I go now?' Then I went out on to the street.

"I wandered slowly along. When I came to myself I stopped walking, because I was already at the edge of the village heading into the country. I don't remember how long I stood there. It was a quiet night, warm and full of stars. The snow was floating down slowly in big flakes, and because of the stars and the white snow it was light. In the distance a strip of woods darkened the horizon. I heard steps; I turned around. It was my friend. She did not ask me about anything, but just quietly came up and stood beside me. We stood there without a word for a very long time."

Perhaps it was the memory of that holiday which gave Lyuba an overpowering impulse to run away to her real home the next winter holiday. Teachers soon arrived at Chernogorsk and attempted to persuade her to return to school but when she refused they did not drag her back.

At home she found "terrible poverty. Often there was hardly a kopeck of money to buy anything." Peter worked in Mine 9 but a substantial slice of his weekly wage was withheld because he did not want Soviet citizenship. Augustina had been forced to leave her job the previous year because the Mine refused to grant five days' leave when the children were ill at Achinsk: it may have been the time when Nadya lost the top of a finger in an accident. Lida had been refused a job; Lyuba tried to get work but was told she was too young to employ. Thus fifteen mouths depended on Peter's truncated wage, and much of that must go on fares to Achinsk and the little presents which mattered so much. At last, on 24 January 1968 Peter complained to the chairman of the city executive committee, Grigorev, and Augustina was taken back at the mine.

The family circle had suffered a sad loss while the girls were at the *internat.* "Uncle" Andrei, Peter's young cousin and foster brother, whom he had left fit on his own release in December 1964, never returned from the Lugovoi labor camp near Reshoty.

The Vashchenkos regard his death as virtually murder. Early in 1966 Andrei had three months to run of his sentence of five years' hard labor for refusing to serve in the armed forces. He was now twenty-three years old and had kept the faith, to the indignation of the labor camp authorities, who several times threatened him, "You will never see home alive."

On a day of deep snow with a frost of minus 45 degrees centigrade, a temperature colder than regulations allow for outside work, he was ordered into the *taiga.* Regulations lay down that a team must not number less than three—one to axe and two to guide the falling tree safely with poles. But only the brigade-leader (another convict) went with Andrei.

Instead of lumber brigades all around, these two worked alone; no witnesses. Telling Andrei to shift snow from the base of a pine tree, the leader began to cut another. It fell on Andrei, pinning his leg, and the leader left him alone in the snow while he went for a tractor to pull the trunk clear. Before Andrei froze into unconsciousness and death, perhaps he sang for the last time on earth one of his favorite hymns, unheard except by his Lord waiting beside him with the martyr's crown prophesied by his mother, Fekla, on her deathbed long ago.

"They informed Grigory by telegram to come and get his body," writes Peter. "We buried him at home in Chernogorsk. Many believers came, even from neighboring cities and villages. The local authorities were uneasy and many of them went along with the funeral procession. When we arrived at the cemetery there were already many authorities there. They were afraid there would be a riot because everyone knew why he had been sent to the camp. But there was no one to complain to and thus it was slipping into oblivion until they began to threaten Sasha with this same outcome . . ." That was twelve years later, in October 1978. Then the Vashchenkos knew for sure that the accident had been contrived. Peter's eighteen-year-old son, serving forced labor for the same offense of refusing to serve in the Red Army, was threatened with "the fate which befell your uncle Andrei."

*   *   *

Early in May 1968 the third daughter, Nadya, ran away from the *internat* in her turn. Her age was only thirteen and three-quarters. She rejected pleas from officials that she should return. Two more years of "serving time," as her mother expressed it, were left, yet the State abandoned the attempt to "reeducate" the third of these Christian girls who, in their eyes, were worse than hooligans. The Vashchenkos were together again at last after six years: all eleven children, the parents, grandparents, Natasha and her daughter and grandchildren; the family choir could again find full voice.

It was now more than five years since Peter had tried to emigrate. The resolve to go where they might worship God freely had not weakened, nor had the intransigence of the Soviet State. Pressure on believers which had lessened after Khrushchev's fall was again increasing. The Politburo in Moscow were well aware that Christianity's revival in the Soviet Union had gathered momentum despite discrimination, propaganda and slander, rules and regulations, legal process, and open assault.

Towards the end of May, Peter was summoned to the city executive committee and confronted with a man who identified himself as Robert Efimovich Golst (well known for a commentary on the law of cults) from the Council of Ministers in Moscow. "He was not the only one there but I do not now remember who else. He proposed many things, that I begin to live as other people lived, that I quit religion and God. When he did not receive a positive answer from me, he said: 'Whether you read the Bible or not, we will imprison you anyway.' "

Peter and Augustina decided to appeal for help from the American Embassy: surely some way could be found whereby they could leave the Soviet Union as a family. Peter sold the cow to pay for the tickets to Moscow and took with him Lida (seventeen), Lyuba (fifteen), Nadya (thirteen) and also Vera who at twelve might be in danger of abduction to an *internat*.

On 29 May 1968 they sought to enter the Embassy. The police refused to let them pass and seized Peter and Lida, at which the other three girls, terrified, dodged the guards and reached diplomatic soil. Two were seized by Soviet drivers working there and dragged back. Lyuba ran into a building and into a corridor. Some women in an office looked up surprised but did not approach her, and as they were talking English, which she could not, she walked on until she encountered a man who offered in Russian to take her to the ambassador. He lightly grasped Lyuba's arm as if to guide her, but when they were out of sight of the women, he twisted it with all his strength, forced her out through the other archway, and handed her to the police.

Peter and Lida had been removed already to the police booth round the corner, where they heard a policeman telephone: "We have taken a mother *(sic)* and a father but the children have run into the Embassy." The two were removed to Eleventh Police Sector station and separated. During interrogation Lida was threatened with a revolver. She answered: "Kill me. I do not know anything and will not tell you anything."

The police held Peter for seven days while they worked out his identity. He was outside the law because he did not carry an internal passport, but on 6 June they released him with orders to leave Moscow at once. They warned him that if ever he spent more than three hours in the American Embassy he would be treated as a traitor to his country.

They said his children had been returned to Chernogorsk. He made the three-and-a-half-day journey home but they were not there and no one, in the family or the city offices, had heard of their whereabouts. A wearisome round trip to Achinsk drew blank. With scarcely a pause he decided to go back to Moscow and seek American aid. Augustina and his sister Natasha came too.

At 10:00 A.M. on 18 June 1968 Peter, Augustina and Natasha approached the entrance of the American Embassy and began to explain to the Soviet policeman why they desired to enter. His reply was to seize Augustina and Natasha, at which Peter lunged past him to safety inside.

The ambassador, the late Llewellyn R. Thompson, and the consul, Samuel E. Fry, treated Peter Vashchenko with practical sympathy. They telephoned a ministry and learned that the children were in the Danilovsky Children's Holding Center in Moscow. An Embassy man drove Peter over in a diplomatic car but they were told a lie: that the girls were not there. Back at the Embassy Ambassador Thompson telephoned a ministry again and was told another lie: that the girls had been sent to Siberia, to the city eastward of Achinsk, Krasnoyarsk, where the Trans-Siberian crosses the broad Yenisei river.

The ambassador then discussed the Vashchenkos' future. And now came a misunderstanding.

This is what Peter understood to have happened: the ambassador told him that he and his family would need a sponsor in America to send an invitation to emigrate. A consular officer thereupon offered his own father as willing to act as sponsor, though it would take a little time to obtain the invitation. The ambassador replied (in Peter's memory): "Why don't you invite them yourself?" The officer agreed and the papers were made out. The ambassador urged Peter to resume his internal passport because without it he could not expect to receive a Soviet exit visa. Peter knew he would be arrested the moment he left the Embassy, for he had been more than three hours inside and had entered without permission, but the Americans promised that his invitation would still be valid when he came out of prison.

Somehow Peter must have misunderstood the ambassador's conversation with the consular officer, for as Samuel E. Fry points out, [1] "Under our immigration laws it would simply not be possible for an American consular officer to 'sponsor' an immigrant visa application." The normal practice in Moscow is to provide the Soviet citizen with information about how to apply for a Soviet

---

1. In a letter to the author.

exit visa and about what is required in an American sponsor, but consuls always take pains not to give the impression that they can assist, in a personal capacity, in immigration cases.

Peter went away convinced that he had been sponsored by an American. What is more, when at length an invitation reached him from America, almost ten years later, he was convinced that it came from the same man, though he was not in a position to check this belief (which was in error) because in 1968 the KGB removed the immigration papers as soon as they laid hands on Peter.

Unaware of any misunderstanding, Peter said good-bye to Ambassador Thompson and the other Americans and walked off diplomatic soil into arrest. He had no idea what had happened to Augustina and Natasha. He was not likely to see them. Imprisonment was a certainty for him, though he did not expect it for them.

*   *   *

His four daughters had been at the Danilovsky Children's Center all the time, unaware of their father's visit. For them, the night of his arrest began a new, sad chapter in their lives. Lida takes up the story from some hours after Peter had left empty-handed after the officials at the Center had lied.

"It was late in the evening," she writes, "when we were told that we were being sent from Moscow by plane to Krasnoyarsk. The plane was to leave Moscow a little before twelve midnight. They put us in a small bus at the Children's Holding Center. Several men and women arrived to accompany us. They tried to seat us separately, but one of my sisters came and sat down next to me. The men scolded us and said we must get back in seats by ourselves, but we threatened to break a window and jump out.

"We were escorted out of the bus and ushered into a police room to await the departure of the plane. Then several policemen came and took us to the plane. When they had put us on it one woman remained with us. During the flight she tried to get us to talk, but we preferred to be silent. Once the plane dropped sharply and I said to her: 'What I want is for this plane to crash and to end all our suffering.' (And that *is* just what I wanted; I did not know that it would still be necessary to live a long time and endure much more.) A look of fright spread across her face and I understood that she wanted to live, but I was already sick of life at eighteen years of age.

"In Krasnoyarsk I don't remember if we were the first or the last to get off, but I do remember that there were no other passengers with us. There were about eight policemen standing on the ground at the bottom of the steps. They made a ring around us, because it was necessary to go through a crowd of people. The policemen kept repeating: 'Get out of the way! Make way!' People looked at us and didn't understand. Some looked with pity, some in bewilderment, some with scorn, and everyone stepped aside. We were put into a car and taken to the Children's Holding Center in Krasnoyarsk. I had the feeling that they had made a hole in my heart with a knife and that it hurt and it seemed that blood was streaming out of it. It was a terrible pain and it intensified with their shallow, mocking questions, and we had no strength to answer them and were silent. We were greeted by rain in Krasnoyarsk. The car window was open and the fresh air beat against our faces. All my thoughts were on home. How were things with them there? We did not know a thing. In Moscow we had been told that the family was no more: father was in prison, mother was in prison, and the children had been put into children's institutions. They said this to cause us pain.

"Our eyes burned as if there was sand in them from the constant crying. And all around there was no one who understood or sympathized; there was only scorn and mocking to be heard.

"When I lay down to sleep I pleaded: 'Lord, let me see the children and my parents in my dreams or end my life in my sleep, because in the morning it does not seem possible that I shall have the strength to go on living.' But it turned out differently. In the morning how I hated to wake up and return to reality, but although my sleep would be troubled it would return my strength to live. Night would be replaced by day with all the difficulties and joys which this day would bring. Once again would be heard the swearing

НАПРАВЛЕНИЕ

Начальнику *Центрального* ДПР
(наименование ДПР)

11 милиции направляет Вам несовершеннолетнего
(наименование органа милиции)

1. Фамилия, имя, отчество *Ващенко Лидия Петровна*

2. Возраст (число, месяц, год) и место рождения *6/III 1951 Советская Гавань Хабаровск. края.*

3. Местожительство *Гор. Черногорск. пос. Шахта 16 1ая линия 3.*

4. Место учебы и № школы, класс. Если не учится, сколько классов закончил, когда *школа-интернат 2 - 8,5°. .. Аненска Ул. Дзержинского*

5. Место работы, должность

(наименование предприятия)

6. Время пребывания в детских учреждениях, какие причины выбытия

7. Родители или лица, их заменяющие. Указать их основные установочные данные и место работы

отец *Ващенко Петр Яковлевич - лишена род прав.*

мать *Ващенко ~~Александ~~ Васильевна*

8. Причины задержания и направления в ДПР *Пытались пройти в Американское посольство. вместе с отцом который направляется в Спец. приемник. 11 о/м.*

9. При несовершеннолетнем имеется (перечислить одежду, обувь, в которые он одет). Ценные вещи и деньги *Светлое пальто классика капроновое синее платье деньги в сумме 10 рублей (десять рублей)*

Начальник _____

(наименование органа милиции)

Подростка _____

(фамилия и инициалы)

с перечисленными вещами и ценностями

Принял _____

(наименование должности и роспись)

Сдал _____

(наименование должности и роспись)

Дата _____

ТВ 5165—65

This undated document is from the Eleventh Police Sector (Moscow) to the director of the Central Children's Receiving Center about a minor, Lida Petrovna Vashchenko, address Chernogorsk, Settlement of Mine 16, First Line Street #3. Item 7 lists her parents and deprives them of parental rights. Item 8 asks for "reasons for detainment and sending to the Children's Center"; the written answer: "She and her father tried to enter the American Embassy." Item 9 lists the clothes and money in the possession of the minor: a light-colored coat, a synthetic blue dress, a 10-ruble note, and one other item (probably some sort of hat).

with the bad, nasty words, the fights, the ridicule. It was as if we were little prisoners. The tears would again flow because thoughts of home hounded us even during dinner when we would leave the table still hungry.

"In this routine our days followed one after the other. It does not matter in what city a holding center is located, the daily schedule is the same, and the children are assembled there for the same reasons. There were girls here who had had more than one abortion. There were children whose parents had provided them with everything and therefore they were left with nothing to do but be occupied with debauchery, thievery, and drunkenness. There were children who had abandoned their homes and run as far as they could in any direction to escape their drunken parents. Some ran to relatives, others simply climbed on trains. That is why the police had brought them all there. There were children whose parents had abandoned them in the station or left them with some passenger. There were kids who had become separated from their parents or from some group. And this is where we ended up.

"Having stayed at Krasnoyarsk some time we were sent to the city of Kansk [about two hundred kilometers east of Krasnoyarsk]. Once again we were taken in a vehicle to a plane. One escort was with us, and at Kansk a truck with an iron covering pulled up to the plane. The windows had iron grillings and we were taken straight from the plane and put into the truck. Once again we encountered the bewildered looks of people and heard: 'Now what kind of young people have come? How young they are and already the police must be occupied with them.' But how could they know what sort of young people *had* come? And besides, what sort of real criminals would require six to eight policemen? Many times during my twenty-seven years I have had to be accompanied by police and I still cannot get used to it. When, once again, I am escorted I become embarrassed and I want to shout: 'People, why are you looking like that? I am in no way a criminal. I do not deserve your scornful glances and mockings.'

"But then I remember Christ and I recall how he did not want to answer questions—not because he couldn't answer and did not want to converse, but because they were not interested in either the question or the answer. They wanted, they tried to accuse him, not only with their questions, but by twisting his answers. They construed everything as Christ's fault in order somehow to indict him and cause him pain. These people experienced pleasure by causing others pain. And it is necessary to encounter such people who are contrary. But they all share the image of God, and the fact that they are men means that they are *immortal*. It makes no difference what a man does, he will give an account to that image which he bore on earth, as to whether he justified in life that name by which he was called and evaluated—man."

*   *   *

As for Peter, he was taken again to the Eleventh Police Sector, where they confiscated the invitation and other documents given him in the Embassy. Sitting in a KPZ cell he caught a brief glimpse of Augustina: she was ascending a staircase under escort when she suddenly turned round and smiled full at him. But Peter did not know that she was in pain, nor could he know why.

Very soon, to his astonishment, he found himself in a Moscow psychiatric hospital at 15 Kashirsk Highway, close to the Leningrad railway station in the northeastern part of the city.

At that time it was not generally known, even within the Soviet Union, that the Kremlin had decided some years earlier that any one who was dissatisfied with the system should be treated as mentally disturbed; the authorities could then claim a total absence of political prisoners. The Kremlin official in 1962 had implied to Peter that if he wanted to emigrate he must have been knocked crazy; and in 1968 the psychiatric doctor left him in no doubt. "By opposing the Soviet State," he said, "you are banging your head against a wall. No one bangs his head against a wall unless he is mad. Therefore you are mad and that is why you are here!"

Twice a day before meals every patient was forced to swallow a handful of pills of various colors—red, yellow, white, blue—kept in an envelope marked with his name: Peter's envelope was among those with a red stripe to denote "Dangerous patient." One orderly poured the pills into his hand, and commanded him to swallow or chew; the second handed him a glass and commanded him to drink; the third inspected his mouth and hands to see he had taken all the pills. These daily swallows did Peter no harm but they affected some who entered sane, yet could be diagnosed psychiatric before they had stayed there long. "Here in this psychiatric hospital," writes Peter, "were not only those who were really ill, but healthy people who did not agree with Soviet reality. With me was a writer, who suffered terribly regarding the future, because he did not know how his situation would work out. He had written a book and wanted to go into the American Embassy to give them the book, but he was taken at the gates. He said that none of the foreigners had noticed or helped him."

Peter's sanity undoubtedly was sustained by his conviction that true madness lies in denying God: "The *madman* says in his heart, there is no God. . . ."

Many sane men who opposed the Soviet outlook found themselves confined in one of these lunatic asylums for months or years, but Peter was discharged to prison on 10 August after one month and twenty days, then returned to Chernogorsk for trial in September. The chairman of the People's Court was S. N. Klepinin; the people's assessors (jurors) were Korotich and Sorkina, a man and a woman. Peter was allotted a woman lawyer and the charge under Article 198 of the Criminal Code was that he had lived maliciously without a passport from 1965 to 1968.

Recalling the ambassador's advice, he pleaded guilty. The official record of the court runs: "He explained that after his liberation from the place of his confinement in December 1964 he got a job in February 1965 and in March 1965 he sent his passport to the Central Soviet Organs of the city of Moscow to exchange it for an exit passport for leaving the boundaries of the USSR. Since that time he has lived without a passport. Many times he was summoned to the organs of the police to receive a passport, but he refused it for religious reasons. After the arrest of Vashchenko he explained that he had changed his mind regarding his position and came to realize his previous errors about keeping the laws of the Soviet power. He considers that he acted incorrectly and declared that he will receive a passport, because to live without a passport is a violation of Soviet laws."

He was sentenced to one year in "strict regime corrective-labor colonies," the sentence to run from 8 July 1968. Once again he suffered the usual procedures: the indignity of having his head cropped to the skin and all his body hairs shaved, and being forced to wear convict uniform. He served his sentence under poorer conditions than during his previous imprisonment. The labor was not so hard but food was scant and the discipline strict. The camp administration had two sets of prisoners they watched and opposed more than any: the *gifrrists* who brewed a highly narcotic stimulant from tea and became virtually drug addicts; and the Christian believers. "If," says Peter, "you only depended and relied on your own strength, then it would not be possible to bear all these sufferings without God As is written in Philippians 4:13: 'I can do all things because Jesus Christ strengthens me.' "

For Peter, the early months were the sorer because he did not know the face of Augustina. And when he discovered, the pain was all the sharper.

14

Augustina's Calvary

When Augustina was seized by the arm and saw Peter run into the safety of diplomatic soil she began to explain to her captor about their search for the lost children, "but he did not want to listen. He thrust my arms behind my back so violently that I could not feel them. They hurt terribly and for seven days after I was unable to move my arms back."

The policeman took her round the corner to the command post, a small booth where sat several of his comrades. He seized her by the hair and began to beat her head against the wall, saying: "Why did you come prying around here to this Embassy?"

"Why are you beating me?" she gasped. "I haven't done anything!"

"You are *not* to come here!" He pushed her onto a bench.

She said: "I didn't come here the time the children were stopped at the gates. But now, who can I ask where my children are? No one knows."

At that, "he began to kick me in the legs as I sat on the bench: many bruises were left on my arms and legs. Then they brought in Natasha, also with her hands twisted behind her back. We were in the booth about an hour, then were taken under guard to the

KGB building, where we were interrogated, then put into a car and taken to the Eleventh Police Sector. Here again we underwent preliminary questioning, seated on a divan in the reception corridor near a policeman."

Several cells opened out of the corridor and after sitting some time Augustina noticed Peter in one of them. Shortly afterwards an official whispered to the interrogator and the women were taken upstairs: Peter was to be moved to the psychiatric hospital and the police wished to prevent their having so much as a glimpse of each other, but Augustina was the last one on the stairs "and when I glanced around I caught sight of him. In the office we were again questioned and then led downstairs into the corridor where we had been sitting earlier. Again we were told: 'Sit here: stay put.' It was only towards evening that Natasha and I were separated; she was sent to one cell and I was sent to another.

"I was alone and she was alone also, but when I began to pray she always heard me and she also prayed.

"We sat in the temporary detention cells (KPZ) for seven full days. I did not want to eat at all and doubted I could summon any appetite. But I took myself in hand, and forced myself to eat at least one meal a day and did not surrender to sadness."

This was a tussle, for her husband was under arrest, she knew not where; her four eldest daughters had been abducted again; at home waited seven more children from Lila, nearly eleven, to baby Paul, about to have his first birthday, which she would miss. And she would miss Grandpapa Paul's eightieth birthday, and he and his Anna needed her and Peter. "How things would work out I did not know; I just turned it all over to the Lord."

The policeman on guard at the cells was a friendly man and would try to reassure her. They conversed through the eyehole. " 'Why are you crying? They will get things straightened out and you will be going home.' He would ask all the time about the family and about what had happened, and he came to the conclusion that I would not be imprisoned."

He could not believe that a mother of eleven children, the youngest a mere baby, would be put in prison for nothing worse than trying to enter an embassy. Augustina Vashchenko, however, was about to taste Soviet justice towards those who offend the ruling ideology. She would not see home again for more than two years.

The cell was in the basement of a stone building and stayed cold even when the streets above were hot in the sun. For seven days she was not allowed out for exercise and at night she had to sleep on bare linoleum, laid on the stone floor, without any covering over her light summer dress except a small jacket, "and thus all night I was freezing while trying to sleep. I would get up to get warm and then curl up in a ball and fall asleep until I woke up cold again, and once more got up." In the mornings her back was so painful that at first she could hardly stand. She has never lost the aftereffects of those nights in the KPZ following her beating at the Embassy gates.

On the seventh night, at 2:00 A.M. Augustina was awakened and told she would be moved, but they would not say where as they led her to join a group of other prisoners. Outside stood a *voronok*. When Augustina's turn came she was astounded to hear the official in charge tell the driver to put her in a section by herself: "She's very dangerous." It was windowless, boxlike and cramping, with hardly room to sit, and induced much discomfort as the drive lengthened until broad day filtered through the cracks.

"We drove for a long time and pulled up to some iron gates. They opened automatically and then closed. We passed through yet another set of gates. The *voronok* backed right up to the doors, and since I was the first to be summoned I got out and waited until the others were taken out. I had the sensation that I had arrived in hell; in front of me through an open door could be seen, reflected in the light of day, a person dressed in a black smock, waving a big bunch of keys.

"I was put in a cell with a woman who said she had already been here five times. She urged me to look at my head to see if I had lice, because if they found anything they would cut off my hair right to the scalp. Although she did not have much hair, her head was dirty, but I did not see anything else. Then I asked her to have a look at my head, because I had braids down to my waist. I explained that as I had been in prison seven days, and on the road almost four before that, there might be something. She looked at me and said that there was nothing.

"When we were called to the doctor, the woman was quickly examined and then sent off, and I never met her again. The woman doctor suggested that I undo my braids and when I had done so she uttered a great sigh at how long my hair was. Then she began to examine my head. She dug around for a long time and then she said that it was necessary to put my head under a light. And I, unsuspecting, said: 'I don't have lice.' Her voice immediately changed and she maliciously said: 'We will see!' When she had put me under a lamp she looked and said: 'No, then what is this white here?' She showed the woman standing next to her whom I did not know. She looked and said: 'This is dandruff.'

"The doctor did not look again, but simply opened the door and screamed, 'To the barber!' A man in a black smock approached and led me to the barbershop and told me to sit on a stool. I asked why. He answered: 'We are going to cut your hair.' I said: 'But there is nothing in my hair.' And he said. 'I don't know anything. The doctor sent you and I am not able to change it.' He began to cut off my hair to the scalp with his electric shears. I wept when I saw the first locks of hair lying on the floor. Even he envied how long my hair was."

This abrupt, tragic and apparently senseless sacrifice of that lovely fair hair, which had never been cut in her life, puzzled Augustina until that night in a crowded cell, "the woman lying next to me asked: 'Why did they cut your hair?' I told her everything and why they had put me in prison. She cursed furiously and said: 'Chignons are in style now! Since the doctor liked your hair she decided to do that. And then she will come and take it, wash it, and she will have either braids or a chignon for herself.' It is true that I myself love braids and the children also wore braids; we did not cut their hair.

"I was terribly grieved over this, but that's all right, I just turned everything over to the Lord, for he sees and knows everything."

The cell contained forty women or more, and was an experience

Augustina will never forget. The Vashchenko household, though poor, was clean despite coal-laden dust, strong winds and water shortage; and if her high-spirited children could be noisy, no one used filthy language, no playful scrapping became a venomous fight. In the cell, however, swearing and acrimony echoed around and at meals it was not unusual for a metal bowl of soup to hurtle through the air, aimed by one angry vixen at another and splashing those between. Augustina preferred to eat the miserably scanty fare on a corner of her plank-bed as soon as she was allotted one; previously she had slept on the floor with the overflow, most of whom would start a fight if trodden on at night by mistake.

Her moment of arrival in the cell is etched on her memory: "In one corner several people were arguing, in another they were reading. Someone else was hiding away from the supervisor's line of vision, knitting with wooden knitting needles carved out of the plank-beds. As soon as I entered I was offered a place near the door. I sat down and immediately they asked why I had been imprisoned. As I began to speak several came over from other corners of the cell.

"I explained that I was a believer who had come from Siberia, that my children had been taken because they were being raised to know God. People in this cell came from everywhere. Some expressed dissatisfaction that I had been imprisoned, while others said that in the Soviet Union people were not tried for religion, you could pray as much as you wanted. When I commented that the Soviet Union permitted only older people to worship, you could not take children, many agreed that they had not seen young children in church.

"Then came discussion and arguments. Some said that it was right to teach children to know God and they pointed at a woman who was sitting not far from me on the plank-beds. They said that she drank a lot, even vodka, and her eldest son and daughter were drunks, her husband drank less than she did. She had been imprisoned and the younger children had been put into an *internat*. Her husband and two older children were still at home. She would have done well to teach her children to know God."

The prisoners' interest in Augustina's faith saved her from the practical jokes which she saw played on the next greenhorn. "I don't remember why she had been put in jail. When those who were interested questioned her they said: 'Write a request to the governor asking that he give you a guitar for tomorrow. After all, tomorrow is Sunday. Then give it to the supervisor.' She wrote, began to knock on the peep hole. When she gave him the request the supervisor cursed her, and everyone in the cell began to laugh at her.

"There was another incident. Everyone took turns as duty person to clean up the cell, and next bathday it was this woman who had just arrived; they took us to have a bath every ten days. She did not know how things were run in the cell, and they said to her: 'You stand last in line. Gather up all the mugs and the tea kettle'—they were all aluminium—'and you clean them in the bath.'

"She got a piece of rope and put all the mugs on it and tied it to the tea kettle. When they ordered us to go to the bath everyone began to line up, she took her place in line with forty mugs and the tea kettle, since there were forty people in the cell! They led us from the cell into the corridor. As soon as she came out the escorts began to let her have it with their cursing and pushed her back into the cell and detained all the others.

"This is the sort of amusement that people come up with because of nothing to do. All day long you just sit there. You get up at six a.m. and go to bed at eleven p.m. In the morning the designated duty person cleans up. Then you wash and have lunch. How time drags until dinner! There is much worthless talk and most of the time they make fun of someone. No one wants to know about God, although the Lord remembers every word. You can pray in the cell only at night, because there are so many people and it is crowded. When everyone has gone to bed, that is when you can pray."

* * *

After hearing Augustina's story the investigator preparing the indictment, V Korolev, was at a loss what charge to write down.

The next time he summoned her he read out the evidence of one of the policemen outside the Embassy, A. G. Lisitsyn, that Augustina had called him a "bitch."

"That is a lie! I am a believer, and we do not use such words."

Korolev wrote it into the record all the same, following the usual procedure in Soviet political trials, that an accusatory statement by an official cannot be removed: it has become a part of the case. The third time, he confronted her with the policeman who had so cruelly twisted her arms and beaten her legs, V. S. Tuvaev. He gave evidence that he had heard the dirty word *bitch* and that she had bitten his hand.[1]

Augustina demanded to see the scar. He prevaricated: "She *wanted* to bite me." Augustina persisted but he refused to show the place and the investigator closed the interview. They got round the absence of proof by submitting a statement from a medical examiner "that I had grabbed the policeman, pulled him, and that he had hit his elbow against the wall: there had been trauma without any bodily disorder." (The official record of sentence says "slightly wounded.")

Investigator Korolev ordered her to sign the indictment but she refused.

As she comments, "No one paid any attention to the questions I raised. The case was predetermined to turn out in a certain way." In an ordinary criminal case the clues are followed and the case is brought according to the evidence, but in offenses against the regime the KGB usually decides the sentence; charges are framed accordingly. Since it is not a criminal offense to *ask* to be allowed to enter an embassy the KGB framed Augustina by saying that she had *attempted* to enter, then charged her with resistance to authority, but in manufacturing the evidence out of the available facts they magnified the case out of all proportion, unless they had intended from the first to impose a savage sentence on the mother of a large family who had done nothing but make an inquiry.

When Augustina received the formal indictment at last, she

---

1. Or arm. There is no distinction in Russian.

found that the first witness would be Peter, and the address revealed
to her that he was in a psychiatric hospital. She wrote at once to
the procurator named in the indictment. "I asked him to arrange
a meeting between myself and my husband, because he had been
completely healthy and I could not understand how he had got
into a psychiatric hospital; at that time I still did not know that
all those considered suspicious or unreliable by the Soviet authorities
are put in psychiatric hospitals. But the procurator did not answer
my letter. I wrote a second time and got an answer, after about
a month: 'Gone on leave.' That's where it ended."

The trial in the People's Court, however, did not go as the
KGB planned The woman judge looked at Augustina and Natasha,
frail and thin after many weeks in prison, looked at the strapping
policemen, and asked where was the third witness—Peter Vashchenko. The procurator said he was in a psychiatric hospital
"and is not responsible." The judge demanded: "Then where is
the certifying document? I will not judge this case." She adjourned
the court for five minutes, which stretched into thirty, and then
a policeman removed the defendants to a waiting room where they
sat until evening and were returned to prison.

More weeks went by. A fresh indictment was served, omitting
Peter's name. The trial took place on 20 September 1968 by Judicial
Consultation in a distant corner of Moscow, before a woman judge
and two jurors (people's assessors). Only one policeman appeared
as witness. Each defendant had a counsel despite refusing their
services.

"The trial began," writes Augustina, "and when they read my
case they did not indicate all my children, but simply said seven.
I said that I had eleven, but they did not want to listen. Then
they began to read a falsified statement from Peter which said
that he was in severe mental shock and that he could not be at
the trial. Asking them why they had falsified the statement, I said:
'Since there is such falsehood here, I will not answer any questions.'
But they went on with the trial anyway."

The woman defense counsel asked the policeman: "What word
did the defendant use when she swore in an uncensored way?"

"Bitch."

"How much education do you have?"

"Ten years."

"And what would you say, as a witness: Is this word a 'censorable' word or a literary one?"

The policeman did not answer and she said that the word was a literary one, heard in many outbursts.

The procurator then dealt with Natasha, and told the court that she had seized a policeman by the leg, ripped his trousers and scratched his shin. This was too much for Augustina, who interrupted: "Why do you disgrace yourself with such accusations? The trousers were not rotten! To have ripped them she would have needed time to find a hole!"

Everyone laughed, yet the court did not reject the evidence. After a brief adjournment the judge announced conviction under Article 191, Part I (Resistance to Authority) and sentenced both women to three years in medium (general) regime corrective-labor camps, the sentence to run from the day of arrest.[2]

Augustina's defense counsel afterwards asked her whether she would appeal. "I replied that I understood that the court had already been told what punishment to give out. She said: 'It is true that the sentence of three years was arranged and that even had you asked them to reduce it, even had you cried, it was not in their power to lessen the punishment. I know that this is not just, but if I complained for you, then I would be here with you, but you are allowed to appeal.' "

Natasha, aged fifty-four and asthmatic, was sent to a labor camp for invalids: her health worsened during the long sentence. After release she never regained her strength and died at the age of sixty-four in November 1978.

Augustina, on a dreary day of snow in November 1968, emerged from a windowless *voronok* at the medium regime model camp near Mozhaisk, a place one hundred kilometers (sixty-two miles) west of Moscow and much colder than Chernogorsk, to serve her

---

2. Literally, "from ring to ring," *ot zvonka do zvonka.*

term; behind a great barbed wire fence stood barracks and a large sewing factory worked by the prisoners.

The camp commandant, who interviewed each new arrival, opened her file, with its red marking to denote "Dangerous Prisoner" and studied the charge; then he looked at Augustina and burst out laughing. "*She* pushed a policeman? He hit his arm on the wall, she scratched him, but without causing bodily harm!" And he laughed the more. Then he saw the sentence of three years, turned serious and assigned her to a work brigade: first she made sheets, then medical caps.

Laughter soon died at Mozhaisk. Augustina entered upon the saddest period of her life, cut off from her children and her beloved Peter, and driven from early to late on a poor diet.

"There was really no free time. We got up at six. Making of beds, twenty minutes of exercises, breakfast, and after breakfast the whole command was led to the working zone. At eight everyone was already at the machines. Lunch was at noon in the dining hall. Work ended at four. At four-thirty training began; some attended a general education school, others trained to make clothes, others to become mechanics for repairing sewing machines. Everyone trained for two hours until six-thirty. Dinner was at seven; then they would assign some to peel potatoes in the kitchen, some to wash the floors in the dining room, and some to do clean up in the area until retreat. If you finished cleaning early the detachment chief would call a meeting, and there would not be time to write a letter home."

The one mercy was cleanliness. "This camp was called a 'model' camp because foreigners were often brought here and shown how prisoners live in the Soviet Union. The cots got clean sheets all the time and every morning we would dust everywhere like in a hospital. When foreigners came, dinner in the dining room would be better than usual. There would be more potatoes in the soup and the *kasha* would be thicker." *Kasha* was the generous name the prisoners gave to the liquid millet at breakfast. Dinner consisted of a soup of boiled sour cabbage with a few potatoes. They had no meat, only bones in the soup, and if Augustina or anyone got a little meat on her bone, a more aggressive prisoner would seize her bowl.

"On one holiday we were given for supper a little piece of herring and a glass of tea, with thickened milk but so little that it was just barely white." Each prisoner was allowed ten rubles worth of goods from the camp kiosk at the end of each month, an essential aid to diet, yet this bonus was forfeit if she had failed to fulfill the very large work norm: the Soviet Union not only makes heavy use of prisoners' forced labor in sustaining its economy but demands it on a nearly empty stomach.

Augustina was indeed descending into the valley of shadow. Although not yet forty she felt old; she was ill; she longed unbearably for Peter and her darlings. In a scant moment of leisure she wrote home, the first news they would have had of her whereabouts since her conviction. She told them to come soon if they wanted to see her alive. At the end of the letter she quoted from memory a hymn based on a verse in Isaiah, "As one whom his mother comforts, so will I comfort you."

> Comfort me, God, with the warmth of Your love,
> Once again I draw near to Your breast.
> Master, I believe what You say.
> I have loved You, my God, since a child.
> Embrace me tenderly, my Savior,
> As a mother embraces her child who is sick.
> I cry, and quietly whisper:
> O God, O God, I love You.

15

Lida the Comforter

LIDA HAD BEEN some weeks in the *internat* at Kansk, certain the authorities had no right to detain her at seventeen without legal process, and conscious of the need at home.

One day in August she received permission to go to the city. "I found the airplane ticket office and bought a ticket to Abakan. After dinner I walked back into town, took a bus to the airport and flew back to Krasnoyarsk; I had to change planes here.

"Our plane had just landed when they announced that all flights had been called off due to an approaching thunderstorm. Sure enough, after some time such a violent downpour began that the men rolled their trousers up to their knees and suitcases were lifted higher off the ground. Torrents of water rushed by. I stood near the window and prayed. Time was passing and soon there would be a check and my sisters would say that I had gone home, since by that time I should have been home if everything had gone as planned, but I was still in Krasnoyarsk and it was unknown when I would fly on

"I prayed very hard, but I don't know how long. People were walking around and pestering the information bureau as to when it would be possible to fly on. I was afraid of running into a policeman; I thought that they had already discovered my absence and had telephoned, and as we wore uniform clothes it would be easy to find me in the airport. Towards evening, planes began to take off. When I flew into Abakan it was getting dark. The buses had already stopped running and I and others with me who needed to get to Chernogorsk were forced to hitchhike. All of us managed to squeeze into one car and there were more in the car than there should have been, but we all got there.

"When I arrived home I found out in detail about the misfortunes which had beset us. Without my parents the house seemed like an abandoned nest and the children like neglected fledglings."

She collected infant Paul from the Chmykhalovs and the others from the various believers who had taken them in. She tried to put the house in order as her grandparents Paul and Anna were too old to do much, and started the children on their lessons again, all the time wondering what had been done to her mother (she knew already about Peter's sentence) and why the Americans had not made inquiries: "We trusted and waited for help from the Embassy. It wasn't possible that someone was not checking, and then the Soviets would be ashamed that they had imprisoned the mother of such a large family, and suddenly we would be saved. But it was not at all like this. Nobody remembered us. Nobody had anything to do with our grief and it was necessary to drink it to the dregs."

Then a group of teachers sent by the education committee and the mine administration arrived. They urged Lida to send the smaller children voluntarily to a home and the older ones to an *internat*. She did not want to listen and they pressed her. She held Paul in her arms and the other children clung to her dress, retreating step by step before the menacing teachers. Lida asked if a fresh water delivery might be authorized, for it was a long haul by the little hand cart.

"That is not possible," they replied. "It is better to give the children up. You are young. What are the children to you? Put your own life in order." Lida felt bitterly that this was a fine thing to say "when they were the primary cause of our troubled family life. How glad they were that we were now in such a position."

True to the wonderful tradition of the Chernogorsk church, believers did their utmost to help, by digging the potato patch and
providing vegetable seeds and sharing the home and nursery chores.
Winter arrived. At last came Augustina's letter. As Lida read it
she began to cry and little Paul, seeing her tears, tried to comfort
her by bringing her his toys and saying, "Don't cry."

"I said to him: 'Let's pray.' He got on his knees, but then jumped
up and began to wipe away my tears. This just increased my tears.
He kept trying to comfort me." Lida decided then and there to
go and visit her mother, and wrote an application. But her grandparents were distressed, certain she would be arrested and returned
to the *internat.* "You will not return," they wailed. "What shall
we do with the children?"

*   *   *

"When I arrived in Mozhaisk," writes Lida, "the snow was mixed
with the dirt on the streets. At the station the policeman on duty
told me where the women's labor camp was located and advised
me to take a taxi to avoid any trouble getting there. I got one
right away. The road went through a field. There was a row of
pines on each side, then the car turned to the left. On the side
where the camp buildings were, a swamp made it impossible to
approach on foot On the other side of the camp were the barracks.
The car stopped near the entry door.

"I went into the building. I did not want to believe that this
is where my mother served time, that it was not possible for me
to see her immediately. A little window opened and I said who I
had come to see. A woman answered that she would give me a
two-hour 'general' visit, that is, in the presence of an escort. I
sat down to wait. It approached dinner time. I had forgotten to
eat breakfast and now as I joyfully anticipated the meeting I felt
hungry. I had put two pastries and several pieces of candy in my
pocket and had just begun to eat when the little window opened
again and I was told to go to the place where passes are checked.
Several minutes later I was in a room with a long table.

"Mama entered with a woman accompanying her, but I stood stock still and could not believe my eyes. My mama's lips were quivering. She came up to me and kissed me. I just kept looking and looking at her. What had happened to her stoutness and her braids? She seemed completely waxen as if there was no blood at all in her. Underneath her hat could be seen a scarf and beneath that her forelock was visible, like the forelock usually left on us children. The woman screamed severely at her and my mother's entire manner was that of a submissive slave. The woman scolded her for coming up to me and kissing me. She said that if my mother did not obey she would deprive her of the meeting. I understood that this violation, had it been committed by me, would have been forgiven, but she was screamed at for breaking a rule of visits.

"We were seated opposite each other at the table. I continued to remain silent and thought to myself, Who had the right to scream at my mother and insult her? She was my mother and why did these people give me so little time to see her and why was it forbidden for her to embrace me? Why was it forbidden even to stretch my hand across the table and take her hand? Why was all this forbidden? For a long time I was unable to calm myself inside and I answered her questions abstractedly.

"I was beyond crying. There was hate in my soul for these people. There was anger from lack of knowledge and from my own helplessness. There was pity for my mother, for my father who was languishing in another camp, and for the children who were in such need of their parents; they were in their home but without the guardianship they needed. Three were in an institution, I had left the rest at home and the youngest was just one year old. I had come to the meeting with my mama to tell her all this news.

"What was there to be glad about? To change the subject I stuck my hand in my pocket and felt a pastry. Immediately I asked 'Mama, can I give you a pastry?' She answered: 'Go ahead.' I chose a moment when the escort woman was not looking and then thrust the pastry across the table into her hand. Mama began to break it up into little pieces and suck it. I had figured that when she was nibbling I would escape the questions which were unpleasant for me, but this grieved me even more, for she ate it so greedily that I realized that she was hungry. Why had I not put sausage or something substantial in my pocket? I had been even unable to feed her a little bit and again I began to blame myself that she would leave the visit hungry.

"We did not talk about anything serious and the two hours passed as if they had been several minutes. Starting next day I had been promised a three-day 'personal' visit—living together privately—but this first meeting was over and I must leave, and there was nowhere to go; I did not know the city. Nothing made sense to me, everything was for the very first time. When they led mama out she cried again. I was able to hold back the tears which had welled up in my eyes and comforted her by reminding her that we would see each other again the next day.

"I had to go into the city to find a hotel. It was here that I felt my strength leave me; I had the feeling that I was doing some sort of hard labor. Having arrived at a hotel, I finally was left alone with my grief within the walls of my hotel room. I undressed and walked over to the window. In the distance I caught sight of lights and they reminded me of mama in the camp and of how I could not be with her now although it had been necessary for me to come six thousand kilometers [six hundred twenty miles] to reach her. On the train I had traveled with a man who was not nice and who conducted himself with undue familiarity towards me. I had to seek help from traveling soldiers.

"And having overcome all this, I had finally reached mama and found her in bad shape. All this broke my strength. Before I went to bed I decided to pray and I got down on my knees near the bed. The scenes of the visit passed before me, with the unfamiliar sight of mama without hair; she had always had braids before. It brought tears to my eyes.

"Here there was no one to be embarrassed and I cried; I cried so hard that my breaths came in gasps. I cannot even describe what was going on inside, the pain I felt in the area of my heart. Apparently I was in a bad way because when I came to myself quite a bit of time had already passed. I threw myself on the bed and slept intermittently until morning. In the morning, not having rested, I left again for the camp after I had gone to several stores to get food, my thoughts already with mama."

A three-day "personal" visit under the Soviet penal system allows the prisoner and relative to live day and night together in a tiny room, one of a row off a long hall, with a communal kitchen where the relatives cook the food they provide. "The three days passed quickly. We talked about everything and then the time came already for us to part. How terrible it is to relive those minutes."

Instead of returning to Chernogorsk, Lida traveled eastward on the Trans-Siberian until she reached Kansk, where it was bitterly cold in mid-December compared with home, and she had not brought felt boots. By the time she had passed the textile factory and entered the huge *internat* (700 children to Achinsk's 360) her feet seemed frozen to the soles of her high rubber boots. She slipped into the building and sat on a window sill at the end of the hall and warmed her feet against the radiator. She asked a passing girl kindly to call "one of the girls named Vashchenko," and soon all three had joined her. She had already bought a railway ticket for Lyuba, whose sixteenth birthday was a few days away, though that was no guarantee of release.

Lyuba had hated Kansk. "It was just like Achinsk, only worse." She had no heart for learning; she rarely smiled, her thoughts wandering continually to her mother's misery and humiliation.

Lyuba agreed with enthusiasm to Lida's plan and found a teacher: "I am going to accompany my sister to the public bath," she said, "as she doesn't know where it is. If I am delayed a long time, you sometimes have to wait in line for two or even three hours." She reckoned they would be beyond recapture by then. This was warfare: these girls, who as Christians would never tell a lie in personal matters, had developed a nice line in strategic deception.

Instead of going home to Chernogorsk, where the police looked for the absconded Lyuba, they traveled farther east and visited their father in his labor camp near Reshoty on Lyuba's sixteenth birthday, 17 December 1968.

*   *   *

On the next visit to her mother, in the spring of 1969, Lida took little Paul. She now had a job at the Mine and the bosses had tried to stop her going; they said they were worried about her. Grandmother had cried her eyes out and at the main line junction little Paul had run after a flock of pigeons and nearly fallen into the path of an electric train. She raced after and saved him but all he did was to cry because she would not let him chase the pigeons.

They went first to their father. There was no time to have a three-day visit with both parents and Lida had decided that her mother's was the greater need. The official at her father's camp expressed surprise that she requested only a two-hour visit and that Peter's wife had not come; when he heard the reason he was shocked that the State should imprison both parents and did the paperwork quickly. "Among the atheists," comments Lida, "are some who are humane and sympathetic." She adds: "In the USSR when the father in a family of Christians is in prison, that is a normal state of affairs. But it is rare at present that the mother should be arrested, even more rare for both at the same time, when there are a great number of children and a nursing infant, and all the children are minors. Even several officials thought that was terrible."

At Augustina's labor camp it was almost more harrowing for Lida than before. Paul lay asleep in her arms when they arrived. She had to return to the station briefly, and when he woke and saw Augustina he yelled and refused to be comforted or amused by his mother, a stranger, yet ran laughing into Lida's arms. "It was difficult for mama to bear this. I could see how she was suffering inside and trying not to show it. When I would be preparing something in the kitchen the first day he would hold on to me. The second day went better. He had become used to mama and already would go to her arms and even kiss her. But the time came for parting. The visit ended. They asked me if I wanted to leave the child in the camp so that he could remain with his mother," but

Lida knew that Augustina could not bear this, for the infants were kept separate from their mothers except at stipulated hours, and Augustina had seen mothers desperately taking peeps through the high fence, and punished for pushing candy through the cracks. On the second birthday a child would be sent away to a home.

"And I did not leave him," writes Lida, "and could not imagine how I could leave him. Mama cried a great deal and so did I when we parted. Only Paul was glad to be able to go outside again. He didn't need anyone since I was beside him, and he had nothing to do with that woman who kissed him and cried. When I cried, however, he noticed and kept rubbing his cheek against my hand. How could he really know what was going on in his mother's heart, what a stab of pain she felt at that moment and how lonely it was for her to be left here among these strangers when her children were going home."

The weary months dragged by for Augustina. Once some Cubans were taken round the camp. The prisoners were warned not to speak to them. "When they came to the working zone I was already behind my machine. While I was sewing I wrote my appeal and explained that I had been unjustly tried. No one said anything to me, but the camp chief looked at me sharply and all the women prisoners said: 'Now you will be put in the punishment cell.' The next day the detachment chief summoned me and gave me back my appeal and she said: 'They read it and gave it to me to give back to you.' But they did not punish me. People are extremely afraid to tell the truth."

Another memory is of the evening when forty new prisoners, each with an infant, were to arrive from a distant camp. The inmates were ordered to stay in their dormitories and go to bed after dinner. "We all looked through the window as they were led through our zone. It made your heart ache. Some could not stand it and cried, and some cursed the Soviet rulers that they tormented not adults only but children as well. The children were all dirty and messy from the road in their mothers' arms. Their faces were thin. They had been bound up for a long time. Along both sides of the road were the escorts. It reminds one of the times when Hitler mocked the prisoners, as they show in the movies. One cannot look at this calmly. Everyone was upset.

"I also had occasion to see things such as this: a mother would have her child die in the camp. She would have seen him only when he was ill and then be told that he had died. She was not told when the funeral was, only later when the one who buried him told her. One woman, who was not a prisoner but worked in the camp as a bookkeeper, cried terribly for her baby and was grieved that she had not been allowed to bury him herself."

In the hot summer of 1969 the women were made to dig ditches to relay the camp water supply but any who took off their long outer garments to get a little sun tan were scolded, and punished for a second offense. That winter, when Augustina had completed half her term, she was offered the opportunity of exchanging labor camp for work on a national project. Those selected had to pass a judicial inquiry to see if they were reformed and sorry for their crimes. "They asked me if I would still believe in God when I was sent on the project. I said yes, and then the judge said that I should not be sent, that I had not been reeducated, that I would preach there." But the camp chief took her part.

Though told they would be prisoners no longer, they were escorted to the train by police with guard dogs and put in another prison, at Perm in western Siberia, then taken to the city of Solikamsk. Here they were distributed among dormitories, told they could walk about the town if back by 11:00 P.M., and not to get drunk or fight. As tomorrow was New Year (1970) they were given pocket money. For most the holiday quickly became a drinking spree. Augustina left the dormitory and wandered all day through the unfamiliar streets. She searched for believers but the Baptist prayer house was on the far side of the city and no passer-by could (or would) tell her where. At 11:00 P.M. she returned to find the dormitory in a drunken stupor: "It is very difficult for a believer in such a society."

Peter, his sentence served, came to visit her in January. He made the best possible use of the time.

The national work project was the building of Solikamsk paper factory, a hard labor indeed. "It was necessary to dig and spread cement by hand, and for a woman this is very difficult work. You have to fill up your shovel and then carry it to another corner of the steel framework. There were two or three floors."

However, three months after Peter's visit she wrote a request to the Presidium in Moscow and was able to enclose "a medical statement certifying that I was pregnant. And in August 1970 I was freed early and went home at the end of the month." On 9 September Sarah was born, their twelfth child.

СССР **572/93** Форма «Б»

МИНИСТЕРСТВО
охраны общественного
порядка

СПРАВКА № 040045

СЕРИЯ АН

Выдана гражданину-ке _Ващенко_

Августе Васильевне

год рождения _25.III_ -_1929_, национальность _русская_

уроженцу-ке _с. Боград Боградский рн_

Красноярского края.

осужденному-ой _Краснопресненским Райнар._

судом гор. Москва.

«_20_» _сентября_ 196_8_г. по ст. ст. _191'2п_ УК

к _3_ годам лишения свободы

имеющему-ей в прошлом судимости _____

не судима

в том, что она отбывал-а наказание в местах заключения

с «_18_» _июня_ 196_8_г. по «_10_» _декабря_ 1969г.

откуда освобожден-а по _Определению Московского_

гор. суда Москов. обл. от 10/XII-69, условно

ко. [?] в.м. 8дн. в соответствии с Указом

[?] СССР от 20/III-64, с направлением на

стройки народного х-ва.

Начальник подразделения

(подпись)

Начальник части

(подпись)

чать

дан билет на проезд до станции _____

железной дороги

деньги на билет в сумме _____ (прописью)

дано денег на питание в пути _____ (прописью)

дано личных денег в сумме _Сто пруадцати двр_
35 ком (прописью)

чие выдачи _____ (сумма прописью)

Главный бухгалтер

Подпись освобождаемого

This document from the Ministry for the Protection of Public Order states that Augustina Vasilevna Vashchenko, born March 25, 1929, is Russian, from Bograd [about 60 km. north of Chernogorsk] in the Krasnoyarsk Territory; that she was tried Sept. 20, 1968, according to St. 191, Part II and given a 3-year sentence; that it was her first trial; that she served from June 18, 1968 till Dec. 10, 1969. The effect of the document is to free Augustina from prison camp provided that she serves 1 year, 6 months and 8 days on a national work project. On the back (see left) the document says that she was given 132 rubles and 95 kopecks.

16

Prison through the Eyes of a Child

IN 1968 ANNA Petrovna Makarenko, Maria Chmykhalov's sister, was aged just forty: tall, very pretty, with light brown hair. Many had wanted to marry her but she preferred to live single with the Chmykhalovs. She worked at the mine until all women were withdrawn; then she shredded mica. She was arrested at the age of forty and endured three terms of imprisonment and labor camp. Each day in camp her beauty slipped away, as she was forced to do heavy lumbering on indifferent food.

Anna was the beloved *nyanka* (nanny, auntie) to her niece and nephews. Timothy, who was six when his aunt was sentenced and just seven when his father was sent to labor camp and his mother spent a month in prison, has provided a vivid account through the eyes of a child, written in the Embassy when he was sixteen.

Anna was arrested at work on a hard winter's day in December, by a policeman named Terskikh, who told her at once that she would be sent to prison. A woman at her place of work went with her to find out why Anna had been arrested. "When," writes Timothy, "she arrived at the police station Terskikh searched her and took her comb and satchel. In her bag was bread and a lunch.

They immediately took all this and put her in jail. This woman took her bag and came to our house. She brought the bag and said: 'Your *nyanka* has been imprisoned.' She handed over the bag."

Shurik (Alexander, aged nearly nine) "took the bag, clutched it to his breast, and fell down on a box and started to sob. He said: 'Auntie, Auntie, where are you now?' And when evening came Shurik sat down in a corner of our garden near the house and cried. He wailed: 'My dear Auntie, how I miss you ' Often Grandmother would come and reassure him and she cried herself. He missed Auntie so badly that he became thin Shurik would often tell about Jonah and Elijah from the Bible, but when Auntie was imprisoned he became sad and did not talk much. Most of the time he said nothing or cried. Everyone tried to comfort him."

Anna was put on trial early in 1969 for passport violation, with several other believers. Timothy recalls how, before the judges entered, policemen and *druzhinniki* (auxiliary police) chased out any children they saw with their parents. "We crawled under the benches, but if they had seen us, men-at-arms would have pulled us out.

"They would say about the accused that he or she was a very dangerous criminal, that he preached heresy, that he or she lived without a Soviet passport, and besides that she wants to go abroad to our enemies. And almost all the people shouted: 'Put her in prison!' Some shouted: 'Shoot her!' Others shouted: 'Send them to the polar bears . . . Let them live with the bears!' " But this was provocation on the part of the people and also on the part of the Soviet authorities. They convicted Anna Petrovna and sentenced her to one year.

"When the judge read the sentence three policemen led our Anna to the temporary detaining cell (KPZ). From the People's Court to the KPZ is about five hundred meters and three policemen led her on foot. One policeman pushed us so that the children would not go with Auntie and another one said: 'Let the kids go.' And all we little ones went together with Auntie and managed to say good-bye. Mama was not at the trial. She stayed home with Grandmother because she was extremely sick; it was her daughter who was being tried, but she was in a bad way.

"All the believers who were at the trial followed behind and cried, both relatives and friends. When Auntie was led through the gates we all stood there behind the gates and cried, but the policeman chased us away and shut the gates. We returned home and went through the streets with tear-stained eyes and broken hearts.

"When she was taken to Minusinsk Prison she stayed there for several months. And during this time we would come and deliver packages for her, but these packages only got as far as old man Misha who worked in the prison and received packages and granted meetings; and he did not permit us a single visit so that we would not find out that he had not passed on our packages during that whole time.

"None of us ate as much as we wanted but sent packages to Auntie in prison so that she could be strengthened and stand her ground, because in prison they feed you very badly. They feed you three times a day. For breakfast they give you tea and three lumps of sugar, and 600 grams [21 ounces] of bread for the whole day. For lunch they eat left-over bread and watery soup made from fine-ground barley groats, because that is the cheapest, and fish which nobody else wants, and water. For supper they eat whatever bread is left over from lunch and if there is nothing left then you drink without bread. Also for supper they give you as much hot water as you want. We don't know exactly. This is approximate. This is what I remember from stories.

"Therefore we collected all the best for the packages—and Misha would laugh and say: 'Put the best things into the package.' He became very swollen from these packages and became fat and full. He let his stomach out and sat waiting for new booty for his fat mouth. . . . We also sent in twenty rubles for her to use in the prison kiosk. This money can be used by one who has sat in prison for a long time without breaking any rules. You can't give this money directly into their hands; you put it on account and the prisoner is given the receipt which indicates how much money he has in his account. But evidently this money which we turned in, Misha took for himself. He did not give it to Auntie and to this day it is not known where it is. We found out only when Vova, Nadya, and Shura went to the camp and Auntie did not know anything about the packages or the money.

"Anna was serving her term in a camp called Reshoty not far from the Tunguska train station; there are many camps scattered through the *taiga* where people serve their sentences.[1] From Tunguska station you can go in a local train with only a few cars which stops often in little half-stations from which you can go to the camps. A van pulled up to the train for food and packages, and when they climbed out of the train and asked a woman at the station she said: 'That van there is going to the camp. Run over and ask.' All three of them went and asked and they were put on board: Nadya and Shura in the cabin, and Vova in the storage part. Shura was still little, eight years old.

"There was a bad storm and it was cold. They arrived at the camp where Auntie was serving her time. They immediately went into the *izba* which was used for waiting, left their things there and went to the camp. Near the camp they put them into formation. They led out five prisoners at a time and they formed into rows. When they led out five more there was Auntie and Shura recognized her and shouted: 'Auntie! Auntie!' and when Auntie saw them, at first she did not believe her eyes. She thought she was dreaming. She was unable to work during her whole shift and cried. When they were escorting the prisoners in formation Auntie cried and went to the administration to ask for a visit. She said that she had not broken any rules and was supposed to have a general visit. Outside the children requested one from the administration too. They also cried. The camp administration humiliated or mocked them until nine in the evening and then gave them a room. Auntie was brought in and Shura had missed her so badly that he immediately kissed her and cried from joy.

---

1. Thus she was in the same neighborhood as Peter Vashchenko, 1968–69.

"In the morning at six they ordered her to go to work. This is what the administration considered a meeting! This was an *all-day* meeting yet they were given only two *nights*, though they had been registered for three *days and nights*.

"When they were leaving from the visit and saying good-bye Shura sobbed and did not want to part from her because he had begun sleeping with Auntie when he was one year old and Auntie loved him very much and pitied him. We used to meet her when she came home from work. She would come with us into the yard; we would sit on the porch and she would give us treats, especially Shura.

"Then they parted: Auntie went into the zone and they went back home. A big storm came up, and Auntie was terribly afraid that something would happen to them on the road. Then she got a letter from them on the way home and calmed down. She was extremely grateful that they had let her know. After that they went home and told everything about their trip."

Timothy's mother recalls a later visit taking Tolik and Shura, when Anna had been transferred to the invalid brigade. The boys crawled through a hole in the fence, dropped into a basement and reached Anna who was sorting vegetables. She was frightened at seeing them, saying, "What have you done? Why have you come here? They will lock you up." A woman prisoner said that she would go out into the yard and take a look, then wave her hand when it was all clear so that they could leave without the guard seeing them. "When they arrived back in the *izba* they were extremely pleased with themselves and happy that they had seen their aunt, talked with her, and hugged her. Anna had raised Shura off the floor in her arms and kissed him and cried."

When Anna's term ended in December 1969 she met inhumane, indeed monstrous behavior from the administration of the camp complex, and true kindness from some ordinary Russians. Timothy tells the story as he heard it from his aunt.

"When Auntie's term was over she was led out beyond the zone and told: 'You will be a Soviet citizen and take a Soviet passport.' But Auntie said: 'I cannot be a Soviet citizen. I am unable to keep atheist law. I am a believer.' Then the camp commandant Blinov said to the escort: 'Take her back into the zone. Let her serve some more time.' Auntie took her things and went into the zone with the escort. Then Blinov screamed: 'Let her go home.' "

Having played this cruel practical joke, Blinov gave her the five rubles for the fare from Tunguska to Reshoty town where, at camp headquarters, she should receive her ticket for the three-day journey home, together with the money she had earned and any she had brought or had been given by relatives. But he did not arrange transport or an escort to the public station at Tunguska: "Let God take care of her," he sneered.

She walked along the light railway track towards the station. All around was dense forest and it began to snow, a heavy snowstorm turning into a blizzard. Timothy quotes her: "I was walking along, crying and asking God to help and preserve me. When I was about half-way I saw ahead, sitting on the tracks, two *muzhiks.*[2] I looked around and there was not another soul. Everywhere snow was piling up. I walked on, my legs knocking and giving way. I said: 'I don't know what is going to happen; You alone know, Lord, my help and defense.' I had to pass by them; there was no place to turn off. I was alone and there were two of them.

"I drew nearer and they were sitting on the rails, a suitcase open beside them. One of them stood up. I got closer and closer. There was no place to run, and no place to turn off because on one side was a precipice and on the other side the *taiga.* Then I began to pass them. They did not move from their places, but watched me and I them. I was bundled up like an old woman— in the camp I had become like a thin, exhausted old woman. One of them asked: 'Is Tunguska close?' And I answered: 'It is close.' And thus God saved me. These *muzhiks* were from the men's camp which was not far from the women's.

"When I arrived at Tunguska there were women sitting there and I sat down. Two children came from the little village. I love

---

2. Literally, peasants, but Anna is using the term in the sense of alarming "roughs."

children very much. The women asked the children for water and they brought it. I had a little candy and a piece of bread. I gave them the candy and asked them to bring me some hot water if they could, and they left. They came back with their mother and the children pointed at me. Their mother came up to me and asked: 'Where are you traveling?' I said that I was from the camp and had arrived on foot to go by train to Reshoty. I told her I was a believer who had served a term. Then the woman said: 'Come to our place to spend the night. The train does not leave until 6:00 A.M. and here it is dangerous and cold.' I went. I had with me camp *valenki* and work slacks which I had been given. I did not wear them and I gave it all to the woman. There were many children and the husband had been killed here—it was not known by whom—and she lived on charity and what work she could do."

Anna spent the night. She prayed and gave thanks to God for protection, safety, and a refuge. Early in the morning she caught the train and reached Reshoty. And the camp administration refused to give anything of what was due to her: no ticket, no earnings, not even the thirty-eight rubles of her own which had been sent from home. They withheld it all, presumably to please commandant Blinov. They said: "Because you have not abandoned God, let God take care of you. And if you go home without a ticket you will be put in prison." Thus, once again in Soviet Russia, a citizen's rights under the law counted for nothing beside the whim of a boss.

Timothy continues the narrative: "Auntie left, and began to pray and ask God for help. It occurred to her to return again to Tunguska. So she went back to the woman at whose home she had spent the night. She was let into the house by the same children and she said Hello, and began to cry. She said: 'I have come to ask you a big favor. If you can, help me, and I will not remain in debt to you.' She began to explain: 'Please can you lend me money for my journey? Or, look, here are two flannel dresses.' These were two dresses which Mother had sewed for her at home and gave to her in prison; they were almost new. The woman took the two dresses and left. When she returned it was late in the evening. Almost all the children were asleep and those who were not told their mother how this woman had prayed and cried. Auntie had laid herself down on the floor, but she had not slept. She prayed to God that he would help her to get home. When the woman returned home she brought money and gave it to Auntie.

"In the morning at six Auntie once more traveled to Reshoty and bought a ticket to Abakan. In the train there was another woman and child in the compartment and this woman asked why she wasn't eating anything and questioned her about where she was coming from, but Auntie said almost nothing. Then this woman said: 'Sit with the child while I run to the restaurant.' She left and bought *pirogi* [3] and something else. She said: 'Have some. In the course of my life I have been in such situations too.' During the whole trip she gave Auntie things and they ate together. In this way Auntie successfully reached Abakan and came home by bus. As soon as she got home she immediately sent money to the woman she had spent the night with, although she had given Auntie no money, but just sold the dresses.

"They would not give Auntie work and she had been home for several months when she was arrested again for the same reason: refusing Soviet citizenship. She was convicted and sent once more to serve her time in this same camp in Reshoty. According to Soviet law they are not supposed to take you to the same camp to serve your time, especially to Reshoty where the camp commandant was Blinov."

*   *   *

" 'You, Petro Chmykhalov, are under arrest.' A month had not passed when policemen came and said this to Papa.[4] Everyone at home fell on their knees before the Lord and prayed, and placed Papa in the Lord's hands for safekeeping so that he would strengthen him to stand firm during these trials. After the prayer the police

---

3. Pastry flaps filled with cabbage or similar.
4. This was actually in May 1969, so Timothy's chronology is muddled; but I have not tried to sort it out since the incidents as he recalls them are what matter here.

put both Mama and Papa in the *bobik* and took them away to the police station. We always pray such prayers and we did so when Auntie was taken both the first time and the second, because we trust in our Savior who is the Savior of the whole world, the Lord Jesus Christ. We turn everything over to him so that he would protect and give strength to remain true to him. He answers our prayer and we trust in him so that even today he will not leave us, but preserve us. And so Papa and Mama were arrested by the police and taken away."

Petro was sent to Minusinsk prison for investigation and Maria to a KPZ at Chernogorsk, where the children went every day to try and see her. They would stand outside and shout, "Mama, are you still alive?" Her voice would come back, "Still alive and healthy. God does not leave me, and helps me. He gives me strength." The police would yell and chase them away and Nadya Chmykhalov, running from a policeman, fell in front of a bus and might easily have been killed. The policeman picked her up unharmed and threatened her with jail. Another policeman chased thirteen-year-old Tolik with threats and Tolik replied with tears. "I don't care if you beat me, but give us back our Mama."

Sometimes the children shouted, "Mama, have they tortured you for your faith in our Lord?" and she called back, "Still alive and healthy," but in fact she nearly died of ill treatment: indeed she heard a warder say as he shut the air hole of the cell, "Let the Baptist woman die. We'll hurry her along." Old man Misha still purloined the food parcels at Minusinsk prison, though the family had complained about Anna's: "We wrote to Gromyko and also Brezhnev and all the rest so that they would get this straightened out," says Maria, "and so that thieves would not be assigned to such positions. But no matter how much we wrote about Misha's conduct he remained in his former position and just grew fat. Thus, there is no one to complain to. Whoever has the least little bit of power does just what he pleases."

Maria'a health deteriorated but not her spirit: "When they questioned me the investigator came in alone and said: 'Do you want me to send you to a psychiatric hospital?' And I asked: 'Who are you that you are able to do this? I am raising five children and am in my right mind. According to what law do you want to do this? Or do you have law like a rope: if you pull it taut you can manage to push through anything, and if you let it drop to the floor you can freely step over it?' The investigator waved at the guard and left. This is the kind of human rights which exist in a Communist country."

Maria received a one-year sentence for passport violation but in view of her health, her young family and aged sick mother, it was suspended and she returned home. Her husband received a one-year sentence for the same offense, though the judge told him flatly he was being tried "because you requested to emigrate." He and one other believer, were sent first to Krasnoyarsk and then assigned to a work project near Barnaul in the Altai Territory, 540 kilometers (335 miles) west of Chernogorsk, living in limited confinement similar to Augustina's on the national work project. After Petro Chmykhalov's release he returned to work at the mine face, but in 1971 he was rearrested and given another year, this time in a hard labor camp.

It was while he was at Barnaul that Maria took the three boys—Timothy was seven years old—for a two-week visit, traveling with the other believer's wife and their four girls aged from twelve to two, and also a boy and a girl who went to visit their grandparents in the city. It was Timothy's first trip in a train. They left late at night in an almost empty carriage and the children soon enjoyed themselves crawling along the berths. The carriage had just returned from the repair shop in a filthy state. "Until midnight we all crawled along the berths and ran through the car until we got tired, and we went to sleep wherever we were. In the morning when it was getting light Mama woke us and washed us because we were like miners—all black. No one would have recognized us: we did not even recognize each other and we laughed at each other because only our teeth and eyes shone. Mama began to wash us, beginning with the oldest and ending with the youngest. We also changed clothes."

They changed trains at Novokuznetsk, waiting a whole day and reached Barnaul before dawn the next morning, and drove in a crowded bus to the visitor dormitory, where the duty person tried at first to refuse to let the children stay.

"When Papa came from work we walked through the woods to the stream Barnaulka, about three kilometers from the settlement. All around was forest and we saw a squirrel and watched it jump from tree to tree. The river was not terribly deep. We swam near the children's vacation camp with me carried on Papa's back where it was deeper as I was unable to swim, and I would shout that I was drowning and we would swim to shore. Otherwise we would have drowned. We often walked to Barnaulka to swim, walk in the woods, and to chase squirrels.

"We also would go to the plant where Papa worked because it was interesting for us to ride around the city in the tram. Papa worked at all sorts of jobs. One time when we were in the tram, rogues or hooligans began to follow us in order to beat us and take our last kopecks. We went from one tram to another and thus we rode around for about four or five hours to get away from them. Then we returned to our room.

"We lived there for two weeks and the time came for us to leave. Papa accompanied us to the train. Everyone said good-bye and Tolik hugged Papa and began to cry. We got in the carriage and everyone began to look out of the windows, to wave, and to cry. When the train pulled away Papa ran along the platform and waved. We screamed for him to stay where he was, but he ran all the way down the platform and when the platform ended he ran a bit further, but then the train began to go faster and Papa was left behind.

"Everyone cried because we could no longer see Papa and he was no longer with us. Probably Papa cried too and his heart began to ache and hurt because that was all, until we met again. This episode was so painful that I want to cry as I recall it. We live together and we do not cause anyone harm and do not offend anyone and are arrested for nothing and condemned just because we believe in God."

17

"Let My People Go!"

THE VASHCHENKOS WERE all together again when Augustina returned from prison, for Nadya and Vera had run away after a year in Kansk, though Vera was only thirteen, and had not been rearrested.

Augustina found terrible poverty at home in the Mine 16 settlement. Lida and Lyuba had been unable to repair the house in Second Line Street which had fallen into decay during Peter's absence, and had bought for a song a pitifully small house nearby made of railway sleepers. A neighbor had rented a bulldozer and knocked the empty house flat, claiming it was dangerous, but really to gain credit with the authorities who had threatened many times to bulldoze it to stop the believers gathering there to pray. Peter had been refused compensation; he was told to sue the neighbor, which he would not.

But they were all together. "Sorrow passes quickly in our family," writes Lida. "This is apparently because our whole lives have been composed of it. A small happiness lasting several minutes brightens a difficult life and then new difficulties and experiences come." They were a united family, looking on all life with reverence, as

God-given, yet to be enjoyed. "This is a warm, happy family," says someone who knows them well. "One senses a great deal of warmth and human love. They laugh—this is a family that is able to laugh and enjoy life immensely."

In 1971 there was another division in the church at Chernogorsk, which now numbered about four hundred members. Like the earlier break after the imprisoned presbyters had returned, this division arose from differing interpretations of the Bible regarding attitudes to the Soviet State. As a result of the breach Grigory Vashchenko, his family and a number of others left Chernogorsk to live in the Soviet Far East at Nakhodka, Primore Territory, believing it would be easier to emigrate from there; and Evgeny Bresenden of Nakhodka succeeded in 1975 but Grigory's application and all but two others were always rejected.

In 1975 the Kremlin changed its policy towards Evangelicals. It eased slightly the pressure on registered churches, told independent churches they might register without being obliged to accept affiliation with the All-Union Council of Evangelical Christians-Baptists and its Pentecostal wing, and increased pressure on those which refused to register. Andrei Miller's group at Chernogorsk decided to register. Apparently the authorities had hinted that the strict conditions imposed on a registered church would not be enforced, yet when members tried to bring their children to church they were obliged to leave them outside or suffer expulsion; many of the believers felt they had been tricked by the State.

The conditions had not changed. Preaching must be confined to the "prayer house," children may not join the church nor go to special meetings; the State authorities may forbid certain subjects for preaching and may remove a leader at pleasure. The members must have the presbyter's permission to visit believers in another community. And, Peter Vashchenko adds, "they must not prevent their children joining the Octobrists, Pioneers and Komsomol organizations of atheist education, which aim to make a child grow up an absolute atheist who is able independently to reject the existence of God and to instill this in others. Every believer must serve in the Soviet Army and defend the atheist system. . . ." In fact, claims Peter, "in registering, believers must give the authorities pledges which conflict with God's commands."

Being well aware of the cruel dilemmas he refuses to judge or condemn; and anyone who has traveled among the registered churches in Soviet Russia must be impressed by the depth of dedication and the beauty of their lives under the shadow of restrictions imposed by the militantly atheist government. Remove the straitjacket and Russian Christianity would bound forward from a strong base.

*   *   *

The Vashchenkos, with their militant Christianity, continued to meet opposition and discrimination at every turn. A harrowing instance occurred when Abel, aged seven, had an accident in 1973, though it lives in the Vashchenkos' memories not for the discrimination but for a miracle of healing.

"It happened like this," writes Augustina. "Mine 9 is now called the Yeniseisk Mine. Semikobyla, the manager of the Krasnoyarsk Coal Trust, arrived to examine good order in the mine and around the mine—where the miners' gardens (allotments) were located. Not far from these we had a garden too. Each person had one, fenced off from each other. And when Manager Semikobyla discovered them he ordered that a bulldozer root up all the fences and put them in one pile and burn them so that these gardens would not be used by private residents and the *kolkhoz* field could be widened. The miners had been planting potatoes for themselves.

"The burning of these fences left a big pile of ashes. The middle of the pile was still hot, but the outside was covered with grey ashes. The children and I went to our field to dig up potatoes. During the work Abel and Dinah ran to a little hill and at its foot was the pile of ashes; they did not know that the inside was hot. Abel decided to run down the hill and jump over the pile, but he jumped right in and burned both feet. When he screamed we rushed to him and pulled him out. He had on sandals and the embers poured on to his sandals. When I took off his sandals his left foot had been badly burned and there were embers between the toes of his left foot and they were all burned. Immediately blisters swelled up, but the right foot was not as badly burned. We picked him up and carried him home in our arms because he could not walk by himself.

"We phoned for an ambulance and I took him to the hospital. They drained the blisters on his foot but the skin on his toes had been burned off. When the doctor came to look at him he began to reassure him sympathetically and asked how this had happened. But then he asked: 'What kind of a name is Abel, that your son has?' I said that Abel was a Bible name, that he was named after Adam's second son. Then the doctor immediately treated me differently. At first he had wanted to put me in the hospital with Abel, since he could not walk by himself, but on discovering I was a believer he decided Abel should be left alone. He said to me: 'Go home. He will lie alone and the orderlies will take care of him.'

"They put him into a ward alone and when we went to call on him a woman was lying with her daughter. She was sixteen yet the mother had been put in with her, and ours was seven, but they would not permit me to stay with him in the hospital when he was so seriously ill.

"He was shy around other people and an unknown woman had to carry him to the toilet, because he could not stand on his legs. The women in the ward began to say that I should come and ask the doctor to let me stay and lie with him, but I said that I had already asked and been refused. They said: 'He doesn't sleep and cries all night.' And when they changed his bandages, he fainted because of the pain. They changed the bandage on the foot which was least burned, but on the one which was badly burned they changed bandages only once in a week and the foot began to suppurate. On top, on the sole, and between the toes was all covered with rot and they put ointment on it once and that was all because he cried from the pain and would pass out, so they decided to change bandages only once a week.

"When we found this out we, on our own without telling anyone, took him home. But the doctors said all the time that there would be infection and that it was necessary to amputate the foot. They said that at home there was not the cleanliness and hygiene that there was in the hospital, but we tried to maintain cleanliness. Since it was summer with the heat and flies it led the doctors more than ever to think that there would be infection. Having taken him home I treated his feet myself and maintained cleanliness and for some time I would leave the feet open, i.e., they were not bandaged. After this we prayed a great deal for his healing. Then the children's doctor came and when she looked at him she wanted to examine his feet. I said: 'You will have to unbandage them.' But when she glanced at his feet she said: 'No, that is not necessary. That is too horrible. I cannot do anything to help. This is a matter for the surgeon.'

"After our earnest prayers Abel began to get better, but no one thought that he would be able to keep both feet because the doctors had concluded that it was necessary to amputate the left one. Of course it was a stubborn struggle for his life. And it was not rare for Satan to use people to frighten us for if God had not healed him and he had died, then they would have tried us parents for it. But we entreated him for a healing and he heard our prayers and helped us. For two months Abel was sick and someone from our family always had to be with him day and night.

"The glory for this healing belongs only to God because if he had not listened to our prayers, there would not have been a single doctor who would have rendered Abel help to save his feet."

* * *

The following year, on 8 April 1974, Augustina gave birth to their thirteenth and last child, a son, two weeks after her forty-fifth birthday. All six sons and seven daughters survived infancy to grow into healthy boys and girls: their births spanned twenty-three years.[1]

---

1. When a friend asked Augustina whether she would have married Peter had she known that the marriage would bring imprisonment, sufferings and hardship, she laughed, and said, "Had I known I should have had thirteen children I wouldn't have married him!" Peter grinned from ear to ear.

Peter and Augustina gave the new baby the uncompromisingly biblical name of Abraham *(Avram)*. It may have been this registration which reminded the local bureaucracy that the Vashchenkos continued to educate their younger children at home, still declining to have them exposed to the atheist school system. The Chmykhalovs, like most other believers, had allowed their boys to resume school after some assurances, but though one or two teachers were kindly, the day came when the class beat up Shurik so badly that he refused to return to school. The teacher never lifted a finger, despite little Timothy's screams that bullies were beating his brother.

The Vashchenkos were determined that each of their children should grow up thoroughly literate, writing a nice hand, and the elder daughters took a share in the teaching. All the family considered that to go beyond a good grasp of the "Three Rs" was a waste of time since higher education was barred. When a believer sought it he would be told that foremen or skilled engineers and such like were essentially educators of those under them, to "reeducate" them into Marxism and atheism: "We do not need educators with religious convictions!" Thus scientific, creative, or intellectual work which requires a higher education is refused a believer, however able, unless he hides his Christianity; at any sign of that, indeed, the authorities swiftly follow up with enticing offers, which can be swiftly withdrawn.

By 1974 six of the children were of school age. The city evidently thought that Sasha at nearly sixteen was not worth worrying about but in the late summer some inspectors came to the house. On 23 September the parents received a strict warning and on 13 November the local procurator, Rezvanov, filed a suit demanding that they be deprived of parental rights over Abel, Dinah, Paul, Jacob and John, "and that the children be turned over for education to a State children's institution." The statement claimed that Peter was unemployed, which was not true, and that the home, outside and in, was filthy and insanitary, whereas in fact cleanliness ranked next to godliness for the Vashchenkos despite their poverty and their animals, and despite the fact that if a small slice of the vast

Kremlin expenditure on armaments and subversion had been used to enlarge the water mains of Chernogorsk, and to renew the pumps, it would have been easier to get water: the main dried to a trickle for months at a time while water often ran down the street wasted.

The trial for depriving of parental rights was set for 30 December 1974 at noon. Peter decided to take all the threatened children to Moscow and once again plead with the American Embassy for help in emigrating. They left on 28 December, shadowed everywhere by the KGB.

The trains to Achinsk were full for the New Year holiday. They had to take tickets on the cross-country line as far as Novokuznetsk, hoping to get the rest of the way from there, but instead found a twenty-four hour waiting list. They tried the airport: no seats for three days—possibly the KGB had seen to that. It was bitterly cold. "We went back home. The appointed time for the trial passed. No one came to see us. The authorities were afraid that if they took legal action to seize our children that we would once more go to the Embassy to complain, and everything would be brought to light, and it would be bad for world public opinion."

Instead they received a summons on 20 January 1975 from the city soviet to attend at Room 15, second floor, at 10:00 A.M. the next day, bringing their adult children, "for discussion."

Nine of them went including fourteen-year-old John. In the office of the deputy chairman, who was a woman named Galina Stepanovna Andriushchenko, they found seven other officials with her, including Procurator Rezvanov, representatives of the KGB, the education department, and a psychiatrist; Peter heard later through someone present that when the officials discussed the Vashchenkos afterwards, this psychiatrist emphatically rejected a suggestion that they were out of their right minds. "You are wasting your time," he said, "trying to find them abnormal or mentally deficient. These people are in full possession of their senses."

The meeting was a session of the Commission for the Observation of the Legislation concerning Religious Cults. "They wished to know why we wanted to leave and live in America, why our children did not attend school, why our children were not able to serve in the Soviet Army, why we would not go to the doctor for help. We answered all the questions. Then the procurator said: 'When we have sent you abroad we will drink a vodka shot to you that you have been freed.' We replied: 'You can drink half a liter, but we will pray for you.' "

They left Room 15 under the impression that the discussion had been a long step towards securing exit visas. They were all the more upset, therefore, when on 7 February the *Chernogorsk Worker* carried a long accusatory and grossly unfair article, "The Narrow Path of the Vashchenkos," by a journalist, V. Nikolaev, who had sat in on the discussion. It began: "There is still a bad taste in my mouth. I try to understand these people, but there is just no way that I can." And it ended, "One shouldn't call you a Soviet citizen, Peter Vashchenko! You are not worthy of that title."

Soviet press articles against believers usually take one of three forms: the lampoon which crudely paints them as clowns; the scurrilous, in which accusations are selected from a time-worn list of alleged crimes or heinous fanatical actions; and the sweetly reasonable, in which the writer shakes his head sadly. The *Chernogorsk Worker* chose the third, subtly mixing falsehoods with truth in the universal tradition of Communist propaganda. Thus V. Nikolaev mentioned that they stole their sick son from hospital, but not the callous discrimination displayed by the doctor; and he claimed, against all the evidence, that Peter was a bad worker. Inevitably, Nikolaev made no attempt to discuss the dilemma that strict obedience to the laws of God involves breaking the laws of the Soviet Union.

Nikolaev gives his own case away in a paragraph in which he says: "In short, God indicates his will and the Vashchenkos simply fulfill it. Such a thing is, of course, to us atheists absurd. But we have always said and say that no one may be persecuted for his faith. Why then aren't the Vashchenkos left in peace? Let's get to the bottom of this. Is it really the fault of faith that this family comes into conflict with the law? After all, in our country there are thousands of believers and the overwhelming majority do not break the laws. And more than that, they participate with us in

РСФСР
ИСПОЛНИТЕЛЬНЫЙ. КОМИТ
ЧЕРНОГОРСКОГО
ГОРОДСКОГО СОВЕТА
ДЕПУТАТОВ ТРУДЯЩИХСЯ
Хакасской автономной области,
Красноярского края

21. 1. 196__ г.

№
г. Черногорск

Защенко Петру Павловичу

Защенко Августе Васильевне

проживающим в поселке шахты № 17, в доме № 3

ПОВЕСТКА

Исполком горсовета ставит вас в известность, что 21 января
1975 года вам необходимо придти /кабинет № 15,II этаж/
для беседы вместе с совершеннолетними детьми.

Исполком горсовета

20 января 1975 г.

Translation:
Peter Pavlovich Vashchenko
Augustina Vasilevna Vashchenko
Residing in Settlement of Mine 17 [sic], house 3

SUMMONS
The Executive Committee of the City Soviet [Chernogorsk] hereby inform you that
on January 21, 1975, you must come with your adult children to Room 15, 2nd
floor, for discussion
Executive Committee of the City Soviet
January 20, 1975

the building of a Communist society. Certainly we try to convince them that belief in God is nothing more than an illusion. We struggle with religious prejudices, but at the same time we treat the believers with the same respect that we treat the other members of our society." Even his immediate readers knew that this was not true.

Nikolaev concluded that the Vashchenkos were motivated by malice against the Soviet State under a veneer of religion. The article had its intended effect. People became nastier. At work and in the stores Vashchenkos would be cut by acquaintances and people would laugh and whisper, "There go the Americans!"

The family were especially upset at the sentence; "Everything, and their children also, they are prepared to sacrifice to God." This, in the context of years of anti-Christian propaganda, would not be read by the populace as it would be in the West, but as saying that the Vashchenkos were prepared to throw a child under a railway train or burn it on a pyre if God so ordered.

Therefore they wrote to the newspaper a five-page reply, dated 6 March 1975, in which they explained the high sense of parental responsibility which is obligatory to a Christian, and then discussed their interpretation of that proof text which the journalist had thrown in their faces with his words: "And if you are going to quote the Bible there are also words in it which say that all powers are established by God and that if you oppose them you oppose God." They also pointed out the unfairness of publishing articles against believers without allowing rejoinder: "People misunderstand and hate believers and won't give them jobs, because of slanted articles." The Vashchenkos ended by threatening to complain to the United Nations, since freedom to defend oneself against accusation is enshrined in international law.

The newspaper sent for the family. Editors showed them the reply set up in type, questioned them closely on their views—and never published one word.

*   *   *

By now the campaign to emigrate which Peter had launched more than ten years before had grown to vast proportions. Pentecostals of the USSR looked for an "Exodus" with the same hope as the Children of Israel of old.

During 1974 the Vashchenkos had petitioned President Podgorny and President Nixon, and in December President Ford. Grigory, once so cautious, was leading a campaign from Nakhodka, where with his neighbor Evgeny Bresenden he signed a long letter to "Christians of the Whole World," pleading for help. Petitions went out from congregations in widely different parts of the Soviet Union. From Chernogorsk eighty-nine church members and their children petitioned President Ford for help to emigrate, accompanying the appeal with lists of names and fifty-four individual letters. The Vashchenkos believed that more than four hundred in Chernogorsk wanted to leave, though some, through fear, pretended they did not.

It was not therefore a matter of complete surprise, though of overwhelming joy, when the Vashchenkos heard a rumor that they would be sent abroad on 1 May 1975. Their invitation having been confiscated seven years before, they hurried to the city's instructor on religious affairs, Liliya Dimitrievna Dugina, to ask if the rumor were true. "She said: 'It is true. You are going on the basis of religious conviction and possibly we will send you by 1 May. You can prepare to leave.' She even became concerned: 'Do the children have clothes?' We said that we would buy them, but we asked: 'This isn't empty propaganda, is it?' She answered: 'No, it is the truth'" They believed her because she was a deputy of the city committee. They wondered whether the confiscated invitation lay in her file She insisted that the Americans had asked for them, and the Vashchenkos noted her words: "You are American citizens and should turn to the American Embassy for everything."

They sold their potatoes but kept the cow, hoping for a better price at the last minute, but did not plant their vegetables. Other believers who were told they were going began to sell up to get money for their fares. All waited the summons to fill in emigration forms.

The May Day public holiday passed. No word came from the city authorities. On 4 May the Vashchenkos went to vice-chairman Andriushchenko and asked what had happened. "She said to us:

'Who told you such a lie?' We said: 'The instructor on religious affairs, Dugina.' 'Well, then,' said Andriushchenko, 'go to her and get this matter straightened out.' We went to Dugina and asked her why she had deceived us.

"And she said: 'We submitted documents for you to Moscow and thought that you would be let out, but they refused.' "

The Vashchenkos went home. The cruel trick had tragic economic consequences, for the family had to restock, buying potatoes at a higher price than they had received; they lived the rest of the summer without essential vegetables which they had not planted. Possibly the city authorities had intended, by their deception, both to punish the Vashchenkos and to weaken their resolve to emigrate.

18

Aaron

THAT SPRING OF 1975 Lida Vashchenko was twenty-four. Fair-haired and gentle, her courage and her loving nature were obvious to all. Refusal to deny her faith having barred her from appointment as a store superintendent, who would have to give atheist lectures to staff, she worked as an orderly in the maternity home at Cherno-gorsk.

Across the road stood the women's consultancy and the abortion section (literally, "criminal section") where abortions were carried out daily by the State, still the most usual form of birth control in the Soviet Union. Babies aborted at later stages of pregnancy were sometimes born alive, in defiance of their mothers' wishes and artificially premature. They would be carried across to the infants' ward of the maternity home where all babies are looked after by staff, the mothers being allowed them only at feeding time and the husbands never admitted, as is the Russian custom.

These "tortured bodies, whom I am forced to swaddle and for whom my heart breaks when I take them in my arms," provoked Lida's indignation, especially as the maternity staff disliked babies from the abortion section and were indifferent if they died within a few hours. Then they were thrown into the stoke hole.

One day Lida came on duty to find a little corpse already stinking. The other women had been too squeamish to take it down to the boiler, yet all of them had had one or more abortions themselves: "You go, Lida." The woman stoker, though in the same case, was equally squeamish. Lida was "repulsed by such hypocritical pity and felt I would have liked to have gone along the beds where women lay who had had abortions, to beat them with the body of this dead baby. Their hearts did not shiver during the convulsions of their child before its death, when it died before their eyes, or when he was pulled out in pieces. They had no pity then, but now, with the body of the baby who was not wanted by anyone, who has no parents to bury him, they shirk throwing the unfeeling corpse into the furnace." Lida shoveled him in and slammed the furnace door. To her, abortion was premeditated murder whether at early or late stage; God had given a life and a mother had killed.

A few days later on 31 March 1975 a tiny male baby barely recognizable as human was brought across alive, after a seventh-month abortion. Lida learned later from the unmarried mother's own lips that "the infant cried when it lay next to her, but even then she did not take pity on him and with great impatience waited for him to die. When she was told that he was alive, she went to the toilet and cried for a long time.

"When he was brought to the maternity home he was placed in the corridor; they hoped he would die by morning, but he rallied and began to pick up and by morning he had not died, but on the contrary was better." Lida saw him "lying there all blue. When I wanted to take him into my arms, I was warned that it was an aborted child: 'Don't touch him, or you will be infected. We don't know what she poisoned him with.'"

All April the mother refused to breast feed and the nurses gave him only *kefir*, a thick substance made of fermented milk, and never bathed him. Lida, however, liked him although he scarcely looked like a baby. "His fingernails were only half formed, the stomach was covered by a thin membrane which was permeated by red and blue veins. His eyes were half sealed over so that the little whites dominated the greater part of the eyes. He rolled them particularly when he was given shots and for a long time they would not return to their former position. I think this was due partly to fear and partly to the fact that he was two months premature." The doctors seemed to have been using some form of acupuncture.

Nobody wanted him. Lida began to think of adopting him but after a while dropped the idea because she did not believe they would give a baby to a recognized believer. After a while he was transferred to the children's hospital, at the opposite end of the city near a small park of pines, and it was when she was passing in a bus that "I distinctly heard in my head his voice, the voice which I had heard in the maternity home. And then once more my world was turned upside down. Why could not I, at twenty-four, take the place of his mother?"

Lida found the woman in a communal living complex. She welcomed the proposal, stating plainly that she did not want her baby, whereupon the maternity doctor said the infant could be registered to Lida, since the real mother had refused to register, provided that the children's hospital director did not object. When Lida asked, the director said she did not mind who had the baby. Finally the mother wrote a formal release in Lida's presence: "I, Valentina Vasilevna Goroshnikova, reject my baby and will not present any future claims."

The maternity home wrote out a certificate of adoption, registered him in the name of Lida's choice, and he was entered in her passport. By Soviet law he became Aaron Viktorovich Vashchenko.[1]

The doctor had suggested that Lida should lie with her baby because he had been neglected and was ill. Then she approached his little bed. "I could not refrain from crying. Before me lay a

---

1. The father is given as Viktor Vasilevich Vashchenko. Presumably the hospital concocted a fictitious forename and patronymic approximating to those of the natural mother, Valentina Vasilevna. The mother is given as Lida Petrovna Vashchenko without reference to adoption. The date of registration was 23 April 1975 at Chernogorsk City Registry office, Registration number: 458. The printed number of the certificate given to Lida is 387754.

pale creature with a bare little head (they had put a medicine dropper in his head). A yellow medicine was bubbling out of his nose. He was completely covered with needle marks and his stomach was like a map of veins. His little buttocks were so pricked that the syringe needle would go in with a crunch, like into wood, and when it was pulled out, the medicine would stream back out because there was no place for it to go. The baby gave off an unpleasant smell; he had not been bathed since he had been born.

"He began to cheep, but he did not cry. Overcoming my squeamishness I took him into my arms and pressed his forehead to my cheek. The baby breathed hard as if trying to get something up, and when I moved him away from me he looked for my cheek again. All at once I forgot my squeamishness, tears welled up in me, and I pressed him more tightly to me. I thought to myself, 'I will never part with him or allow wrong to be done to him.' "

She took Aaron to bed with her in a ward, and the mothers said, "At long last he has found a mother." Then she gave him a bath, his first, but before she could dry him fully a nurse took him away from her, saying it was time for the medicine dropper. After an hour Lida peeped in and saw her baby, unclothed, with the windows open because the nurses wore warm clothes. She decided that Aaron "would not be healthy here, quite the contrary." When the treatment ended, Lida warmed him by holding him in a towel over a pot of boiling water, and resolved to get his discharge as soon as possible. She said aloud, not so much "to comfort him as myself, 'Don't cry, Aaron. Be patient a little longer. We will soon leave, you will be great. The whole world will find out about you!' I surprised myself by these words and pondered them, because I had said them without thinking."

She slept in with him for three nights. His temperature dropped to normal but they insisted on continuing the treatment, pricking him all over with needle marks until one mother in the ward exclaimed that the doctors were just like the Fascists who did experiments on children.

With the Victory Day (9 May) holiday approaching, Lida decided to flee with Aaron, and left on 7 May. Leaving hospital without authorization was not uncommon, "but for some reason they only chased after me," for the very next day the director and another doctor called at the Vashchenkos. Rejecting Lida's pleas that Aaron be examined at home, they claimed he was very ill and removed him by car. To lie with her son again Lida had to walk back to the hospital, where the director, who had herself granted the adoption, said severely that she would make sure Lida did not get Aaron if she left again without authorization; indeed, "I will do anything so that you do not get this child."

Lida read this as a threat to Aaron's life and was distressed beyond measure: "After these words I decided to abandon such a hospital altogether in order to preserve the life of the child."

*   *   *

Peter, Augustina and all the Vashchenkos were delighted when Aaron came into their home, almost exactly a year younger than Lida's youngest brother, Abraham. "We greatly pitied this baby even though we had our own thirteen children. He was not one too many for our family." They found a wet-nurse and they kept Aaron warm by holding him much of the time over the stove. Lida had resigned her job to devote her whole self to him. "I did not know what he would grow up to be—an atheist-Communist or a Christian, but I always asked God that he grow up into a fine person who could accomplish much for God in his life." From being a scrap of sick humanity he grew stronger and healthy "and had already begun to laugh," when they learned that the city executive committee wanted to remove him.

Liliya Dimitrievna Dugina, the instructress of believers who so recently, for whatever reason, had cruelly misled the Vashchenkos about emigration, was furious at the implications of Aaron's adoption. The committee summoned the children's hospital doctors and berated them for giving the child to a believer, and a Vashchenko at that: "They will take him to America and raise him as a spy!" The doctors promised that such a puny infant would soon die, so the committee decided to wait, and then to put Lida on trial for causing his death by leaving the hospital.

When Aaron did not die the authorities decided to get him back. In Lida's opinion they cared not a rap for babies aborted or abandoned, "but everyone noticed when Aaron ended up with me," she wrote a few weeks later.[2] "All the medical personnel of the city gathered and said that I wanted to 'sacrifice' him to God. Yes, Satan knew that he would be brought up for God, and that is what he was afraid of above all else. . . . Not a single one of these children did they pity, but to my Aaron they showed an excessive 'pity'; they saw at once that he alone, out of the darkness which engulfed these children, was joyfully greeted into a family and warmed by its fifteen members."

First they summoned Peter and Augustina and asked whether their daughter had motherly feelings towards the boy. Her parents' strong affirmative destroyed any such excuse for removing Aaron. Next they sent officials posing as doctors wanting to take Aaron for treatment, who when refused admittance, "called us foul, dirty words." Then they decided to deprive Lida of parental rights by court action and subpoenaed her to appear.

She fled. Dressed as a boy, traveling by horse-drawn cart, with Aaron in a barrel, she reached friends in the countryside, and when she jumped down, the neighbors thought she was one of her brothers. But it was easier to look after him at home and after a while she returned by bicycle, once more dressed as a boy, with Aaron in a sleeping bag.

Her reappearance was soon known to the police, who haunted the house just as in Lida's own childhood. She foxed them when exercising Aaron in the baby carriage by pushing her baby brother too. Once she and Sarah, five years old, had to take Aaron some two kilometers. "Several times we stopped and I gave him a bottle; he would then go back to sleep. There were two ways you could approach our house. When the time came I decided to ask Sarah, 'Which way shall we choose, the shorter or the longer?' Sarah thought a bit, and it was obvious she was tired. Then she proposed

---

2. This and several other quotations in the chapter come from a long appeal, describing the case up to that date, written by Lida and Vera to the United Nations, dated 19 August 1975.

the way which was a bit farther. I was surprised. 'But you're tired,' I said. 'Why do you prefer the long way?' 'I don't know.' I decided to go the way she preferred. When we approached the lane we caught a glimpse of the back of a police car going to our place. If we had gone the shorter way we would have arrived at the house at the same time and they would have taken the baby, but now we just waited until they left and then returned home."

The executive committee at length decided to remove Aaron, by force if necessary. The Vashchenkos afterwards discovered that at the committee meeting, which included the KGB, not everybody voted that he should be seized, but the family believe that the decision was submitted to higher powers and endorsed. The authorities had to find a way which would look genuine and be within the law. They therefore sought out the natural mother, Valya, and frightened her with stories that Lida intended to kill the baby as a sacrifice. As Lida comments, "So often I have had to observe how the good intentions of a Christian are always distorted and it is painful to listen when you want good and strive for it, yet are deliberately slandered."

Valya refused to ask for him back and threatened to harm him if compelled. Eventually they wore her down. "She was forced to play the role of a broken-hearted mother, and she played it very badly," as Lida was about to see for herself, in one of the most frightening hours of her life.

*   *   *

About noon on 17 July 1975 nineteen-year-old Vera, who with Lida and Nadya were the only Vashchenkos at home at that moment, was preparing to go to the store. "I had put the money on the table," she wrote when the memory was still fresh,[3] "and Nadya had returned from the night shift and had gone to bed. Lida, the mother of Aaron, was rocking him gently in her arms, four and a half months old and fast asleep. Hearing a knock on the gate and the dog bark, I went outside."

---

3. Quotations from Appeal to the United Nations, August 1975.

She saw with Dugina the instructress, Rimma Alekseevna from the executive committee and a third woman, whom she did not know. Vera asked through the narrow slit in the gate what they needed. They said: "Let us in. The mother wants to see her child." The third woman was Valya, who had aborted Aaron. "But I refused to let them in because they are deceivers and we, since childhood, had seen their falseness and injustice and we know that with them everything is built on deception and violence."

Dugina shouted that the mother was broken-hearted and just wanted to look at him. Rimma Alekseevna said: "When will your conscience finally awaken? The mother comes to you blinded with tears and asks you to show her her baby, her own son."

Valya stood impassive, silent. Vera, seeing no tears, shouted back: "And where was this mother's bleeding heart when she had an abortion? And when she got out of her bed and refused to nurse, and abandoned him, and left the hospital?

"They were infuriated and began to scream: 'Open up to us or we will climb over the fence!' I walked away from the gate, took the dog off his leash and let him into the house. Then I took a lock and locked the entrance to the house from the outside. During this time one of them went for the car full of people, mainly men, which they had left in a side street in order not to frighten us away. It pulled up to the house and men jumped out. I walked to the other end of the yard. One of the police investigators (as we later found they were) grabbed hold of the fence and shouted: 'Open the gate!' And another poked his documents through the fence at me (apparently he had received them not long ago) and shouted: 'Have a look at my documents.' "

The uniformed assistant chief of police, Vasilev, climbed up on the fence and shouted: "We are representatives of the Soviet power!" Vera, in a desperate attempt to save Aaron, recalled Dugina's remark that they should consider themselves Americans, and answered: "We accept only the American authorities, since we are American citizens." She tried to explain.

Vasilev called across to Dugina, who was telling the gathering crowd of curious neighbors that the Vashchenkos had stolen the baby and refused to restore him to his legal mother: "Is it true that they are American citizens?"

"Yes! But this is the sort of situation in which anything is allowed."

A policeman shouted to Vera, "Well now, pretty one, give me the key or open it yourself." She refused. He forced the gate and others swarmed in. Vasilev walked up to Vera, and asked: "Where is Lida now?"

"She hasn't hidden just so that I can tell you where she is!"

Dugina screamed: "Why listen to her? Remove the window pane and crawl in." When Vera warned them that they would complain to Moscow, they sneered, "Watch out for yourself, but what you won't tell us we will find out anyway!"

Vera tried to push them aside from the window but was seized and her arms twisted behind her back. "Having freed myself, I again rushed to the window where a robust fellow was crawling in and had stuck in the window. I wanted to pull him out but Vasilev twisted my arms behind my back and pushed my nose in the fence."

Lida had been hiding inside, holding tight her beloved Aaron, who slept peacefully, while she listened to Vera's spirited defense. Then Dugina caught sight of her and yelled, "Your sect always does this. This is the humanitarianism of the believers You try to catch a person in your nets when he is in misfortune. When you should have been helping Valya in her grief, you trailed after her and bought her child."

*   *   *

Lida takes up the story of this forcible entry which took place when the high representatives of the Soviet Union were at Helsinki to sign the Agreement on Human Rights.

"I, Lida, am now writing what happened before my eyes. They took the large window pane out of the window and pushed Valya Goroshnikova to the window. The first thing I heard from her was: 'You are a scoundrel.' This curse I took to be entirely the work of the Chernogorsk executive committee, who taught her to say it and brought her under escort to do this robbery under the pretext of being the mother. At first she even forgot what she was supposed to say and they had to help her get into the role."

Lida asked, "Why am I a scoundrel?"

"You did a mean thing."

"What did I do?"

"I did not know you were such a person."

"What kind of person?"

Valya made no reply. Then she said: "Give me my baby."

"Valya, what is he to you?"

Valya stood silent, picking at the ground with the tip of her shoe.

Then Valya repeated: "Give him up. I need him now."

"Since when did you begin needing him?" asked Lida.

Valya lapsed into silence again but Lida heard Dugina and Rimma shout hysterically that the mother's heart was bleeding, that she was completely blind from tears and had come to them begging that they return her baby to her.

"And," writes Lida, "here we continued to stand at the window, I in the room, Valya outside. All of a sudden she made a move to step aside, deciding she had finished her part; but Dugina pushed her from behind toward the window once more and tried to force her to climb in where the window pane had been. But she did not move from her place, and I warned her, and those standing with her, that it would be better for them not to climb in the window, because that would be an illegal act. In one hand I held a cane and in the other my baby and I wanted to use the cane to defend myself against the louts. She stepped away from the window and stood off to the side at a distance."

The abductors now seemed nonplussed and retired for conference. Dugina said it was pointless to argue with the Vashchenko girls: the police must act. Valya continued to stand listless.

The uniformed policeman pulled out a gun and jumped at the window. Being a small man, he managed to crawl through it, while the police chief shouted at him to shoot the dog if there was one: fortunately Mukhtar was safe behind another door. Nadya stood in front of Lida, trying to shield her. Then another man appeared at the window but, recalls Lida, "since he turned out to be rather large, he could only shove in his head and his legs up to his knees and the rest of him hung outside on the other side!"

Finally they pushed this man in, while Dugina kept shouting: "Take the baby away from her!" One of them twisted Nadya's arms and dragged her into the kitchen. Ripping herself free, she shouted: "Why are you twisting my arms? I still need those arms to earn our bread and to feed myself and you, you parasite! I have just returned from the night shift and you burst in here and won't let me sleep." The man twisted her arms still harder and screamed: "Shut up!"

Lida continues: "I was occupied with the other two. In one arm I held my son, Aaron. The other arm was put behind my back by one of the men. The other grabbed hold of my hair and beat my head against the wall. Then Nadya from the kitchen screamed out: 'Why are you pulling her by the hair?' Then I realized that it was me that was being pulled by the hair. After that I ended up on the couch, but I continued to hold on to my son in my arm. Once more they pushed my free arm behind my back and pressed me to the divan on the arm with which I held my baby. Finally I collapsed."

Before the policeman seized him from her arms, Aaron woke up and looked around with a scared look. She kissed him. She last saw her baby in the hands of the policeman as he rushed to the window.

He emerged holding poor Aaron head downwards and handed him to Valya, the mother, who continued to hold him upside down. They led her away by the arm. Lida learned afterwards that Valya was upset by what she had seen, and took a long time to recover.

In triumph, Dugina jumped into the car with Aaron and the police and Valya and speeded away to the city.

19

The Ultimate Horror

"I ASK YOU in the name of our whole family to grant us this request for the sake of God: Take us away from here. And help me find and recover my son. For Christ's sake—the poor beg for bread, and we, for His sake, ask you to intervene on our behalf. May He help you do this. *Lida Vashchenko, August 16, 1975.*"

Thus Lida appealed to the United Nations, in vain, four and a half weeks after Aaron's abduction, in her long account of the whole incident. Every effort to trace him had failed. She heard that the natural mother, Valya, who had held Aaron upside down when forced to take him back, had refused to keep him but was rewarded with a nice apartment for her part in the abduction.

Lida realized that any appeal to the city authorities would go unanswered, and they had spread a rumor that she had beaten a policeman but would not be prosecuted because her mother's imprisonment had been disgrace enough. "The city executive committee suggested that I find a job. I told them that if I knew where my baby was I would get a job there cleaning the floor, but in the meantime I would not go anywhere. For some reason this seemed very funny to them."

On 22 August Lida, her father, the two elder boys and one of her sisters went a considerable distance by overnight freight train to a place in the forest where they could pick quantities of wild berries. "It was the first day I was able to forget my grief a little, although not completely because my thoughts from time to time would return to Aaron. In the forest I noticed that summer had already passed and I had not seen it. No one asked me how many berries I had gathered; I was left to myself. It was the first day I had begun to laugh and generally forget myself, escaping reality.

"On the 23rd thoughts of Aaron never left me and I constantly prayed for him silently."

They returned home on the evening of the 24th by overnight train, traveling on an open flat-bed freight car. It was drizzling and they were soaked. During the journey an extraordinary incident occurred. "All of us were overcome by such fear that several of us began to cry, especially me. When they asked me what was the matter I answered: 'I'm afraid.' I did not know who or what I was afraid of, but I felt as if there was a gigantic force crushing down on us in the car. When I tried to creep towards my father I realized that he too sensed something and probably was crying, because he hid his eyes and would not admit that he too was frightened and had a foreboding of something bad. Each person wrapped himself up in his raincoat and quietly prayed. Morning approached and little by little the fear which had gripped us dispersed. And after we were back on the ground each of us admitted that something had happened which it was impossible to understand or talk about, although each felt the presence of Satan. We thought that something had happened at home, but when we reached home we discovered that everything was all right there."

Weeks later they discovered that this was the hour that Aaron died.

At the beginning of September, before Aaron's fate was known, they decided to appear once again to the American Embassy. The parents and five of the children, with some friends from Chernogorsk, caught the train from wayside stations in independent little groups. The three-and-a-half-day journey passed without incident: Lyuba says, "It was obvious that God was accompanying us along the way. On 5 September at the Embassy, the police stopped Augustina and John as the others walked in, but American officials came out and brought them in. The Vashchenkos told about Aaron, and the deception over exit visas. Once again they received immigration forms to use as soon as an invitation came from America, and were told to return if they met obstruction. They were handed a document to show the police at the gate and a telephone number to call if they were stopped. As they were afraid of arrest on leaving the Embassy, a consular officer escorted them to the pedestrian subway."

They were now shadowed everywhere by KGB men and women, on the metro, the escalators, even into the toilets. "They were easy to spot," says Peter. "They were always standing there with their rolled-up newspapers or pretending to read one, but they tried very hard to hide. Some are very clever in their work, others are not. For seventeen years we have struggled with them and we immediately and clearly recognize them. On the way home, we were already approaching Bogotol, about forty kilometers west of Achinsk, when the former Chernogorsk KGB Chief, Kolpakov, came into our car pretending that he had not expected to see us. He asked where we were going. We said: 'Visiting.' But he needed details. We understood each other; he accompanied us to Achinsk and then turned us over to other escorts. Thus we traveled under KGB escort, only they were dressed in civilian clothes."

Once again a visit to the Embassy seemed to cause a change in Soviet official attitudes. When the Vashchenkos called at the offices of the city soviet, the vice-chairman of the executive committee, Galina Andriushchenko, who had not been present at Aaron's abduction, at last disclosed that they had taken him then to Abakan children's hospital: "He is having treatment with expensive medicines. I am paying for this myself," she said, which sounded odd since treatment is free in the Soviet Union. She told Lida: "Come back alone in three days. I will arrange things and tell you." In fact, she was dissembling.

Three days later Lida returned carrying some of Aaron's clothes.

"When I entered her room she rushed to meet me, took me by the hand and invited me to sit down. But I intended to see the baby and I refused to sit. She tried to lead the conversation into unrelated themes—'Why are you so beautiful today? Who did your hair?' etc. I answered her: 'Have you really forgotten why I came? What do you have to say regarding my request?' And then, as if continuing our conversation on a pleasant topic, she said: 'The fact of the matter is that Aaron is no more. He died.' "

At first Lida thought Galina must be joking, for when abducted Aaron had been perfectly healthy; from a barely living premature birth he had grown into a sturdy baby. Galina repeated her statement. Lida felt concussed.

"My head began to ring and only with great difficulty was I able to leave the office. My thoughts raced. 'I am too late. He is no more.' I was crying, but I intensely wanted to hide my tears from her and quickened my step. As I left I heard her say after me: 'If you want us to, we will show you where the grave is.' But I did not want anything more than to get home. There it would be clear. And it didn't matter anyway—there was no point in rushing.

"I remember that on the bus everyone noticed me. Somebody gave me a seat. Then at the front of the bus when a baby started to cry, I could bear it no longer. From time to time I would get hold of myself and stop crying. My father was at home and I told him and he began to reassure me, saying that they were probably just trying to deceive me, that he was still alive. We got on the motorcycle and went to the cemetery.

"We went up to the old woman who had worked there many years. She said that several days ago a baby without parents had been buried by order of the executive committee without any certificate. She was told that the child had been found by the police in a field and was already beginning to decompose. Nothing was known about the parents or about who did it, although it was probably some robbers. She led us to a grave which had a dirty board driven into it. The old woman explained that this was in order not to get it mixed up with another grave; usually a numbered board is put in, but for some reason with this baby they had forbidden her to give it a number.

"As I stood over this little fresh hill of earth I felt, with all my heart, that they had not deceived me, that it was indeed Aaron who lay here below this thick earth. My heart hurt so much that I was ready to dig up the earth with my fingernails. Then the old woman turned to me and said: 'And what connection do you have with this child?' I answered: 'I am the mother.' To this day I have not forgotten the way she measured me with her eyes and the words she said: 'And where were you that you did not notice your baby's absence for such a long time?' She continued, but I was no longer able to listen, and having started to cry I moved away from the grave.

"My father caught up with me and we went to the office of the Bureau of Technical Information, where they keep a list of all who die without relatives. When we asked about the baby we were given the death certificate, and it was for my baby. I recopied it. It was then that my father became convinced of Aaron's death. Until then he kept thinking that they had deceived us. When we left he couldn't get the motorcycle started for a long time because his hands were shaking. Then he drove so fast that I thought we would be killed.

"The old woman had also told us that the coffin-maker, 'uncle' Sasha, had brought the baby to be buried. We found him planing his next coffin. He asked: 'Do you need a coffin?' I said: 'Yes.' He asked: 'For whom? What size?' And then I notice the frightened gaze of my father which was fixed on me and stopped. We called the coffin-maker to the side, because people were beginning to listen in on the conversation. 'Did you bury a little boy?' I asked. He said: 'Yes.' 'Did he look like me?' 'He looked like you. The same light hair that you have, but it was already impossible to make out his face—there was no nose and his eyes had disappeared. I was told to go to the morgue to take him for burial. He was naked, but some woman who signed him out of the hospital left the little boy an old shirt and I put him in a coffin and took him here. Now, don't you worry. We buried him as prescribed. Here, the woman who works in the storehouse tore off a meter of red fabric, because he was just lying there in the shav ngs with only his little shirt-vest on. We covered the shavings and laid him in the coffin, and then we took him and put him in the ground.' "

Lida then took a terrifying decision and the family backed her.

"Early on the morning of September 16, well before the break of day, we went to the cemetery to dig up the grave. As we live in a settlement twelve kilometers west of the city and the cemetery is just beyond the city to the north, we went with a side car in which Vera and I sat while John and Father rode on the motorcycle. As we dug up the grave there were already women driving the cows out to pasture and a shepherd was standing on a hill and looked down at the visitors who had come to the cemetery so early. He couldn't understand what was going on. The child had been placed in an adult's grave, so it was necessary to dig around with the shovel in order to find out in which corner of the grave the coffin was.

"We opened the coffin in order to make sure that it was him. It was true indeed that from the face nothing could be determined, but the forehead, the hands, the legs, and especially the fingernails, were his. Without a doubt it was him and we took him home in order to bury him according to Christian ceremony. We had to fill the grave back up quickly because it was already getting light. The wind rustled the paper wreaths. The metal monuments were gleaming and the tin wreaths knocked about giving off a monotonous sound. It seemed that everything was alive, moving according to its own imperceptible laws. There was a warmth which emerged from the turned upside-down grave, and from the coffin—a smell."

The condition of the little corpse was nauseating. Allowed to lie in the morgue for two and a half weeks following an autopsy, it was barely recognizable as human. Later, at Abakan, though chased away by an angry woman doctor, Lida discovered that, whatever the cause of Aaron's illness, the authorities had forced the natural mother (who in fact had no legal rights after the adoption) to sign authority for an operation, under which Aaron died. Lida does not wish his fearful state to be described in detail yet. Enough that Aaron when torn from her arms was ruddy-cheeked and healthy; if a baby who needs constant, detailed care and love is cast into unfeeling institutional hands, his survival will be perilous at best.

In the cemetery that September morning "it was cold and all of this created an atmosphere that was so frightening that one's hair stood on end. Everyone was breathing very loudly and everything sounded noisy in the midst of this eternal quiet, although we worked very carefully and quietly, and hurried so as not to be caught at the grave. But the fact that before me was really a dead baby, that I had not mistaken him for my son, that he lay in this coffin disfigured—this feeling of grief was stronger than any feeling of fear. I was driven by the desire to take him away from here to the land of the living as soon as possible, as if he were still alive.

"I sat down in the side car of the motorcycle and was given the little coffin. And once more I forgot that he was dead and I tired to make sure that he did not get bumped, that we drove carefully. In thousands of ways it seemed to me that we were once more together and that I was taking him away from people who wished him evil. We would get home as soon as possible, there I would pray, and then he would live again, as in one of the miracles in Christ's day; I simply did not want to believe that he was dead and not alive.

"But even if such a miracle did take place, they would just take him again and once more torment him. Why should he have to travel that tortured way again? Now he is with God and is resting from all his earthly sorrows. When I reason and cry father says to me: 'Don't cry, for he will not come to you, but you will go to him.' And I think—if only it could be at once, but that is not the way it is, and then it becomes even harder."

While a corpse lies unburied in a Russian Christian household, whether Orthodox or Evangelical, no one sleeps that night. The family and close friends pass the hours in hymn-singing and prayer and the reading and expounding of the Word. On the night of

16 September 1975 the Vashchenko home in the Mine 16 settlement near Chernogorsk echoed to the sound of solemn music, sometimes their own voices only, sometimes as they joined in the hymns broadcast in Russian by Christian stations abroad, audible above the jamming; "and on the radio, as if especially for us, were many funeral hymns:

> *The Sons of all the earth*
> *Cannot describe Christ's love,*
> *'Tis higher than the furthest stars*
> *Deeper than depths of hell.*

And again I began to cry during the singing of this hymn and I thought—then why, if he loves, did he allow this to end in death? Then I remembered those moments in life when the hand of God was clearly evident."

Aaron was a martyr. "The infant had not lived long enough to do anything bad or good. His torments were undergone for God because he ended up in a family of believers and had it been a family of nonbelievers, then he would have lived and grown up. From this it follows that he bore his suffering for God, although he was unconscious of this fact because still a baby. He will inherit life eternal among the firstborn. Those who abducted him do not believe in life beyond the grave, but their victory was in this life only. The devil has suffered complete defeat."

They placed Aaron reverently in a new coffin and the following evening took him back to the cemetery, to bury him in a different secret grave they would dig themselves.

Lida was dressed in a rather full, sleeveless coat. "I held the coffin under my coat in my arms. All of a sudden unexpectedly, I saw about five steps away to the side a man and a woman sitting near one of the graves. Out of fright and surprise I almost dropped the little coffin. It could be distinctly seen underneath my coat. I had to pass by them. Gathering up my strength I began to look in front of me so that they would not see my eyes which would have given me away. I walked by them quickly. I had the sensation that hot water was pouring out of my head. When I passed them it was as if something heavy had slipped from my shoulders.

"We began to dig and again there was a terrible fear. After all, this was forbidden and if they saw us they would put us in prison; there would be no need of evidence or witnesses, everything would be clear without words.[1]

"Finally, when we had placed him in the grave and put the earth back, my heart became lighter. Aaron was where he should be. 'Dust you are, and unto dust you shall return,' God said. A calm returned to my heart which I had not known since he was taken from me."

---

1. In fact Procurator Rezvanov threatened to imprison them for exhuming Aaron and then not giving the authorities the body. He said that it was now clear how they lived, by digging up other people's graves. But he did not prosecute, probably for fear of bad publicity.

The window where the police broke in to steal Aaron, July 1975.

встречи что почувствовала голод? В кар-
мане пальто я нащупала яблечко
и несколько конфет я только хотела их
скушать, как вдруг открылось окошко
и мне сказали чтоб я подошла к
пропускному пункту. Через несколько
минут я оказалась в комнате с длинным
столом, а еще через несколько минут
вошла мама с женщиной сопровождав-
шей её. Но я стояла неподвижно
и не верила своим глазам, губы её (мамы)
задрожали и она подойдя ко мне
целовала меня, а я всё смотрела и
смотрела на неё. Куда девалась её полно-
та, коса, вся она казалась восковая,
как будто не было в ней крови совсем.
из под шали виден был платок, из под него
выглядывал небольшой чубок, обычно у
нас детям оставляли такой. Женщина
строго покрикивала на неё, а она всем
своим видом показывала рабскую покор-
ность, женщина ручалась что она подошла и поцеловала меня, сказала что
лишит свидания если не будем слушать-
ся. Я теперь понимаю что это нару-

Right:
Lida's handwritten account of her visit to her mother in the Mozaisk prison camp.

Below:
The Vashchenkos mourning Aaron in 1975. *Front, l to r:* Vera, Sarah, Lida. *Middle,* Abel, Paul, Dina. *Back,* Peter, Augustina, Abraham, Jacob, John, Lila, Sasha. (Nadya and Lyuba absent.)

The younger
Vashchenkos mourning
Aaron. *L. to r:* Dinah,
Abel, Sarah, Abraham.

The Vashchenkos left
in Siberia
mourn Peter's
sister Natasha,
November 1978.

Below: The Seven in
the Embassy
shortly after their
arrival.
Standing l to r: Peter,
Augustina, Maria.
Sitting: Lyuba, Lida,
Timothy, Lila.

Top: Peter and Augustina Vashchenko *Center l to r:* Lyuba, Lida, Lila
Bottom: Maria Chmykhalov and Timothy

20

Lyuba's Feet ·

WHEN PETER RETURNED from labor camp and obtained work at the mine, and Augustina came back from prison a year later and could look after the children, Lyuba sought a job so that she could swell the family budget. She was seventeen, fair-haired, slender; and clever with needle and thread, her ambition still to be a dressmaker.

Every place refused her, "not because I was too young but because they recognized the name Vashchenko. 'We don't need any workers.' 'But the newspaper says they are needed here.' 'They were, but not now.'"

To a boss, "Vashchenko" at once spelled "Believer." He might take on a believer unknowingly but anyone known to be Christian, like the Chmykhalov boys and many others in Chernogorsk, found difficulty in getting work; and evidence accumulates that this discrimination occurs in cities and regions throughout Russia. Lyuba's experiences from the time she sought work can be paralleled again and again.

Rebuffed everywhere, she went to the young people's office of the police, she went to the city executive committee, and at last landed a job at KSK—the extensive mills and workshops which formed the Worsted Cloth *Kombinat,* the largest enterprise in Chernogorsk city; many of the Vashchenko family worked there at one time or another. Too far to walk, it meant a tedious journey on two buses, changing at Chernogorsk 1, the former Mine 9 settlement. The buses are so crowded that the driver cannot shut the doors, and specially in summer the crush and heat is suffocating.

Like everything, the worsted enterprise is State-owned. Lyuba's recollection of this Siberian factory of the 1970s suggests a Victorian poor-law workhouse smothered by an army of bureaucrats. "There were many teenagers who worked there, even those who were just fifteen; they worked five hours a day until they turned sixteen. From sixteen to eighteen they worked seven hours a day, and from eighteen a full eight-hour day. My work was hard. The department was very noisy because of the large number of machines and equipment. My job consisted in rewinding yarn from cops onto bobbins. For eight hours during my whole shift I would be standing; often I would not sit down for a single minute.

"There were a great many administrators, who came in at intervals. First there would be the head of the entire *kombinat,* with his retinue of secretaries and assistants; then the administrators of the industry, also with their huge retinues of secretaries, and later the heads of the departments with their assistants. They would be followed by the shift foremen and their assistants and then the instructors and the brigade leaders." The factory operated night and day in three shifts of eight hours, with twenty minutes for a meal. Each shift had its full complement of instructors (overseers) and since Lyuba's department contained five *komplekts* or sections, there were five instructors, five brigade leaders, a shift foreman and his assistant, twelve persons in all; a total of thirty-six supervisors keeping watch on the workers in that department alone, during the twenty-four hours.

"In the section of machines where I worked there was an instructor who was very severe and aggressive against believers." She flew into a temper if she even thought that Lyuba might be about to rest on the edge of a box of yarn, yet would tell anecdotes to the next girls though they were sitting comfortably on boxes. "She did not consider believers to be people. In her opinion, believers should take jobs which paid little and were dirty, which other workers would refuse." The woman deliberately gave Lyuba any bad yarn instead of sharing it round, and then deprived her of an *upriazhk* on the score of bad work; an *upriazhk* was the credit for the eight-hour day. Without it, the worker was counted as truant and received no pay and lost bonuses. Lyuba thus earned very little, yet her instructor refused to listen to reason; she delighted in her arbitrary power over a fellow mortal.

Discrimination against believers was common, as Lyuba knew. Nadya Chmykhalov, for instance, worked in another department where they wound the thread onto the conical balls called "cops." Not only was Nadya always given the worst thread, involving more work to achieve a good result, but was marked down as reponsible for every defective cop in the shift, thus losing pay. Even worse, she discovered another girl, under direct orders from the instructor, turning out shoddy work which she then marked with Nadya's number. Complaint to the city executive committee stopped this mischief for a while.

At regular intervals the eight-hour shift was followed by a "voluntary" Komsomol lecture. "I remember," writes Lyuba, "a time when they were going to have a Komsomol meeting. Our department had three doors which the administration could lock and this is just what they did. One door led to a storage area and then into another department, and two doors to the corridor; they were all locked. However, there were two large exits which had no doors. So the administration put people at these passageways to let no one out, and directed everyone to the 'Red Corner' for the Komsomol meeting. These 'Red Corners' or rooms are in every industry and are for conducting Communist and Komsomol gatherings. Several women swore, and asked that they be let out because they had husbands who must go to work, and this would leave small children at home alone; or someone had a child at a neighbor's apartment and the neighbor was unable to take care of other people's children past a certain time. But the administration were not open to appeals. They considered that the Komsomol meeting had to take place and that everyone of Komsomol age should be present."

Lyuba declined these voluntary meetings on principle, because the lectures were an important part of reeducation into an atheist outlook totally incompatible with Christian teaching. Nor would she sign a pledge to fulfill her "socialist obligations" which meant promising to fulfill a certain work norm within a month or a year; a section seldom achieved its norm (although some individuals, including Lyuba, did so) and public regrets for such failure were part of the usual round. If a section achieved it, the factory bosses increased the norm.

Lyuba explained to the authorities that she could not predict a month or a year ahead because health and life were in God's hands, not her own. "Besides, I do not desire to help in building your society," dedicated as it was to the conquest of the world for atheism.

For the same reason Lyuba and many other believers never turned up at a Communist *subbotnik* (or Red Saturday) when workers "voluntarily" surrender a free day and instead do a normal eight-hour shift for nothing; their wages are sent by the State to a designated cause such as arms for Vietnam or Angola, or simply to forward the building of Communism. In Peter's words: "This labor is wholly dedicated to strengthening the atheist order; people work without pay because they want, by their labor, to strengthen our atheist society. But we do not respect it and do not want to strengthen it. Therefore we do not devote our labor to *subbotniks.*"

The alert, informed Christian in the Soviet Union is placed in a dilemma. His natural patriotism and desire to make his native country a better place conflicts with his awareness that in helping to build the Soviet social order he makes the atheist way of life more powerful, with its emphasis on struggle, and hatred, and its avowed aim to destroy religion and non-Communism throughout the world.[1] Leaders of the registered churches, however, teach that the building of society is a civic duty, that the believer is not

---

1. The situation is different in a satellite country within the Soviet bloc, since building society there may make it stronger for the day when the nation is again sole master of its destiny.

called upon to judge its nature publicly by avoiding *subbotniks* or displays of solidarity. Such believers are less repressed.

Lyuba and those like her, on the other hand, were treated as truant for not attending "voluntary" *subbotniks* and Komsomol meetings. Lyuba was mocked, called names and, although she never skimped her work or failed to fulfill her daily norm, they deprived her of bonuses due to her. Once she was actually told that the bonus was withheld because she was a believer. "It is part of your religion," said the instructor, "to do your work well; it would be 'sin' not to. Why should you receive a bonus?" Yet only the bonuses make the pay tolerable for an honest worker who abhors graft or theft.

*   *   *

Lyuba suffered from headaches. One day her head ached so badly that she went to the medical room.

The doctor put routine questions. "When she asked my name and heard Vashchenko she immediately changed her tone and said: 'Go to the first floor. There's a small pharmacy there. Buy these tablets. And—*pray less!*' Back in the department I told the instructor that I had not been given permission to leave, but I could not work because my head was so bad. She said: 'Since the doctor has not authorized you to leave, this means you must work. I cannot let you go home.' She advised me to go to the city hospital the next morning.

"When I was in my fifth year at the worsted *kombinat* my legs began to hurt terribly and to swell. A time-keeper position became vacant. The work was not complicated and the instructor herself offered me the job; at this time we had a new instructor and she was a bit humane. As the pay was much less, since the work was easy and you could even sit for a while in the course of a shift, I had in mind this table job for a few months, resting up, and then to go back to my machine job, because our family is large and we live on what we earn in industry.

"I wrote a transfer request to the department head, Lipotenko. I saw him when he was walking around the department and went up to him. He did not take the request but said: 'After work, come to my office to see me.' "

Lyuba then embarked on the misery of extracting a decision from a Soviet bureaucrat. She stood a long time on her poor legs, after eight hours' work, outside his door, for waiting rooms are almost unknown in the Soviet Union; the applicant stands in corridor or hall in the hope that his or her turn will come before the office closes or the boss starts a two-hour lunch break.

Admitted at last, Lyuba handed in her request but Lipotenko merely said he would let her know, and when she went up to him next day he mumbled feeble excuses, then barked, "Come to my office after work."

A second long stand, then Lipotenko told her she lacked enough education. She disposed of that, and of his remark that she would be inefficient; he even had to admit she worked well and honestly. "But," he said, "a person in that position must take on increased socialist obligations, work the *subbotniks*, grieve over the fulfilling of the plan, attend lectures." He told her to return next day.

After another wait outside his door she received her request with "Rejected" scrawled across it. She asked why.

Lipotenko replied: "Because you are a believer and we don't trust you!"

She asked to be transferred to weighing but he rejected her on the same grounds.

Having foreseen the outcome, Lyuba handed a paper to Lipotenko: "I request that I be given my final pay since for reasons of health I am unable to work in this place, and because of the fact that a believer will not be transferred to more appropriate or easier work; all sorts of excuses are given. I ask you not to reject my request. 13 March 1974." [2] He took it and dismissed her without signing it.

Two days—and two waits—later he returned it for her to take to the head of personnel for the entire worsted enterprise. "His name was Kruglov. Near his door too I stood for several hours

2. Translated from the actual document.

after work, because for some reason he was never in his office; either he had a conference, or had gone somewhere, or it was not a day or hour when he was receiving, though every Tuesday he was supposed to receive workers in his office for a total of two hours, and whoever was not received had to wait until the next Tuesday.

"Finally, after long days of waiting I got into his office. I went up to his desk and put before him both requests. He did not begin to read either one, but asked: 'Do you have a statement from the doctor that you cannot work at a machine?'" Lyuba began to explain it would not be given her but he cut her off and hurled her written requests at her head.

Lyuba therefore exercised her legal right to give twelve days' notice. Once notice is given in due form and worked out a boss may not dismiss the worker for truancy, but must sign a certificate of release, though he may endorse it with a note of disagreement with the resignation. Lyuba stopped work on 29 March 1974 but received no certificate of release nor final pay; whenever she asked they merely made fresh calculations in her log book and sent her away. At last on 29 August she received a certificate stating she had been dismissed for truancy.

This was contrary to law. The Vashchenkos complained to Moscow, writing many letters until the Presidium dispatched a commission of investigation which removed the stigma of truancy. "We wrote to Moscow," comments Lyuba, "because a believer has no freedom at all. The Soviet government shouts that the Soviet Union is the most democratic country of all, but believing people do not have the opportunity to exercise the same rights as the rest."

After leaving the worsted enterprise Lyuba had again failed to find a job before her mother fell seriously ill in June, two months after the birth of the thirteenth and last child, Abraham. Lyuba took him and raised him herself. For eight months she could revel in the joy of exchanging the shouting and cursing and noise of the factory for the warmth and happiness of the crowded home, desperately poor yet close-knit, high spirited and full of fun yet always ready to turn to singing and prayer.

In February 1975 Lyuba fulfilled the ambition of her life. She was taken on for a trial week at the dressmaking shop which she had often looked at longingly from the bus.

The girls received her in a friendly way and admired her skill, but this was the month of the libelous article in the *Chernogorsk Worker*, and after a day or two, when they found out her surname their attitude changed a little. However, the brigade leader had seen how good a seamstress she was, and recommended Lyuba to the supervisor. Yet at the end of the trial period she was fired; she overheard the supervisor tell the girls: "Although Vashchenko works well we don't want her. These are the same Vashchenkos described in the newspapers." Lyuba went back to Abraham.

"Sewing," she sighs. "This is an occupation which I have liked ever since I was at school. I have dreamed a great deal about it and now I had worked a whole week in a real dress shop and had really *worked*. I had realized that I could achieve success in this business. If only . . . and how many 'if onlys' there have been."

And so it went on. Her father puts his finger on the problem. "People do not look on believers favorably. Those who work with them in industry notice that they are honest and do their jobs well; then lectures begin on the radio to set the people against believers, frightening them by saying that they have connections abroad. Of course there are those who do not think that believers are bad, but they keep quiet. There are very few new converts now."

At one time Lyuba was reduced to cutting wood in a saw mill, outside in the bitter winter cold, but at last she was taken on again in the sewing enterprise though not in its dress shop. Within two months they fired her. She had declined to "volunteer" to spend her vacation building Communism on a *kolkhoz* and the supervisor ordered the girls in her department to demand her removal.

Thus she was unemployed and able to join Lida and her parents when they went to Moscow to seek the American Embassy's aid in discovering the fate of Aaron. The official result of that visit made all the difference, for Moscow ordered Lyuba's reinstatement; the city executive committee's representative even scolded the supervisor in frcnt of the workgirls. He assured Lyuba that *kolkhoz* work was indeed voluntary.

That December of 1975 Lyuba had a great opportunity. "The holiday of Christmas was drawing near," she relates (and the Russian term *Rozhdestvo Khristovo* means literally, "the birth of Christ.") "The workers in my brigade wanted to know what this holiday was and on Christmas Eve they asked me to tell them about this historical event. They suggested that I sit down in a chair in the middle of the department so that each worker could see me from behind her sewing machine. One of the women cffered me her handstitching and took over my machine so that I could be just sitting there if someone from the administration came in.

"I began to tell them everything from the beginning, how Christ was born and about the wonders that he did when living on this earth, and up to the suffering of Golgotha. They all listened very attentively. And little by little the machines were turned off since they made a great deal of noise. And then followed many questions. I answered their questions and they said that we would continue this discussion further next time."

It was a heartening yet dangerous hour. Peter says: "The administration watch very closely to make sure that you do not talk to anybody about faith in God. If they catch you, you will be reprimanded or even fired if it occurs again. My daughter Vera lost her job as a sales clerk in a store because of this."

Nadya, the sister next in age between Lyuba and Vera, came up against the administration of the worsted enterprise that very Christmas of 1975. It fell that year on a workday but they refused to give her leave of absence although she offered to work on an earlier free day. She stayed away, therefore, to celebrate it with the church, and afterwards sent a written explanation of absence: "I cannot come to work on this day because this is the day when our God, Jesus Christ, was born. It is our holiday and I must observe it."

The head of the department summoned her to his office. Peter tells what happened: "He had a large nose and he always liked to use it: 'There is the smell of anti-Sovietism which comes from you!' He jumped out from behind his desk with a madman look and said: 'What is this you have written?' Nadya answered: 'You asked me to write an explanation on why I was not at work yesterday.' He said: 'Get out of here!'

"All day long he ran around the department with her statement in his hand and many people looked at the statement and laughed, because it seemed stupid to them in the fifty-ninth anniversary year of the October Revolution to observe the birth of Christ. Several people from the administration would come up to Nadya, glance into her face, and laugh, calling her a fool. It was surprising that a young person of twenty-two would write a statement about some Christ; it would be forgivable if it were a *babushka* [old woman], but for a young person to speak of God—that was barbarous in an atheist society. Because she did not come to work on Christmas they took her bonus away and declared her truant which affects her monthly and yearly salary."

21

Sasha's Trial

ALEXANDER (SASHA) PETROVICH, the Vashchenko's eldest son, was a metal craftsman in the railway repair shop at the open cast mine, servicing electric and diesel locomotives. Sasha's character is an intriguing mixture. He could have gone far in sports had there been no discrimination against believers. Mechanically minded and cheerful, he also loves music, and is a deeply affectionate person, delighting to buy his small brothers and sisters something interesting or tasty on his way back from work, and liking it also when his mother strokes his forehead or caresses him as if he were her youngest.

On 22 January 1976, when he was still nearly three months short of his seventeenth birthday, Sasha was summoned to the military enlistment office in Soviet Street, part of the police building, for the usual first stage of conscript enlistment. As he was a minor he exercised the right to bring his father to the interview.

Sasha said to Major Schuvalov: "I am a believing Christian, and I fulfill God's commandment, 'You shall not kill.' I cannot break this commandment."

The major did not reply, but instead went up to Sasha's father and grabbed him about the chest and tried to push him out of the door, shouting: "You have taught your son to lose his head with his God! We are going to draft him and reeducate him. Then he will understand everything and he himself will deal with you."

"If you reeducate me so that I kill, and give me a machine gun," said Sasha, "I would shoot you first!"

The major did not record in the call-up papers that Sasha had attended the interview, and the boss of the railway workshop marked him down as a truant, withholding his bonus.

Once he had passed his seventeenth birthday on 7 April 1976, Sasha was frequently summoned to government offices in attempts to bully or persuade him to take the oath, and every time, says Peter, "he was marked down as truant and deprived of bonuses. Once he did not take his summons and go. Then his boss Bulecha-kov would not allow him to come to work for ten days! We went to the city committee with a complaint—such a big family and the oldest son not allowed to work."

The Vashchenkos were not pacifists: Sasha would have been ready to serve in defense of the truth but not for the fatherland of atheism which is ready to unleash its vast armed forces to secure the supremacy of atheism on the entire planet. Thinking like that, Sasha knew he had a hard road to travel.

After his eighteenth birthday he fulfilled a great ambition, by learning to drive during the summer of 1977 and securing a job as a driver at the Vehicle Transport Organization—ATK 40. But bosses are scolded if they have a believer in their ranks, and to show a correct front to their superiors they discriminate, as Sasha's sisters had discovered. He was allotted an old defective vehicle which he had to repair, buying the spare parts from his own money, before he could drive. The military had passed his case to the city procurator. Whenever Sasha was summoned (and it meant hours away from work), the boss gave the car to another youth who could be relied upon to drive carelessly enough to smash a bumper, which Sasha must repair, and wages were given only for hours spent driving.

"For four months he was tormented like this. He was not given the work he was supposed to have, there were no earnings, and he had no rest. Everyone else came home from work at five, but he would have to stay until ten in the evening repairing his car. It was old and quickly went wrong." Peter adds that he and Augustina often urged Sasha to get another job but he liked being a driver; besides, advertised posts had a habit of being filled already, once a boss heard that an applicant's name was Vashchenko.

"One day," continues Peter, "Sasha did not return from work in the evening and we thought that he had remained once again to repair his vehicle. At ten in the evening he still had not returned. We waited until midnight and then went to look for him. The buses no longer ran and we had to go on foot to the city police—twelve kilometers [about seven miles]. There the policeman on duty did not want to talk to us. He was lying on a divan."

Peter had long learned how to deal with policemen or any Soviet official: Never take the inevitable *"Nyet,"* "no," for an answer. Peter said: "Why are you lying around and not answering anything when we ask you questions?"

The policeman jumped up from the couch, and said: "Yes, the Baptist is here—he is in jail here." They found out that he had been arrested at noon, dinner time, but they had not been told and thus had to search for him at night. They walked the twelve kilometers home, arriving as dawn broke.

Next morning they took him clothes, since he had been arrested in his working uniform, and food, which the jail refused to allow. A day later he was home, having signed a promise to return for his trial.

Before the trial, however, the Vashchenko family suffered a great sorrow which turned into a triumph for the gospel.

Peter's aged parents, Paul and Anna, had taken a trip with Natasha to see Khariton, who was frequently ill, in the Caucasus. Anna was eighty-four and still cheerful, though suffering from dropsy, but on alighting at the railway station an hour from Khariton's home, she lost her footing and fell the considerable gap to the platform. She dislocated her right hip, and could never stand again.

They returned to Siberia, to the little *vremianka* or temporary annex to Natasha's daughter's home, round the corner from Peter;

the grandparents and Natasha lived in this lean-to, and Katya, her husband and seven children in the house. Anna was mentally alert until the last, and prayed much and listened to sermons on radio. Peter's children took turns to help Natasha with nursing, day and night.

One October evening it was the turn of Vera (twenty-one) and Dinah (twelve). Their grandmother asked for warm water and then sent everyone to bed, saying, "Don't talk, I need quiet." At 4:00 A.M. on 9 October 1977 "they woke up, and mother had already slipped into Eternity."

Anna had said that she did not want to be buried with wreaths, but with texts from Scripture, for wreaths are perishable, "but I go to receive from God a wreath which will not perish." Her instructions were obeyed. At the head of the procession, in front of the funeral car with her body, marched young believers carrying placards.

"It was the first funeral in Chernogorsk with placards and the local authorities had not expected it. The nonbelievers who lived nearby thought that a strike had begun because of a poor supply of food products! But when they came to look they saw that it was a funeral procession, with placards in front. People and cars stopped and everyone read them, the testimony of the passing of a believer into Eternity."

And thus in October 1977, after a faithful witness of more than half a century, Anna Vashchenko gave a resounding last message to the atheist Soviet Union, with its strict ban on public Christian teaching, as the procession marched slowly through the city to the cemetery on the north side. They had chosen the placards carefully, such as: "For as in Adam all die, so also in Christ shall all be made alive." . . . "I have fought the good fight, I have finished the race, I have kept the faith." . . . "Henceforth there is laid up for me a crown of righteousness which the Lord, the righteous judge, shall give me at that day." . . . "And not to me only, but to all those who love his appearing." . . . "Blessed are the dead who die in the Lord."

Anna's Christian reality blew away Soviet myths. Not Lenin,

but Christ matters at the last hour; not materialism but faith; not pleasing the bosses but the Lord.

*   *   *

Two months after his grandmother's death at eighty-five, Sasha stood trial at eighteen years and eight months, for his refusal to serve in the armed forces.

It was the first trial of its kind since that of Sasha's "uncle" Andrei, the martyr, twelve years before. This was partly because many Baptist youth accepted the teaching that civic duty includes service in the armed forces, and they must survive as best they can the pressures on their faith; but partly because the enlistment office tricked young men like the Chmykhalov boys into believing that if they allowed themselves to be drafted they could serve in a noncombatant capacity on a national work project. In the event, they found themselves in what virtually were penal battalions. "It was terribly hard for them," writes Maria. "The authorities tried to 'reeducate' them in all sorts of ways so that they would move away from God." Frequent transfers, constant threats, "what they went through, only God knows."

Sasha's trial was set for 9 December 1977. All the Vashchenkos were sad as they prayed and wept and knew that only God could help. Sasha had composed some rhyming verses to be remembered by, and recorded them on tape:

> *To all my friends, and all who hold me dear,*
> *All whom I love, good-bye in Jesus' Name.*
> *Be not downcast for me: be of good cheer;*
> *Good news of Christ continue to proclaim.*
>
> *There in Reshoty we shall meet once more.*
> *Exiled for Jesus, He is my reward.*
> *We will be true to Him though lions roar,*
> *Faithful to follow Christ our living Lord.*[1]

---

1. English paraphrase kindly written by Timothy Dudley-Smith from a literal translation.

Nadya composed an answer in verse to his poem; she promised that they would never forget him in prayer with God, nor abandon him in his plight.

The Vashchenkos had two fine German shepherd dogs, Palma and Mukhtar.[2] Mukhtar "loved Sasha a great deal, and before Sasha left home the dog wailed for a long time. You would go out and scold him and he would stop, but then he would begin again. He howled day and night. When Sasha left home to go to the People's Court Mukhtar put his paws on Sasha's shoulders and for a long time gazed into his eyes. No one could look on this scene calmly and everyone began to cry and Sasha was crying. These are horrible memories which cannot be recalled without beginning to cry."

The whole family except the smaller children went to the court, carrying a bag of food for Sasha, since all knew he would be taken straight to prison and labor camp, following the steps of his martyred "uncle" Andrei. They entered the large courtroom, which holds two hundred sitting and standing. Three witnesses, from the military and Sasha's workplace, sat apart to one side in a row; the usher placed Sasha by himself and Peter took a seat at the front as his defender. The public well of the court was full and they recognized many friendly faces.

As Judge Ustyugov entered with the two people's assessors or jurors the usher cried: "Stand up! The court is in session."

The entire public well of the court stayed seated.

"Stand up!" yelled the usher. Not a soul moved. Every place had been taken by believers.

Peter rose, his heart sore for Sasha, but lifted by the spontaneous gesture of the Christians. He explained why the court had not been honored in the customary way: "Every one here understands that the court is composed of people who uphold the ideology of atheism, which is the spirit of the devil; and that the ideology of the believers is the spirit of Christ or his Church. These are two

---

2. Both dogs were shot dead by vandals in the autumn of 1978 while guarding the empty home, which had become unsafe owing to mine subsidence. The remaining members of the family had moved to Lyuba's house in Chernogorsk 1.

opposing parties with different views on earthly and heavenly life. And therefore those who believe in Christ do not give a salute to the other party. However, the Scriptures, at Matthew's Gospel, chapter 5, verse 47, tell us: 'If you salute your brethren only, what do you do more than others?' In the spirit of that verse, we greet you as individuals." The court received this in stony silence and the trial began.

Procurator Podkolzino demanded a sentence of three years deprivation of freedom. The enlistment officer, Borisenko, gave evidence of refusal to accept the draft notice and said to Sasha, "Why don't you enlist and go to a unit where you can serve without an oath and without a gun?" At that, one of the Chmykhalov boys rose and, from his own bitter experience, challenged the officer to say where was this unit where a man could serve without taking the oath or carrying a gun. The officer, his bluff called, blushed, turned his head away and made no reply. Chmykhalov told the court he knew there was no such unit. Then the witnesses from the Transport Organization testified that Sasha was a hard worker with nothing against him except refusal to join the Komsomol.

Peter, as defender, had already submitted a written statement which he intended to elaborate in his speech, emphasizing a point which should have been accepted without question: that Soviet law allows a court to release from military service the breadwinner or the "first helper" of a family which would suffer materially by his being drafted. Peter would have spoken of their home containing many young children and also a crippled believer. This man had been rejected by his son, so the Vashchenkos gave him a home. In addition to the importance of Sasha's wages and his daily aid in bringing up their large family, he would be needed to help build a new home now that their home at Mine 16 was no longer safe owing to subsidence and they had been officially told to move. The law was clear about an eldest son.

The court, however, did not call upon the defense. Thus Peter was muzzled. Instead, Procurator Podkolzino asked for a private consultation with the judge and jurors, who recessed, but did not summon Peter to their conference as should have been his right.

A few minutes passed. Then followed an extraordinary episode which, with its sequel, forms an eloquent commentary on the sixtieth anniversary year of the Communist revolution: the believers turned the atheist People's Court into a prayer house.

Everyone began to sing, and the first hymn they sang was that magnificent marching song of the Russian evangelicals, *Forward after Christ*, with its rousing refrain:

> *Like a loving happy family*
> *All His folk are one,*
> *Following with one heart and soul*
> *Forward after Christ!*
> *Forward all, Forward after Him!*

Verse by verse for twenty verses the sound of the hymn swelled out into the street and round the statue of Lenin:

> *The fight is hot, the flames are fierce,*
> *There are times we waver;*
> *Hold the banner higher*
> *Of the Victor—Christ!*

The court still did not return, and the believers sang hymn after hymn. Later they discovered that the judge, hearing the singing, feared a riot and had sent for police reinforcements.

At last the court reconvened and the judge read out a sentence of three years.

As Peter says, "They did not take into account anything, not the big family, nor the fact that our circumstances had been complicated by the housing problem, nor that as eldest son he was 'first helper.'

"When the sentence was read of three years of deprivation of freedom for an eighteen-year-old youth, all in the court room were greatly grieved. Everyone began to go forward to say good-bye to Sasha. The judge wanted to get him away from the people and suggested that he come to his office; behind the doors in the corridor the police were already standing and outside was a *voronok*.

"But Sasha did not come.

"The police poured into the chamber and began to break through the crowd to Sasha. Some they grabbed by the arms, others they pushed from behind as they led him out of the court room.

"People rushed in a crowd to the door and blocked the passage through the doors so that neither they nor the police could leave the chamber. The police had closed a second door earlier so that no one could get out by this door. The police used force on whomever they pleased in pushing people away from the exit. One policeman hit our son Jacob (fifteen) in the chest and our daughter Dinah (twelve) was hit in the teeth with a fist. But since believers cannot use physical force the police had a 'good time of it,' as they say.[3] So many policemen showed up that you could not help but think of how many there were when they came and took Christ like a robber.

"Only, when a robber is tried there are less policemen."

Sasha was taken to Minusinsk, to the old prison where his father and his "uncle" Andrei had sat before him, and then, in March 1978, while the snow still lay on the ground, he was transferred to a medium regime labor camp, one of several near the end of a special branch line, about eighteen hours northeast by train from Chernogorsk.

And thus, as Augustina writes, "At the age of eighteen he went out amidst a debauched society to suffer for the sake of Christ. He was still a child, but the battle had to be waged with the devil as if he were a grown-up."

---

3. The verb used means, "to swing about," implying free use of their punches.

Part Three
SUSPENSE

22

The Selma Invitation

In the spring of 1978 the Vashchenko family, bereft of Sasha, remained closely united in affection, faith and purpose. Loved and respected by his thirteen offspring, who now ranged in years from twenty-seven to four, Peter never demanded slavish obedience; he encouraged debate before any decision, accepted criticism and wanted all matters prayed about freely.

Nadya, a weigher at the worsted cloth enterprise and a hard worker both there and about the house, loves music and singing and writes verse. One of her delights is to gather the smaller children round the divan to tell them stories or read aloud. Vera, also at the worsted enterprise as a weigher, was a clerk at a store, a profession she loved but lost her job for blaming the system when an irate customer asked why something was in short supply. Vera has a ready tongue. Set to the menial task of serving a waiting line at a canteen, she was given a list of those who might be dished out sausages. When the rest protested she said: "We have beautiful sausages but not for you!" This, overheard by a KGB man, was rated an anti-Soviet remark because it revealed the presence of a VIP list, and she was dismissed.[1] Vera is the family precentor, and sings either soprano or alto. She is not very fond of cooking yet prepares most tasty meals.

John loves sports. He dreams of being an air pilot. But selection for training as a regional or national sportsman, let alone as a pilot, is barred to any who refuse to be reeducated towards atheism. He is more masculine in character than his elder brother and does not like to be cossetted, especially when sick. Like Sasha, he has a good voice but neither of them will sing solo. He wants to learn the guitar and tinkers with motorcycles. A great talker, he will pursue a topic until the other understands it perfectly, especially if it is a Bible theme. He has physical courage—which he was to need in good measure in 1978—and more than once has been attacked when rescuing somebody being beaten. He is strong and fights back and is highly respected by the local thugs, both for his unashamed Christian faith and his skill with the fists if fight he must.

John is a lathe turner and Jacob (sixteen) works as his apprentice. Jacob loves sports too. He is very shy but likes to keep his small brothers and sisters in order if left as the eldest at home; they must jump to his command and have everything spic and span. He can even cook their dinner, but he rarely sings in the family choir. Fourteen-year-old Dinah is happiest looking after small children, tirelessly dressing and redressing them and washing a baby at the slightest sign of dirt. She likes to create order in the house and the older ones laugh at her treating her smallest brothers and sisters and their playmates as if they were dolls.

Abel (twelve) and Paul (nearly eleven), act as the family stockmen like their brothers before them. They take turns grazing the cow and calf, but are quite different: Abel silent, Paul talkative. Paul is like Sasha, very affectionate; he loves flowers and to watch Lyuba sewing and cutting out. Abel is more like John and Jacob,

---

1. This is reminiscent of a joke circulating widely in the Soviet Union in 1979. "What is 500 meters long and 3 meters wide and eats cabbage?" Answer: "A waiting line for sausages."

and loves to hang around as they mend their motorcycles; he would never burst into tears at difficulties as Paul does.

The two smallest, seven-and-a-half-year-old Sarah and four-year-old Abraham are, say the older ones, "like all children." They delight in puppies and kittens, in dolls or toy cars according to sex, and take turns riding the bicycle to fetch water, arguing if one thinks the other has had more turns. Both like to listen to the children's programs from Christian stations abroad, though these come in the middle of the night and are severely jammed, and says Lyuba, "they probably love to sing more than anybody in the family."

In 1978 Peter and Augustina longed as much as ever that their varied family should live where the Christian faith may be freely practiced, where believing boys or girls, men or women, may develop according to their gifts and, if prepared to work hard, may make the career of their choice and glorify God thereby.

The Vashchenkos still sought emigration. The Soviet Union showed no signs of relaxing the straitjacket which allows little true freedom of worship. All the resources of media, schools, bureaucracy and favoritism remain firmly behind atheism.

In Chernogorsk, the weight of the law was again being felt against the unregistered churches. For a time fines had ceased, but in the spring of 1978 the Vashchenkos' and Chmykhalovs' pastor, a man of about forty-five going bald at the top, not very literate but of deep faith, was fined three times. The police would march into a service and say: "You are meeting illegally like an underground organization. Disperse, or be punished according to Soviet law."

The congregation would reply: "Do not interrupt the sermon. When the meeting ends you can talk." The police would leave, decently enough, and collect evidence from around, not returning until the congregation began to go. Then they would read out their notes as "Children seen entering." . . "hymn-singing heard." . . "the sound of prayer." . . etc., etc.

The pastor was fined fifty rubles and the meeting's host twenty-five rubles. Each week they came, fining the pastor one hundred rubles in one month, subtracted from his pay in the factory, but no receipt given lest he use it as evidence for a complaint. The congregation raised the money and repaid him. The first three fines were imposed almost like parking tickets, but then he was summoned to the People's Court. To the authorities' surprise, nearly two hundred believers from all the churches filled the courtroom to support him. This demonstration, and an earlier one at the procurator's office, saved him a prison sentence; he was fined another hundred rubles instead.

The Vashchenkos were hemmed in. On the one hand stood the barrier of the State's refusal to allow the freedom to emigrate enjoined by Articles Thirteen and Fourteen of the Declaration of Human Rights. On the other hand, and indeed all around, lay the discrimination suffered by all believers without exception, and the extra repression experienced by unregistered Pentecostals and Baptists throughout the Soviet Union; overwhelming evidence of this was compiled by Alexander Ginzburg and his friends of the Helsinki Monitoring Group before Ginzburg's imprisonment.[2]

All believers in the Soviet Union are effectively second-class citizens. Those whose conscience forbids them to register suffer harassment. Those who wish to emigrate suffer more because, as they found in Chernogorsk, "When it comes to rights and privileges the authorities say we are 'Americans' and withhold them; when it comes to punishments they say we are Soviet citizens and inflict them."

The Vashchenkos had stopped going to Soviet doctors since Aaron; the family's experiences had been bad enough over Jacob's legs and Lyuba's feet. Lyuba and Vera had suffered discrimination in getting jobs; their parents were now reduced to poorly-paid, dirty work, processing rags in the city's refuse and garbage dump. It was even worse for Petro Chmykhalov. After his second imprisonment for his faith he was refused work and then taxed as a "parasite who did not want to work." His sons Tolik and Shura, released

---

2. In a dossier entitled "Come out of Babylon, my people," which the Helsinki Monitoring Group sent to the West on 2 December 1976. See also a very full account in the Hearings before the U.S. Senate Commission on Security and Cooperation in Europe on Religious Liberty and Minority Rights in the Soviet Union, 27, 28 April 1977.

from penal service in national work projects for their conscientious objection to bearing arms in the Soviet forces, were reduced to tears as they shuttled up and down the city between bureaucrats and the bosses who did not dare take them on. And their Aunt Anna Makarenko was refused the pension she was entitled to after twenty years in the mine: the authorities covered the discrimination by losing her records and then quoting a law which prevented her attesting the facts.

The law could be made to do what the bosses wanted, as one of them admitted. At a meeting when Chernogorsk believers complained to the city vice-chairman, Galina Andriushchenko, she told them: "The law is like the front of a cart—wherever you turn it, that's where you go."

The laws are framed and used to ensure that the Soviet Union may boast of its citizens being free to believe or not to believe, yet the State authorities may attack religious belief and direct it along the atheist path. "If," writes one of the Vashchenkos, "you do not travel along their path then there is one solution—you are doomed to death or gradual rotting in prison. In this country it is not liked if someone raises his voice for truth or justice. He is put away so as not to disturb the building of a 'radiant future'— he has become an Enemy of the People."

Atheism is the very heart of Soviet Communism. Therefore, while respecting Christian believers who knew that God had called them to stay, Peter Vashchenko and his family were sure God called them to go—to take "the Road."

* * *

In March 1978 Peter and Augustina received permission for a first visit to Sasha in his labor camp (medium regime) in the mountains east of Krasnoyarsk. They boarded a train at Abakan at 3:45 P.M. and travelled all night by the new trunk line which runs northeast. At eight next morning they reached Khairyuzovka where they had to wait with relatives of other prisoners until the arrival of the school bus bringing officers' children, which then took the visitors back some fifteen kilometers into the *taiga*.

Sasha ate and lived with them, in the usual way of prison visits, but camp chief Gutnik arbitrarily reduced the promised visit from three days to two.

Sasha told how there were many criminals of the roughest kind. They tried their usual trick with new arrivals, attempting, as he lay in his bunk, to slash his wrists with jagged glass, as an initiation to put him in healthy fear. Sasha had thrown them off, three or four of them, and grabbed the piece of glass and warned them that if they attacked him they must take the consequences. After that they left him alone. He was widely respected for his open honesty about his Christian beliefs, for the others knew what that could cost; the camp authorities gave no toleration to "outworn religious prejudices." He had found six other believers too.

The prisoners' food was bad, without meat or anything sweet, and the work in the forest hard. On 7 April, Sasha's nineteenth birthday, five of the family again made the overnight journey, but were allowed to speak to him only through a thick glass panel fitted with a telephone. "We asked if we might give him a bar of chocolate for his birthday, but this was not allowed."

Ten days after getting back to Chernogorsk the Vashchenko family received through international mail on 20 April 1978 what they had longed for: a *vyzov* or invitation, to America. It came in the name of the Reverend Cecil J. Williamson, Jr., pastor of Crescent Hill Presbyterian Church, Selma, Alabama. Peter was convinced that this was the same man, then a consular officer, who had sponsored him, as he had supposed, in the American Embassy ten years before.

In fact Williamson had been a pastor all along and never in Moscow. A visiting preacher had emphasized the plight of Russian evangelicals. The church offered to sponsor any one of the many Pentecostal families wishing to emigrate. The Tolstoy foundation in New York informed Williamson, late in December 1977, that his church had been assigned the Vashchenko family of Chernogorsk, Siberia. The church officers filled in the necessary papers.

The invitation took four months to reach the Vashchenkos. Twenty-one other Chernogorsk families received invitations, mainly from Califorr a and there was reason to believe that more *vyzovs* arrived at the cty post office but were confiscated and destroyed. Eleven families applied for exit visas, enclosing their invitations. Each received _ verbal rejection, and the invitation and the fee were not returned. Peter determined that his own family's invitation should never leave his hands until it was honored by the Soviet authorities who had frequently told him, "If only you had a *vyzov* we would not stop you leaving." The experience of others convinced him that without the American Embassy's intervention he would never lead his family to freedom, and since in 1975 the Americans had provided a pass to show the police at the gate, and the consular documents included a printed note bidding an applicant report the Soviet decision on his case, he felt entitled to call for their aid.

The Vashchenkos fasted and prayed and decided on a final expedition to Moscow for the end of June, when Peter would be on vacation from the refuse dump. Lila and John would be on vacation, Lyuba would have just returned and her absence would not reach the KGB's ears at once, and Nadya could work Lila's shift.

Meanwhile a last attempt to hand in their Soviet citizenship papers and obtain forms for exit visas proved fruitless. Chernogorsk told Peter that no emigration papers would come through. Abakan referred him to Krasnoyarsk, the territorial capital, and though he knew what it meant when officials passed him from office to office, he decided to go. On Wednesday 21 June Peter and Augustina flew to Krasnoyarsk, shadowed by the KGB for the entire double journey.

A woman official, Kozenets, told them flatly that no one would be leaving; she asserted that the invitation was a trick.

They had bought one-way tickets to Moscow at the advance window in Abakan. Peter gathered the family together again to seek God's guidance. After prayer they were in no doubt; indeed they had a strong sense that God not only intended them to go to Moscow but had a definite purpose; in sending them he would help all believers who wished to emigrate. Should the Americans secure the exit visas the advance party would not return to Chernogorsk since they knew that the rest would follow abroad without difficulty. Nobody planned to seek asylum in the Embassy.

They gathered in the little house which Peter had bought for Lyuba in Chernogorsk 1, Twentieth Khakassian Year Street. The Chmykhalovs were just down the road, and although lacking an invitation to America, Maria decided to come too, with Timothy. The KGB had recently threatened to imprison no less than five Chmykhalovs, and Timothy was shortly due to be registered for military call-up. Maria did not feel that the cheerful, intelligent Timothy, with his buoyant Christian faith, had the stamina or nerves for the rigors of a labor camp. And she had never seen Moscow.

On the evening of 23 June they left their homes by stealth to fox the KGB and not to attract the attention of neighbors sitting on the benches watching the traffic. John loaded up his old motorcycle, which he had adapted for diesel since petrol was short, with the bags of food for the journey. He picked up Timothy and rode off towards the country station of Tasheba about eighteen kilometers away. Augustina walked down to Maria's.

The three girls were to cross the fields on foot to another road. Lyuba liked to be the last to leave the house, and she had a little private habit the others knew nothing about. Before catching up her sisters she did what some of Christendom's evangelical saints of old did: "When I am alone I open the Bible at random. I read whatever two or three verses my eye falls upon and I consider that this is God's answer to my question to him, 'What kind of trip will it be? What awaits us?'

"And here is what my eye fell on before this trip—Isaiah 43:3–5: 'For I am the Lord your God, the Holy One of Israel, your Savior . . . Since you are precious in my eyes and are much valued and I have grown to love you, I will give other men for you, and peoples for your soul. Fear not, for I am with you; I will lead your generation from the east and gather you from the west.' [3] And to this day," wrote Lyuba seven months later in the Embassy,

---

3. This translation follows the Russian version.

"I believe that it was not an accident that it opened to that place."

The girls crossed the wheat field and were walking along the road when a passing car offered them a ride: "We saw the hand of God in this," because time was short. Back in Chernogorsk 1 Maria and Augustina set out. "As we reached the water fountain," recalls Augustina, "Sarah and Abraham caught up with us and asked: 'Mama, will you come back soon? Let's kiss you.' But this would have attracted attention, so with an aching heart and a lump in my throat from the tears I softly whispered: 'Run back home.' And I did not say good-bye as they had asked." She had decided against taking Abraham. If all went well she would see him again soon, and if they were arrested he would be thrown into a children's home.

All, including Jacob who was to take the motorcycle home, reached the country road. John picked up two of them, rode four kilometers while the others walked, then doubled back for the next pair. Thus, walking and riding they reached the station on time and caught the Moscow through express undetected. They were not recognized by the KGB manning the train. The two families pretended to be unacquainted but on the third day the KGB identified the Chmykhalovs.

As they drew near Moscow, writes Augustina, "our two friends were already on the KGB's leash and one man followed them everywhere they went. At the station we went into the women's toilets, and Peter, Timothy and John into the men's and we lost our tail. When we came out he had gone. We went to the metro and no one followed us."

23

"Who Shall Deliver Us?"

As THE VASHCHENKOS and Chmykhalovs drew near to the American Embassy, intending a brief conversation, they had no idea that 27 June 1978 would be "one of the most terrible days in our lives."

The Soviet policeman refused them entry. They dashed for diplomatic soil. While under the archway they heard cries and thuds and looked round to see John on the asphalt, apparently being throttled. They ran on, greatly agitated, into the yard, shouting and pleading as Americans looked up and surrounded them but were unable at first to understand their trouble.

A consular officer shepherded them in visible distress to the consular waiting room and tried to calm them. At first he said he could not complain to the police about their handling of a Soviet citizen; but in 1975 two of the Vashchenkos had been detained outside yet an American had brought them in, and at length the officer tried to find out what had happened. John had disappeared. The police refused to answer questions.

Peter Vashchenko told Consul Gross, whom he knew from 1975, that they would remain where they were until apprised of John's fate. Had he been returned they would have left at once. The hours passed and with them, mercifully, the moments when the Americans might have ejected the Seven without more than a ripple of world interest. Once the news of the sit-in had reached journalists, any action out of tune with President Carter's recent stand on human rights would have provoked anger in the United States and the world.

Peter was now certain they would be arrested as traitors since they had been more than three hours inside, and that night they were allowed to sit on the divans in the consular waiting room. They held a prayer fast for John. Their feelings were numb. "If," wrote Lida three months later, "you ask someone who is lying in a coffin or buried alive in a psychiatric hospital about his future, what can he answer you about his plans?"

The first days dragged by. Members of the Embassy staff cooked them food. Journalists interviewed them, the news rang round the world. Peter had a New Testament and they spent much time reading it but they sought to be quiet and still, only moving their stiff limbs when the office closed. Each day consuls urged them to leave but did not force them out. Unlike Ambassador Thompson in 1968, Ambassador Malcolm Toon, acting no doubt under instructions, took a policy decision not to meet them at any time. Consuls arranged for someone sympathetic to interrogate them.

On 6 July the Embassy sent a telegram to Vera in Chernogorsk. No answer came, and it was learned later that Vera had been chased out of the post office. Four days later they made a connection by telephone. Vera told her parents that John had been returned in great pain after a severe beating; he had been given tortures "almost up to the 'electric chair' " and had a kidney injury. His passport had been in his mother's handbag but he had plainly stated his age, to no avail. "If," said Vera, "they do that to a minor, what will it be for you? Don't leave the Embassy! Whatever you do, don't leave."

That same day, 10 July, at the Vashchenkos' request, the vice-consul sent a letter to Pastor Cecil J. Williamson, their sponsor in Selma, Alabama. In the course of this he wrote that political asylum never could be granted except in circumstances of grave civil disorder and danger to life. Therefore the families "are at present stymied in their effort to emigrate."

The Soviet Ministry of Foreign Affairs refused to discuss the case positively while the families remained in the Embassy, or to give any assurances, although a consul brought their petition supported by evidence of the long fight for emigration. On 27 July the Ambassador met Minister Korinenko who asserted that they would not be repressed while the case was examined, but they needed an invitation from a relative. Meanwhile, the celebrated Soviet dissident, Andrei Sakharov, who had told them early on that the Americans could do nothing, returned and said they had better stay. He promised to write to Brezhnev.

After a month of sitting all day, as still as they could lest they be a nuisance, they almost lost the use of limbs when they first moved. Worse, thirty-four days had passed since they had left home and had enjoyed their last shower. Lida wrote: "It is terrible. In the morning people arrive for work all fresh, cheerful, using some mask to stuff up their noses when they walk past us." The Siberians washed their divans with damp rags from the toilet each evening but having always taken pride in personal cleanliness they felt humiliated until at last they were allowed weekly showers. "There are many who pass by with contemptuous glances which show their hostility and disgust. They do not understand that our fate hangs by a thread and depends on them and that no one cares how the Soviets treat us."

Jews walked by, all smiles because they had brought their exit visas, yet the Seven were blocked: the problem here was that Soviet bureaucracy reckons "Jew" a description of race, not religion; "Jew" was entered in a passport, and the Kremlin had decided four years previously to permit increased Jewish emigration. But the Seven were Ukrainian or Russian.

By now they were profoundly disillusioned with the American officials. Not realizing that an ambassador and a consul act under higher instructions, they felt personally injured; but they had discovered among the Embassy families several believers with whom they reached a deep level of brotherhood, and they knew they would not be forgotten. At this stage some forty people were easing their lot by cooking for them in turns, chatting, bringing them Bibles and books in Russian, and writing materials or games; they specially enjoyed a Russian "Scrabble."

Washington feared that if the Seven continued to receive encouragement or sympathy, the Embassy would be inviting further sit-ins. Soon after their arrival an Armenian woman with two small boys, whose mother had emigrated to California, dashed by the police and joined them. The Seven at first believed she was a KGB plant and the ambassador no doubt wondered how many more were on their way. In countries where local police do not restrict citizens' access the entrance to an American embassy is simply manned by a Marine, and in Moscow it had long been the policy not to have armed guards to "repel boarders" (in Ambassador Toon's words to *The Economist*).

In mid-August, therefore, instructions were handed down that the Embassy staff were not to fraternize. And on 25 August came a terrible moment in the Vashchenko and Chmykhalov story.

At 8:15 P.M. an Embassy couple who had become particularly friendly were ordered to leave by the Marine guard, who stated that they had no authority to be there. The political officer, accompanied by the consul, entered at 8:30 P.M., saying that instructions had come from Washington, and read out a statement. The ambassador, he added, had supposed the Siberians were honest people but they had turned out not to be, because they would not go. Their presence hindered their own case and slowed the emigration of believers. The Seven must depart that very evening. "And now quickly gather up your things and leave 'with God.' I will accompany you to the gates."

The Seven reacted in deepest distress, especially in the light of all that they had endured down the years, including mocking that "the Americans don't want you."

"We answered that we would not walk out with our own legs and that if they wanted us to leave the Embassy they would have to drag us out and turn us over to the Soviet authorities for extermination."

The officers withdrew. Next evening came the same demand: Depart forthwith. But a *voronok* waited round the corner. Maria was "terribly worried for Timothy," as she wrote that very evening, "because he is not courageous and is gentle and is going to a suffering which is for an adult. His interrogators will probably torture him, and also the people are cruel in prison and he is inexperienced. My Timothy will perish in prison because he is not brave; he is tender and can't stand up for himself. Thus, he will not be able to endure it. We are going to suffer; probably there will be torture." She was especially concerned because the Chmykhalovs had no invitation from the United States; an invitation came later from Mrs. Gordon Lindsay, president of Christ for the Nations in Dallas, Texas.

Once again, after argument, the officers left. The next night, 28 August, the Seven were ordered to collect their things.

They believed the last hour had come and summoned all their courage and faith but felt utterly abandoned by man. To their surprise, they were not thrown out but led to a little basement apartment near the barber shop and the western gate, looking on to the road through a heavily barred window. In the past used by U.S. Marine messengers, it had two beds, a small stove, a refrigerator and its own bathroom with shower.

That night they hardly slept, but prayed; they had decided to keep a three-day prayer fast, whether in a KGB cell or still in the Embassy. Their friends found ways to sustain their hope and courage, but for at least two weeks the Seven expected to be expelled any hour and only slowly emerged from a state of shock.

The room became their home. "It is true," one of them wrote on 15 September, "that it is crowded with ten people [1] and at night is very stuffy and we must open the door for ventilation, but that's nothing. We could stand anything if we thought it was moving us nearer our goal."

---

1. The Armenian and her two sons left the Embassy on 31 October for her home. It was reported early in 1979 that she had been able to join her mother in the U.S.

The Embassy assured Pastor Williamson of Selma in September that they were free to remain until they decided to leave.

* * *

Back home in Chernogorsk came evidence that the Seven's presence in the Embassy was helping believers. A statute had been selected to convict the pastor but the trial never took place, and various shadows over other believers loomed less heavy.

Sasha, however, in his labor camp was threatened by a Moscow official with the fate of his "uncle" Andrei.

Sasha replied "Do with me as you like, but reunite my family and let them go abroad."

"That's not much of a sacrifice if you alone suffer for the whole family. It would be easier for us to collect all of you who are left, take you into the forest, and bury you under an old fallen tree."

Soon afterwards, during September 1978, Sasha returned late to the barrack room after a night shift. Finding, as he thought, the other prisoners asleep, he took out a manuscript page of the Gospels, which was contraband, to read before he went to sleep. Another prisoner unexpectedly came up to borrow a needle and thread. When he returned he asked what Sasha was reading and Sasha told him. The man asked to see it; Sasha lent it, and fell asleep.

He woke up to find prisoners discussing his page from the Scriptures. Everyone wanted to see it. Knowing the dangers, Sasha agreed to let them pass it round the circle. Just as the last man finished reading, the camp director of the daily routine, Ovginnikov, walked into the room. He seized the page, saw what it was and ordered Sasha to follow him.

When they reached the office Ovginnikov roared, "You are conducting agitation here!" He beat Sasha until he lost consciousness, brought him round and threw him, welts and all, into a solitary punishment cell, the dreaded *shizo* where the food is bread and water, and every other day a bowl of watery hot soup. Sasha stayed there fifteen days.

*   *   *

In the Embassy room, as the weeks passed from autumn to winter, life centered round different circles of relationships. At the heart was the Seven's strong sense of the presence of God.

They had a strong sense too of being a part of their absent families whom they missed grievously. At intervals Vera was able to telephone her parents. Early in November she brought little Abraham, four and a half, to the telephone: "The girls won't take me to Mama," he said, "so I am coming by myself!"

"But you have no money!"

"I'll sell my bike," his greatest treasure.

Vera reminded him that the back wheel was broken, so no one would buy it.

"I'll take it to the junk yard. Surely they will give me something and I'll come to Mama." On another occasion Augustina broke down after talking to Abraham. Both mothers missed their other children grievously.

Psychological pressures built up at times, but mutual Christian love withstood a test which probably would have wrecked unbelievers in similar confinement, and the two families in the little room each remained united and Timothy was like a brother to the girls. Days were made harder by the Embassy policy of discouragement. Visits were restricted to a short list. Though letters by the thousand were mailed by well-wishers, those sent by American diplomatic pouch had to be returned as violating a Soviet-American agreement, and few slipped through the Soviet censorship of international mail. Copies of many hundreds of the rest reached the Embassy but were seldom passed on, lest they encourage. A radio was allowed from 12 November but not short wave, lest preachers in the West send messages urging them to stay, nor a television set.

The families found it hard to believe that the senior staff cared, even when a consul brought them a Thanksgiving turkey and showed them how to prepare it in the traditional way. In contrast they were warmed by a small circle who became their close friends: the Protestant and Roman Catholic chaplains, a defense attaché and his wife; an interpreter; a secretary whom the Embassy deputed to do their shopping. The young son of a diplomat came daily to teach them English; Lyuba grew the most proficient. They used their time well, turning their room into a pocket university, and, when given the opportunity, enjoyed open air in the yard under escort. They played basketball and Peter was seen kicking a tin can in an attempt to play soccer. Then the winter cold and snow, and a lack of warm enough clothing, limited their activities; it was only after a Christmas press interview in the yard that the Embassy presented them with warm boots.

Their window on Tchaikovsky Street showed a little of the world beyond. But sometimes in the middle of the night the police kicked cans against the grating to disturb them, or yelled in the early morning, "Get up and pray, you cockroaches. Come out and we'll get even. Toads! Dogs!" The police spat, and let cigarette butts blow in smoke

The window disclosed harrowing scenes. A young man in a hat of rabbit fur and a dark coat approached with a document he wanted to hand to the Americans. The Soviet police pounced on him, twisted one arm behind his back and pulled the other back over the shoulder and clamped a hand on his mouth as he cried, "Help!" Another morning a man was led by with hands twisted behind his back. From her own experience Augustina knew the terrible pain though he did not scream.

After several such incidents the Vashchenkos composed an appeal to the United Nations Committee on Human Rights, pleading that they stop such abuse.

*   *   *

By New Year 1979 many people were pressing the Kremlin to grant the Vashchenko and Chmykhalov families their rights of emigration, enshrined in the Declaration of Human Rights signed by the Soviet Union in 1948 and endorsed at Helsinki in 1975.

Two young American visitors to Moscow, strangers to one another, offered to marry a Vashchenko girl as a means of rescuing the family; the marriage would have been invalid under Soviet law. Apart from these bizarre suggestions, the Kremlin persuaders resolved into two schools of thought: the school of quiet diplomacy, and the school of maximum publicity.

Quiet diplomacy was pursued by the ambassador, the secretary of state and presumably President Carter, who sent Dr. Olin Robison, president of Middlebury College, on two confidential visits to Moscow expressly to negotiate exit visas for the families: all he extracted was a verbal promise that the Seven would not be prosecuted for the fact of their stay in the Embassy. They must leave, and their case would be studied once they had reached Chernogorsk. Reeducation lectures in the mines and factories announced that they would return shortly; however, the Seven did not feel they could trust such thin assurances.

Dominating the quiet diplomacy school was the prior claim of high politics. Nothing must prejudice SALT II [2] and the most favored nation trade treaty. Even the National Council of Churches in America decided to hold back open support until SALT should be signed and ratified.

The maximum publicity school, on the other hand, wanted to exploit the recognized fact that the Kremlin does nothing unless it will bring ideological, political or diplomatic gain; humanitarian motives are excluded but the wish to create a favorable impression, and dislike of adverse world opinion, if strong enough, form one of the few levers that can be applied to the Soviet leadership. Therefore the more publicity, the quicker the Vashchenko-Chmykhalov case would be resolved, for it damaged the expensively contrived illusion that all is benevolent, fine and happy under the Red Flag. If, runs the argument, the American government and Embassy had been strongly supportive of the Seven and had applied diplomatic pressure, exit visas would have been processed in a hurry.

The maximum publicity school's campaign for the Seven grew in momentum during the autumn of 1978. A Washington demonstration, press articles, worldwide organization of letters in support, appeals to the Soviet and American leaders (15,000 to the Presi-

---

2. The second Strategic Arms Limitation Treaty.

dent), and questions at White House press conferences formed a part of it. A Soviet diplomat in Washington telephoned a congressman to stop people flooding the ambassador with protests; he received in reply a lecture on American freedoms and a suggestion that the best answer was to let the Seven go. In Europe, the Zurich-based organization, Christian Solidarity International, stirred up much support.

Early in 1979 the two families composed appeals to the Queen which were translated and forwarded to Buckingham Palace. Constitutionally she could do nothing in person but the Palace sent the appeals to the Foreign Office. Release to British territory would by-pass the impasse between the Soviet and American governments. Lida had dreamed about the Queen when still in the consular waiting room.

Life in the small room continued its monotonous way as the weeks crept past a year's stay. Sometimes came frightening moments, as when a young sailor, a would-be emigrant, blew himself up within their earshot after the Soviet police had been asked to remove him as a danger to the Embassy and had opened fire. The Seven froze at the reminder that police could be summoned any hour to remove them.

There were encouragements too. Two believers from Nakhodka bluffed the Soviet and Embassy authorities into believing they would urge the Seven to leave. Instead the two men urged them to stay and showed them proofs that their stand had benefited believers throughout the USSR.

And certainly the Vashchenkos have thrust important issues before the world. In the early 1960s Peter had been a pioneer by his discovery that complaint to the West can ease repression within the Soviet Union, a role of historical importance. The pages of this story of the Seven compel both East and West to consider whether atheism must be always a component of a collectivist society, or whether a way can be found for freedom of religion to flourish. The story demands how soon the Soviet Union intends to grant in practice the rights guaranteed by the Constitution, or whether believers will always be second-class citizens.

The pages pull aside the curtain. Tourists in Russia are like visitors to a zoo, suggests Lida. "A zoo has rules for the animals which do not apply to the visitors (except Don't litter, Don't smoke, Don't feed the animals what is forbidden). Therefore the visitors come and they go. What more can they know about the lives of the animals?"

        *   *   *

Efforts to extricate the Siberian Seven from the Embassy and the Soviet Union continued throughout 1979. In May 1979 an American lawyer tried to negotiate a "stateless" status for the Seven, so that they could be free to go straight from the Embassy to the airport, joined later by their families. The exchange of Georgi Vins, the Baptist leader, raised their hopes, and so did the announcement of a summit between President Carter and President Brezhnev, when their release could have been a gesture of good will.

In America an organization was formed at Selma under the title SAVE—Society of Americans for Vashchenko Emigration. SAVE held a demonstration on the steps of the Alabama State capitol on the first anniversary of the day the sit-in began. In September two Montgomery women were admitted with the congressmen into the Soviet Embassy and presented a petition signed by thousands.

In Europe a British Member of Parliament who had been allowed to meet the families tried unsuccessfully to raise the matter in the House of Commons in July. But in October, at Strasbourg, he moved a resolution in the Parliamentary Assembly of the Council of Europe which called on the Soviet Union to grant them exit visas.

The living conditions of the Seven became easier in the later part of 1979. An accurately researched article in the *National Review* of 31 August had revealed the restrictions they lived under, and brought widespread criticism on the State Department. Soon the Seven were allowed to attend the weekly Sunday service held in the Embassy compound and mingle with worshipers from many countries at the refreshments afterwards. Journalists might interview them in the snack bar instead of in the cold or wet playground. The Embassy widened the list of regular visitors. Staff who shopped for the Siberians could now use the diplomatic food store instead of waiting in Moscow queues.

U.S. Senators and Congressmen who visited the Seven at this time urged the Soviets to grant exit visas, only to be told blandly that none had been applied for in writing. This reply ignored the flow of written applications from Chernogorsk. On 20 September, Ambassador Toon, soon to retire and be replaced by Thomas Watson, discussed the case with the deputy minister of internal affairs, the minister being on vacation. Toon received the same reply, and next day, for the first time, he visited the families in their room. He shook hands. He promised to take applications himself and pressed the Siberians to return home while their papers were processed. Vashchenkos and Chmykhalovs alike sensed a Soviet trap, because word had been spread in Chernogorsk that they would all be imprisoned, and Grigory Vashchenko in Nakhodka had been told that his brother Peter, once out of the Embassy, would be "put in a bag like a cat."

Away from Moscow other members of both families suffered many difficulties. In mid-September 1979, Nadya and Vera took the smaller Vashchenkos for an authorized two-day visit to Sasha in his labor camp. The KGB and the commandant, Gutnik, played a cruel cat and mouse game, and only the girls' courage and persistence won Sasha his visit, which was vital not only for morale but as the only time he could feed well.

He looked thin. He had been beaten again. Gutnik had tried to force him to sign a document stating that he would refuse to leave the Soviet Union if his family went. Letters addressed to him were torn up in his presence before he could read them and he was deprived of his legal right to post letters home. He smuggled some out through visitors. He was caught, deprived of food packages, and placed in the dreaded punishment cell shortly before the family came again in November. He was released for their visit, then returned to the cell for fifteen days. He is convinced that Gutnik hopes he will contract tuberculosis and die; the other seven believers in the camp, all of whom are Seventh Day Adventists, suffer similar persecution. One already has developed T.B.

At Chernogorsk John and Jacob were harassed at their factory.

They were put on different shifts. John was badly beaten up and injured on his way home alone at night, and he was convinced that the hooligans acted under instructions from the KGB.

As for the Chmykhalovs, Alexander suffered a motorcycle accident but could not secure good treatment at the hospital because his mother and brother were in the Embassy. And Vladimir was denied the right to register his two children, on the ground of his conscientious objection to holding an internal passport. Officially, therefore, he and his wife are a childless couple and pay extra tax.

All the Vashchenkos and Chmykhalovs, and their friends, increasingly look to world opinion as the key which will unlock the door to freedom. The more the publicity, the greater the hope of speedy release; and if those in the Embassy must return home first, the world would no longer allow them to be lost to sight or punished.

October 1979 provided a prime example of the power of international pressure on the Soviet government. The Congress of the United States passed unanimously, through both Houses, a resolution condemning the non-delivery of international mail in the Soviet Union; the supporting evidence came mainly from the statistical contrast between the handful of letters delivered to the Seven in fifteen months, and the thousands mailed by members of the public who sent copies to monitoring organizations such as Christian Solidarity International. This resolution was incorporated into the debate at the Congress of the Universal Postal Union held in Brazil that same month. The very next week the Seven received between ten and twenty letters, and a similar delivery week after week thereafter.

Agitation for the families' release came from groups, congregations, and individuals rather than great organizations such as the Governing Board of the National Council of Churches in the U.S.A. This, early in November 1979 in New York, refused to pass a draft appeal urging President Carter to request Brezhnev to grant the Siberians their visas. The Pentecostal World Congress at Vancouver in October showed an even more negative attitude; its leaders not only refused to support their own co-religionists despite strong demonstrations n the congress grounds, but sidestepped the very question of religious persecution in the Soviet Union, no doubt being anxious rot to embarrass their Eastern European colleagues. It was left to the celebrated dissident Vladimir Bukovsky, not himself a Christian believer, who happened to be in Vancouver at the time, to shame the delegates by pleading the Siberians' cause on television. He had already done so in important speeches elsewhere, and continued to be one of their most vocal advocates.

Their story is not finished at the moment of going to press. It had seemed unthinkable that the Olympics could begin successfully in July 1980 under the Smiling Bear symbol while the Siberian Seven languished nearby in the heart of Moscow; then came the Soviet invasion of Afghanistan, and all that followed it.

But their trust is in God, not man. "In all our difficulties," they say, "big and small, God's help has always been obvious. We do not seek a good life, to work less hours or have easier jobs. We do not seek earthly riches. We seek only the freedom to keep God's law. 'Come unto me, all you that labor and are heavy laden, and I will give you rest. Take my yoke upon you and learn of me; for I am meek and lowly in heart: and you shall find rest unto your souls. For my yoke is easy, and my burden is light.' This is the teaching of Jesus Christ. These words should be in the conclusion on the last page of the book. This is our request."

Appendix I

Principal Persons

Note on Russian names: A Russian name consists of the given first name followed by the patronymic, followed by the surname. The patronymic has the father's name followed by *-ovich* or *-evich* for a male, *-ovna* or *-evna* for a female. Many given names have endearing diminutives (e.g., Sasha for Alexander). Russians are frequently referred to by their given name and patronymic without the surname. Strictly, many surnames have a different ending for a female, but for clarity among English readers I have usually ignored this. I have also given the usual English equivalent for a name of Christian origin.

THE VASHCHENKOS

First generation

Four brothers born in Ukraine, in Vaski, including *Paul Antonovich*, b. July 18,1888. Married *Anna Sviridovna*, 1892–1977.
Lavrenty, 1893–1943(?). Married *Fekla*, d. 1942.

Second generation

The children of Lavrenty and Fekla include
Grigory, b. 1927. Pastor of Chernogorsk church. Later moved to Nakhodka in Far East. Married *Olga*, and has many children.
Andrei, 1939–62. Killed in labor camp.

The children of Paul and Anna:
Natalia (Natasha), 1914–78. Divorced by her husband. One daughter, *Katia*, married.
Ivan, b. 1922. Married.
Khariton, b. 1924. Married *Anastasia (Styura)*. Ten children, including *Valya, Peter, Tanya*. Moved to Caucasus.
Peter, b. 1926. Married Jan. 1, 1949, to *Augustina Vasilevna Konovalov*. Thirteen children (see below).

Maria, b. 1929. Married. Ten children, all girls.
Daniel, 1930–32. Died of hunger and cold during forced trek.

Third generation

The children of Peter and Augustina:
Lidia (Lida), b. Mar. 6, 1951.
Lyubov (Lyuba), b. Dec. 7, 1952.
Nadezhda (Nadya), b. Aug. 7, 1954.
Vera, b. April 25, 1956.
Lilia (Lila), b. July 16, 1957.
Alexander (Sasha), b. April 7, 1959.
John, b. Feb. 26, 1961.
Jacob, b. Mar. 9, 1962.
Dinah, b. April 30, 1965.
Abel, b. May 1, 1966.
Paul, b. July 2, 1967.
Sarah, b. Oct. 9, 1970.
Abraham, b. April 8, 1974.

THE CHMYKHALOVS

Peter (Petro) Sergeivich, b. June 22, 1926. Married *Maria Petrovna Maka-renko*, b. Aug. 28, 1922, daughter of *Peter Mitrofanovich Makarenko* (d. 1942) and *Elena* (or *Yelena*) *Fedorovna Sanzhanov* (1894–1972). Maria's sisters, *Anna* and *Yelena*.

Peter and Maria's children

Nadazhda (Nadya), b. July 17, 1952.
Vladimir (Volodia or Vova), b. June 6, 1954. Married Oct. 9, 1976. Has two children: Vladimir, b. July 29, 1978; Elena, b. Sept. 7, 1979.
Anatoli (Tolik), b. Sept. 27, 1956.
Alexander (Sura or Shurik), b. Jan. 9, 1960.
Timothy (Tima), b. April 30, 1962.

SOVIET OFFICIALS, ETC.

Alekseevna, Rimma. Member of the executive committee of the Chernogorsk city soviet.
Andriushchenko, Galina Stepanovna. Vice-chairman of the executive committee of the Chernogorsk city soviet.

Blinov. Commandant at Reshoty labor camp.

Borisenko. Army enlistment officer, Chernogorsk.

Bulechakov. Boss in railway repair shop at open cast mine, Chernogorsk.

Dugina, Liliya Dimitrievna. Instructor on religious affairs, Chernogorsk city soviet.

Golst, Robert Efimovich. Official of the Council for the Affairs of Religious Cults (government department).

Goroshnikova, Valentina (Valya) Vasilevna. Mother of baby (Aaron) adopted by Lida.

Grigorev. Chairman of the executive committee of the Chernogorsk city soviet.

Gutnik. Commandant, Sasha's labor camp.

Ignatov. Assistant to Kazarin in KGB, Chernogorsk.

Ikonnikov, Ivan Romanovich. Head of KGB in Chernogorsk until 1963.

Ishchuk, Sofie Grigorevna. Director of the *internat* (boarding school) at Achinsk.

Kazarin. Head of KGB in Chernogorsk after 1963.

Klepinin, S. N. Chairman of People's Court in Chernogorsk in 1968.

Kolpakov. A former KGB chief in Chernogorsk.

Korelov, V. KGB investigator, Moscow.

Korotich. A people's assessor (juror) in Chernogorsk in 1968.

Kozenets. Woman official in Krasnoyarsk.

Kruglov. Head of personnel, Worsted Cloth Kombinat, Chernogorsk.

Kuznetsov. Minister of Foreign Affairs Ministry, Moscow.

Lipotenko. Head of a department in Worsted Cloth Kombinat, Chernogorsk.

Lisitsyn, A. G. A Moscow policeman in 1968.

Misha. Gatekeeper at Minusinsk Prison.

Podkolzino. Procurator, Chernogorsk.

Rezvanov. Procurator, Chernogorsk.

Schuvalov. Major in military enlistment office, Chernogorsk.

Semikobyla. Manager of Krasnoyarsk Coal Trust.

Sokolov. Head of mines fire and rescue services, Chernogorsk.

Sorkina. Woman people's assessor (juror) in Chernogorsk in 1968.

Terskikh. Policeman in Chernogorsk.

Tuvaev, V. S. Policeman in Moscow, 1968.

Ustyugov. Judge of People's Court, Chernogorsk.

Vasilev. Assistant chief of police, Chernogorsk.

Volkov. Procurator, Chernogorsk.

Appendix II

Chronology

1888   Paul Antonovich Vashchenko born in Vashki, Ukraine.

1912   Paul marries Anna.

1914   Paul a prisoner of war. Converted.

1921   Paul returns to Vashki.

1926   Birth of Peter.

1927   The fire. Family emigrates to Siberia, near Omsk.

1931   Collectivization. Paul, Lavrenty and their families expelled from village.

1931–33   The trek, ending at Gorlovka.

1939   Peter starts work as a plowboy.

1942   Death of Aunt Fekla. Uncle Lavrenty missing, presumed dead in labor camp.

1944   Peter in coastal defense, Soviet Far East.

1949   Peter marries Augustina.

1950   *April:* Ivan imprisoned for preaching. Peter first visits Chernogorsk

1952   Peter discharged from Navy. He and Augustina make their home in Chernogorsk. Peter gets a job as coal miner.

1953   *January:* Augustina's conversion. *Summer:* Grigory (cousin) settles in Chernogorsk. Revival begins.

1954   Peter baptized in the Spirit. The Vashchenkos form a Pentecostal church. The Chmykhalovs converted.

1961   The Great Persecution begins.

1962   *New Year:* Peter withdraws children from school

        28 February: Peter and Augustina deprived of parental rights for three eldest children.

        15 June: Lida abducted by the State.

        July: Lyuba and Nadya abducted by the State.

        August The three girls removed to Pioneer camp and then to *internat.* Parents not told of whereabouts.

        September: Message from the cook. Augustina and Anna visit children at Achinsk, followed later by Peter (incident of the funeral). Peter decides to emigrate with all his family.

October: Peter sells house. First visit to Moscow.

14 December: Peter arrested.

29 December: The Thirty-Two leave Chernogorsk.

1963   *3 January:* The Thirty-Two, led by Khariton, at the American Embassy. Subsequently returned by KGB to Chernogorsk.

March: Renewed attempt to get help in Moscow. Khariton arrested.

21 March: Peter sentenced to two years' imprisonment; Khariton gets five years' exile.

1963–64 Secret meetings with the children.

1964   *December:* Peter released.

1966   Andrei killed in labor camp.

1967   *March:* Lida released from *internat* on reaching age of sixteen.

November: Lyuba runs away from *internat*.

1968   *May:* Nadya runs away from *internat*.

29 May: Peter and four daughters seek to enter American Embassy. Girls abducted by Soviet authorities.

18 June: Peter, Augustina and Natasha (Peter's sister) seek to enter Embassy. All arrested. Peter incarcerated in psychiatric hospital. The four girls sent to *internat* at Kansk.

September: Trial and sentence of Peter.

20 September: Augustina sentenced to three years. Lida runs away from *internat*.

December: Arrest of Anna Makarenko.

1969   *May:* Arrest of the Chmykhalovs: Timothy's father sentenced to labor camp for a year.

December: Peter Vashchenko released.

1970   *August:* Augustina released.

1971   Division in the Chernogorsk church.

1973   Accident to Abel; miraculous recovery.

1974   *September–December:* Threats by State to remove younger Vashchenko children.

December: Abortive attempt to reach Moscow.

1975   *21 January:* The Vashchenkos examined as to why they wished to emigrate.

7 February: Libelous article in *Chernogorsk Worker*.

April–May: Cruel trick by authorities about emigration. Lida adopts Aaron.

July: Aaron forcibly removed.

August: Death of Aaron.

5 September: At the Embassy again.

16 September: Aaron's body secretly exhumed by family, and reburied.

1977 *9 October:* Death of Anna, Peter's mother, aged eighty-four.

9 December: Sasha tried and sentenced for refusal to serve in armed forces.

December: Selma, Alabama, Presbyterian church formally dispatches invitation to Vashchenko family.

1978 *20 April:* Selma invitation reaches Chernogorsk.

21 June. Vashchenkos fail to obtain exit visas at provincial capital.

23 June. Six Vashchenkos, two Chmykhalovs, leave Chernogorsk secretly.

27 June. Moscow. John seized by police, rest reach Embassy. Sit-in begins.

26 August: They refuse to leave; are given a room.